Oral History and the Local Historian

Stephen Caunce

Longman
London and New York

Longman Group UK Limited,
Longman House, Burnt Mill,
Harlow, Essex CM20 2JE, England
and associated Companies throughout the world.

Published in the United States of America
by Longman Publishing New York

© Longman Group UK Limited 1994

First published 1994

ISBN 0 582 07294 8 CSD
ISBN 0 582 07295 6 PPR

British Library Cataloguing-in-Publication Data

A catalogue record for this book is available from the British Library

Library of Congress Cataloging in Publication Data

Caunce, Stephen.
    Oral history/Stephen Caunce.
        p. cm.——(Approaches to local history)
    Includes bibliographical references (p.) and index.
    ISBN 0-582-07294-8.——ISBN 0-582-07295-6 (pbk.)
    1. Oral history.   I. Title.   II. Series.
D16.14.C38   1994   93-26417
907'.2——dc20   CIP

Set by 13TT in 10/12pt Times

Produced by Longman Singapore Publishers (Pte) Ltd.
Printed in Singapore

Contents

List of Illustrations

Acknowledgements

A book of this sort owes a great amount to a multitude of people, many of whom will not be aware of the contribution they have made at different times as I have refined my views on oral history over the years. It is impossible to acknowledge all such debts, but my thanks go especially to David Hey for commissioning the book and for reading the various drafts it has gone through, and to those whose testimony forms the basis of it all. Anyone interested in the East Yorkshire quotations will find short biographical details on the contributors in *Amongst Farm Horses*. I also thank those involved in oral history who set time aside to discuss it while I was writing the book. Of the farming photographs, plates 1.1, 1.2, and 3.1 came from Mr Walker; plate 3.2 from Mr Playforth; and plate 8.1 from Mr Baines. I gratefully acknowledge permission to reproduce Jack Hulme's photographs, that is plates 1.3, 3.3, 4.3, 11.2, from the Yorkshire Art Circus; from Artivan of Huddersfield for plate 10.1; and from Express and Chronicle Newspapers of Holmfirth for plate 7.2. Kirklees Cultural Services gave assistance with locating the last, as well as plates 2.2 and 8.4, and 4.4 is from their collections. Bradford Heritage Recording Unit provided plates 4.1 and 11.1 (photographs taken by Tim Smith), 7.1 (by Sean O'Neill) and 4.2; and plate 10.2, which was taken by Simon Warner, came from the Major Road Theatre Company.

Editorial Preface

In the past thirty or forty years historians have developed many different ways of looking at the history of ordinary men and women – the 'fourth and last sort of people' as William Harrison classified them in his *Description of England* (1577). This professional interest has been matched by the enthusiasm of groups of amateurs who have met together in every part of the land to research the history of their local area. Their emphasis has been on people as much as on place, and they have turned to every sort of evidence that they could find. For the late-nineteenth and twentieth centuries, no approach to this sort of history has been more productive than that which has become known as 'oral history'.

The approach was pioneered by George Ewart Evans in *Ask the Fellows Who Cut the Hay* (1956), the first of his many books to use this technique. Evans was interested in 'the prior culture' of a countryside that was farmed by hand tools and horse power. His informants had all begun work late in Victoria's reign. It seemed a matter of urgency to record their memories before it was too late. No written sources could possibly provide the understanding of the old farming economy that personal testimony could bring. His books made it abundantly clear that personal memories could not be dismissed as mere 'hearsay'; when it came to describing such everyday matters as working practices and domestic arrangements, such testimony was an unrivalled source. It also made compelling reading.

Stephen Caunce was inspired by Evans's work in East Anglia to make a comparable study of farmworkers in East Yorkshire. Rather to his surprise, as his work progressed, he found that whereas in Suffolk the horseman's job was the most prestigious on the farm, one that was performed only by mature farm labourers, in the East Riding the task of working the horses was left to the young, unmarried farm servants.

As in so many other matters, British experience was subject to much regional variation. Stephen Caunce went on to unravel the implications of these different methods of organisation and to analyse the whole farming economy and society in his book, *Amongst Farm Horses: the Horselads of East Yorkshire* (1991). He used documentary sources, where they were available, but his study was underpinned by oral history. Only the men who had worked as horselads could truly inform.

Oral history has sometimes been described as 'alternative history' or 'unofficial history'. It is emphatically not a fringe activity peddling nostalgia. A great variety of topics can be explored by the use of oral evidence, but in practice it is the life experiences of ordinary men and women that are treated in this way. Personal testimonies give a new dimension to our understanding of the past. But to be worthwhile, oral evidence has to be treated as rigorously as any other source of information. It is not an easy option.

In this book, Dr Caunce draws upon his own experiences as a researcher, writer, museums officer and university teacher to illustrate the potential of the approach and to offer sound practical advice to the beginner. Many local historians are convinced of the value of oral history but are hesitant to begin. This book starts with the premise that anyone can contribute to oral history. It encourages the reader by admitting the author's own early mistakes. Its avowed aim is to involve far more people in this sort of activity, for Stephen Caunce is a proselytiser whose commitment shines through every page of the book. He believes, rightly, that, 'oral evidence from ordinary people is an essential part of understanding our total history'.

DAVID HEY

Introduction

My involvement with oral history began in 1972 at Leeds University, when I recorded the reminiscences of elderly country people from the East Riding of Yorkshire as the basis for a PhD. Initially, I had no practical grasp of what I was undertaking, and though oral history has now been around for long enough for the majority to have some concept of what it is, many conversations have convinced me both that this lack of certainty is still widespread and that, in many people, it defeats the intrinsic attraction of a particularly intimate type of history. My memory of my own first sessions is of setting out with great trepidation, especially because of the personal contact that is the essence of this way of working. I was scared of making a fool of myself: would I come back with tapes that had nothing on them, or would the recorder itself cause people to freeze and say nothing? Could I think of appropriate questions and keep the talk going? Could I keep the conversation on topics that were relevant? Would contributors later regret confiding in me and find my work patronising or offensive? I suspect the vast majority of these fears are general, and that those who do not share them at all probably will not make very sympathetic collectors of reminiscences.

I needed practical advice given in a supportive manner when I started and if I can fill that need here for others, I will feel satisfied. Perfection is impossible when starting out, and there is plenty of room for argument about what constitutes perfection in any case, so I have tried always to give realistic advice and to avoid creating the feeling I sometimes still get when reading guidelines, of having forgotten a multitude of essential things. I certainly made mistakes in my research and there are many things I would now do differently, but it cannot have been disastrously off course because it led eventually to a PhD for me, and it has been published as a book, *Amongst Farm Horses: the*

Horselads of East Yorkshire. I do not write as an expert to whom recording is a way of life, for those three years at Leeds were the only ones when it was at the centre of my work, and even then actual recording was a very small part of the time I spent on the whole project. After that, wrestling with the vast accumulation of oral material that resulted from such a seemingly slight basis had to be fitted in round full-time work in museums between 1975 and 1988. I became involved periodically in other smaller oral history projects as part of my work, however, and this has continued to the present. I therefore feel I have enough experience to be able to help others, and yet little enough still to share some of their fears. My own research is used throughout this book to give a sense of reality rather than theory, but I have tried to incorporate lessons learned from my own mistakes then, from other projects since, from contact with other collectors, and from reading other people's books.

Working in museums helped develop my views on oral history and the contribution it can make, for in those years museums were the centres of many government-funded employment schemes for collecting oral history, whereas academic historians found it hard to raise funds for their projects. They also provided a dire warning against the risks inherent in a boom based on enthusiasm rather than foresight and planning. A parallel surge in interest in material culture in the early decades of this century had been the force behind the creation of many local authority museums, yet by the 1970s they seemed like its victims rather than its beneficiaries. Inadequate buildings and facilities, hopelessly low staffing levels, and utterly unplanned collecting of objects had made many resemble rubbish heaps rather than treasure houses, and yet it had all begun with the best intentions. Oral history is at a point now where it should learn from this experience, for the parallels are clear: preserving the past of the local community in a time of great change came to mean grabbing any relic of the past that came to hand, and not fretting too much about what it was or who would look after it, for there were always more relics to be saved from destruction. The result was chaos, and over the years, far from being preserved, most of those objects either rotted, were lost, got broken, or became unidentifiable and so useless. It must not happen to oral history tapes.

Museum work also allowed me to develop my long-standing interest in local history and its links to local environments, which reinforced my belief that oral evidence from ordinary people is an essential part of understanding our total history, not a nostalgic fringe activity. Much oral history is concerned with ordinary people, who see themselves as lacking the type of skills and knowledge historians are interested in, but are the experts on most local and practical subjects. A museum display of old tools or household utensils, for instance, is meaningless without an explanation, and only one group can really supply that: those who used them. Most – if not all – of the people I collected material from will be dead when you read this book, but it passes on their thoughts and memories. The interest that can be aroused by such displays and by local oral history publications shows that this is a branch of history that can be genuinely democratic, appealing to all types of people, and it is always a source of surprise and regret to me how few local historians see oral collecting as one of their natural tools. There is no need to be a specialist and few methods of working allow a local historian to make a more distinctive and valuable contribution to history.

Oral history is capable of contributing to many types of academic history too. Realising the full potential of my research depended on turning the evidence I had collected into an analysis of an economic and social system of great complexity. It centred on the experience of those who worked with horses on farms before tractors took over. They were young and single for the most part and they made up about half the labour force on East Riding farms. They were boarded and lodged where they worked, which made their lives very separate from the married farm workers – mostly labourers who lived in cottages in the villages – and also from the rest of the rural community. A purely nostalgic period piece would have been easy to write, and in talks to all sorts of audiences I have seen the evidence that it has a natural appeal many historical topics lack. Historians, however, must move beyond this in an effort to really understand the everyday workings of our rural past. Working out why the system functioned as it did, how it had developed, and how it functioned in a national context gave this subject interest outside the county and made it a serious contribution to agricultural history.

Other people have also written extensively about rural life and its links to a traditional past so I have tried to show the variety of approaches possible for different people with different styles even when covering closely related material. It is possible to work on many different levels, so there is no need to feel intimidated by a lack of experience or of desire to write anything large or momentous. It is not essential to write anything at all as long as recordings are placed where others can use them. Subjects that have nothing to do with the countryside or tradition as it is usually understood are also covered, for otherwise a reader would have no idea of how wide ranging oral history has become, both in looking back at the past and in collecting records of events as they happen, as a kind of instant history. Anything that people now living have been involved in can be a valid subject for oral history, and collecting oral traditions handed down, sometimes for generations, can push the limits further. Urban areas, all classes, and most economic activities have been covered by oral historians somewhere in some way. Women's experiences and those of ethnic minorities have all been investigated to break through the lack of conventional data that normally hinders historians. Yet the surface has barely been scratched and there is so much work to do that there is room for a vast expansion of the numbers at work. Anyone can find a niche of some sort, suited to their abilities, the time at their disposal, and their ambitions.

I do not attempt to justify oral history. There are certainly historians who are not convinced that it does produce valid history, but this is probably because there are very different views on the nature of history itself, and what seems self-evidently valid to one historian may seem equally self-evidently useless to another. The debate between these schools of thought is worth conducting, and it forces those of us who uphold oral history to define why we do so, but it is not relevant here. For those who want to try their hand, to discover if they find oral history worthwhile and practicable, such discussions simply distract. The results that have come from oral history are sufficient cause to accept it as far as I am concerned, and I hope they speak for themselves here. Those who want to follow this up can find plenty of discussion of it elsewhere: this book is intended to complement those already in existence rather than to duplicate them.

Precisely because oral history is developing all the time, there is no case for setting clear limits to what can be done and no room for dogmatism about methods. Collectors and contributors are involved in a personal and dynamic process unlike any other form of historical investigation. To make it work in all its different settings, with all its various end products, and all the different personalities involved, the key must be diversity of approach, not uniformity. If you feel you would like to try some oral research, whether alone, as a historian in charge of a project, as a teacher, or as part of a group recording its own experiences, try it. If this book has one underlying message, it is that there is so much scope for filling gaps in the historical record that anyone with a desire to be an oral historian can do worthwhile work, as long as they are honest in their dealings with their contributors and willing to learn on the job. Remember that all the early efforts in this field were conducted without guidelines, and by people whose basic resource was themselves. This book is a menu you can choose from, not an instruction manual. It should be something you can return to for help with a change of course or to direct you to other books where you can find more single-minded consideration of particular methods of working, of the nature of oral history, and of the results you can get on particular subjects. Take everything that seems valuable, but don't let the urge to try oral collecting for yourself shrivel as excessive preparations convince you of your inadequacy. You can do no real harm by experimenting as long as you respect your contributors and what they tell you. As far as the basic collecting goes, you are likely to surprise yourself with your innate skills for many of them are the inter-personal skills that we all use every day and of which we are barely aware.

CHAPTER ONE

What is Oral History?

My father was a coal merchant to the villagers. He had a bit of land,
kept two or three horses. Mostly allotment land. As we grew up there
was only one thing for us and that was to go on farms. Seven
brothers, five sisters. I was the fourth child. I was the second son....
The youngest one – he was at home so long, helping my father, my
father was getting on, then he went to Wakefield for a policeman, so
long. He wasn't there that long anyway: he turned tail and came back
home, and then he took my father's business over when he died, that
was the youngest. Now all us others, we never looked for anything
else. When we got old enough we knew there was only one way for us
– to go on farms.... I left school when I was thirteen....
In winter time our hours was seven to five, you started work at seven,
you did your horses, you fed 'em, mucked 'em out, groomed 'em,
geared 'em, before breakfast. You went in to your breakfast about
twenty minutes to seven. You were supposed to be out by seven and
then you went to work in the fields.... A lot of places they had to go
out at seven, that was the time, maybe dark as pitch.... Now when
days began to get a bit lighter you edged on a bit, say about
February, about half an hour a day, you kept making 'em longer and
longer till about March.... You went out to work from six, come in at
twelve, fed your horses.... You'd no time to sit down – soon as you
got in you fed your horses and then you swallowed your dinner, you
hadn't much time, and then you came out, fed your horses again, you
had your corn to fetch in from t'granary, you had your straw to fetch
in out o' stackyard for bedding and generally by that time it was one
o'clock and they were very strict on time, a lot on 'em. Dead at one,
not a minute past. You stayed out till six and you came in, you gave
your horses a feed, you went in and you had your tea – supper they
called it.... And you were supposed to put two hours in before
breakfast with your horses, you were supposed to put two hours in
after tea. (Tape 5/1)

This was William Johnson's introduction to work in 1906, described in his own words. It was in no way exceptional for someone born, as he was, in the East Riding of Yorkshire in the late nineteenth century. Apart from army service in the First World War, all his working life was spent on farms in the county. He died in 1976, but his experiences, his encyclopedic farming knowledge, and his old skills are not totally lost: the quotation comes from the hours we spent between 1973 and 1975 in his daughter's house in Leeds recording his reminiscences. He eventually became a farmer in his own right, which was rare, but it was expected that, on leaving school, most boys would be hired as farm servants, as he was, which meant living on the farm. Mostly they looked after and worked the horses, though a few had more general duties or worked with the other stock. Their contracts ran for a year at a time, and were legally binding, so they had to stay on one farm for the whole year. The labourers who did the work that did not require horses, such as hedging and ditching, were paid weekly like most other manual workers of the period, but servants were paid just once a year, on Old Martinmas Day (November 23rd), when all their contracts expired, then after a week or so at home, a new year's work began in exactly the same way as it had innumerable times before:

> You went to plough – if t'weather was right, if it wasn't too wet or hard, frozen hard or owt o' that ... Chiefly, that was your winter's job ... Well, they were called ploughlads, that was his job.
>
> *How long would you be at that?*
>
> Oh, it depends on the weather, and condition of the soil, and whether your farm's clean. You see, if, for corn, if your land's fairly clean, there's no point in getting it ever so deep, just a nice fine top to keep your *frostmould* . . . But if your farm's, you know, if it has a lot of rubbish in, well, I mean, you have to do a bit more at it, and that prolongs the job a bit. It's a matter of what a man thinks, you see, some farmers, he's a bit rough, well, you know, 'Oh, it'll do', maybe wants another time over. I've heard it said a lot of times, 'Oh it wants another time', you know, more doing at it before they drill it. 'Oh, it'll go over in time'; yes, but then that farm gets worse and worse and worse, you see, and it gets rougher and rougher and more rubbish in. Today it doesn't matter so much because they just put insecticide and weedkiller on and that does it, but ... there's so far soil wants working – nicely cultivating, I think. (Tape 15/1)

Such memories interest many people and though they are hardly the stuff of which history has traditionally been made, oral history is based on the use of such personal reminiscences as a source on which to build history as an alternative and complement to the documents on which historians normally rely. Through memories like those of Mr Johnson, groups of people who had previously been considered too unimportant to merit much attention since they were too ordinary, or who were not seen as feasible subjects for historical study since they rarely left behind the kind of documentation on which historians rely, have become widely written and read about. Does it matter how farmworkers were hired on East Riding farms and how they ploughed the fields, however? Is it worth recording?

Implicit in the massive recent growth of local history is a recognition that every family and every place has a history of its own, and one that can contribute detailed knowledge to the study of wider themes. Most lives are lived within a local framework, and, as part of groups and communities, every individual has played a part in moulding our present society and economy. Most of us lead ordinary lives no more or less special than that of Mr Johnson, and we cannot understand the way society really worked in the past if we ignore our equivalents from days gone by. If history has managed without this type of material so far, this is often because historians have never been able to avail themselves of it. This is most clear when we look some distance back: J.F.C. Harrison in his book *The Common People* makes no bones about his feelings. 'The inner world of medieval peasant belief is to us a closed book. The same is true for the craftsmen and the townsmen. We can study the institutions of society within which the common people lived; but their thought systems are much more elusive.'[1] The records that would tell us how an average family of the Middle Ages farmed, what they hoped for from life, what they felt about the way society was organised, or almost anything else, were simply never created. We know little enough about the higher reaches of this society, so there is scant chance of ever penetrating the veil of obscurity that surrounds everyone else. He has written the best history he can in spite of this, but he clearly regrets that things are not different.

I have never forgotten the thrill I got on reading for the first time from the transcript of the Putney Debates (reprinted in *Puritanism and Liberty: Being the Army Debates 1647–1649 from the Clarke MSS*). This is a verbatim recording of discussions held at Putney in the autumn of 1647 when the king had been finally defeated in the English Civil War, but the rank and file of the Parliamentary army and its high command could reach no easy agreement as to what kind of settlement was to follow. The soldiers, feeling that they had contributed heavily to the victory, were attracted to the programme of the Levellers, who sought a much greater voice for ordinary people in the running of the country. The generals agreed to debate the issues involved at least partly to win time while they regained control of events, but the results were not charades. Subjects were thoroughly discussed that never

Plate 1.1   An East Riding farm servant, or horselad, in the fields with his team during ploughing, which was the biggest single job of the year. The land to the left has been ploughed but the light, flinty soil of the Yorkshire Wolds does not retain the clear furrow pattern seen on heavier soils. Note his distinctive dress, with flared corduroy trousers and a double-breasted waistcoat. Taken at Manor Farm, Thixendale, probably in the late 1890s.

usually came near the surface of a society like that of seventeenth-century England, with its strictly hierarchical politics and an assumption that ordinary folk preferred to be led rather than make their own decisions. Here we have the words of men who would normally have gone to their graves without leaving any trace:

> Really I think that the poorest he that is in England hath a life to live as the greatest he; and therefore truly, sir, I think its clear, that every man that is to live under a government ought first by his own consent to put himself under that government: and I do not think that the poorest man in all England is not at all bound in a strict sense to that government that he hath not had a voice to put himself under.[2]

Colonel Rainsborough's famous speech demanding the right of all men to participate in government is often quoted, yet it is something that could never have been recorded in the type of documents on which we generally base our knowledge of his times, except perhaps as evidence in a trial for subversion. This was not a man reading from a prepared script, but one putting his case in spontaneous words as part

9

of a dialogue. The transcript records the responses made to it, so we can get some sense of how different people felt about it. It must be the nearest we can get to seventeenth-century oral history and its power proves to me how much we lose because there is not more of it. Giving voices today to those who normally do not speak on the record may similarly preserve opinions that those in power would often prefer to ignore. A conservative historian can make just as committed a contribution on the establishment side, however, by taping contributors chosen for their support for the status quo. The words of the generals at Putney, who feature prominently in standard histories, fascinate as much as those of their opponents.

Oral history often has a rather subversive image in this country, which probably reflects the fact that documentary history already serves elite groups adequately, so the impetus behind its use comes from other directions. Oral histories about them will only add to what we know rather than radically alter it, and this image is in any case no criticism of the mere collection of data through reminiscences. In the USA, at an academic level, oral history has always been dominated by elite projects, such as the Kennedy oral history project, which is part of the enormous archive set up to further study of President Kennedy. In the 1970s, the largest American project in existence was the Marine Corps Oral History Programme, and in Britain the Imperial War Museum has similarly been a driving force behind oral research in this country. The rural past, moreover, is often seen as a haven of stability, deference, and order, so collecting the memories of people like Mr Johnson does not lead automatically to left-wing history. Books like *The Country House Remembered: Recollections of Life Between the Wars* (1985), edited by Merlin Waterson, show that sympathetic treatment of a subject so stereotypically conservative is perfectly compatible with oral methods. Contributors and collectors alike came from the upper echelons of society, with Mary, Duchess of Buccleuch being recorded by Lady Tomkins, for instance.

At times in the following chapters, thé many approaches to oral history and its many uses will seem too varied for my earlier brief definition to hold up under the weight. Nonetheless, there is a unifying bond that ties together all the divergent branches. A common willingness to use oral history methods has bred a sense of shared purpose and philosophy among most of its practitioners, even when they disagree violently about what it is that they share. There is a British society, *The Oral History Society,* which holds an annual conference for oral historians of all types, and which publishes a journal, *Oral History.* Much is written about the special nature of oral history, but to me oral material is not an end in itself and the very name can mislead in implying a particular type of history. Oral history is rather a method of gathering material, a contribution to the general process of making sense of the past so that we can better understand the present and plan for the future. It is one type of historical source among others, albeit an intrinsically interesting one, and a very neglected one that has needed to have a spotlight turned on it to make people aware of it. It may be that if oral history becomes completely accepted, the concept of a unifying bond will come to seem outdated, but this is a long way off as yet.

The range of subjects already covered is truly vast, however. A recent guide listed, among many others, collections of varying size and seriousness on advertising history; Lancaster hospital; bobbin and bonnet making; Buddhism; cider making; the Everest expedition of 1953; the Ford Motor Company; the Luton hat trade; the Co-operative Movement; ballet; radio manufacture; crime in Ilfracombe; the Sainsbury family; the experiences of the blind; gun-running in Northern Ireland; Christmas festivities and computer history, quite apart from the many wide-ranging local history collections.

One of my favourite pieces of oral history is Kevin Brownlow's massive study of the silent cinema between 1916 and 1928, *The Parade's Gone By . . .* It illustrates perfectly the way that even high-status and highly visible sections of society can benefit from oral research. The silent cinema was the origin of all the visual mass media of today, but little notice is paid to it, and most of that is purely artistic. Kevin Brownlow felt that the only one way to find out about the early days was to ask those who were there. The title, he wrote,

> sprang from an interview with Monte Brice. Brice, who had been a writer and director of silent comedies, told me of the time he watched the shooting of *The Buster Keaton Story*....
> 'They had it all wrong,' said Brice. 'I tried to tell them that things weren't like that in the twenties, but they wouldn't listen. I remember the assistant, a young guy. He said to me, 'Look, why don't you go away? Times have changed. You're an old man. The parade's gone by...'[3]

It is staggering how many survivors of the very earliest days of the silent cinema Kevin Brownlow was still able to talk to in the 1960s, and the secretive and chaotic way in which the industry functioned as it underwent explosive growth is revealed, confirming that documentary sources alone cannot hope to show us what was happening then, since much was simply never written down, even as business records. He overturned completely the idea that silent films were mere bumbling precursors of today's superior products, and the descriptions of technical achievements made on minuscule budgets by today's standards are truly eye-opening. Simply projecting silent films at the right speed, to avoid the manic movements that result from modern projector speeds, has contributed to restoring their reputation, but the book's strength lies in establishing them in the context of what audiences expected and what theatrical tradition suggested acting should be. A genuinely silent form of drama developed, and the mature silent film cannot be judged as a talkie that has no sound, which is why they look alien today. Kevin Brownlow has re-awakened serious interest in these films as a result and his reconstruction of Abel Gance's *Napoleon,* which he regards as the greatest of the silents, has now been shown to modern audiences to huge acclaim.

Most books on the cinema are basically promotional works, and most contemporary interviews were dishonest to some degree, for film people above all others are both skilled in and used to manipulating the faces they show to the public. This book transcends these difficulties and offers genuine insight into what was being done, how, and why, as with this reminiscence from Louise Brooks, which touches on the nature of creativity and inspiration:

> A director works fast who knows everything ahead of time. He sees the picture finished, whole, cut, titled. Pabst would take one shot, bang – that was it. I remember I was going to do my famous Follies-girl walk across the stage in the theatre scene of *Pandora's Box.* I'd planned it all out. I took four steps on stage and Pabst said 'Cut.' That was the end of it. I had given him all he wanted.
> Those young comedy directors – Eddie Sutherland, Mal St. Clair – they thought they were geniuses, like Chaplin and Sennett. What they didn't know was that when they were out drinking and playing around and dancing all night, Chaplin and Sennett were thinking about tomorrow. Chaplin would think about a picture for years. I went down with him once in 1925 to a Hungarian restaurant in the Jewish Ghetto in New York. He went there every night. God knows why; nobody knew why. He would get the violinist to play, and give him five-dollar bills. And how many years later did he do *Limelight?* And there was the scene. He was the violinist.
> But Mal St. Clair, who worked at Sennett, and Eddie Sutherland, who worked with Chaplin, imagined that Sennett and Chaplin really did think up their scenes right there on the set. And Mal and Eddie would try to make pictures that way, with large hangovers to boot. When I was married to Eddie Sutherland, he was having a lot of trouble on *Fireman Save My Child.* He'd done no preparation. If he wasn't inspired on the set, he would think of a reason why he couldn't shoot. He would say 'That building is too close to the camera. Now move that building back and we'll shoot tomorrow.'[4]

Documentary evidence records only a thin slice of life, and if it cannot accurately represent an industry like the cinema, it is much more true for lives like Mr Johnson's. Even though record offices have multiplied in recent years, and now preserve small business records, trade union records, club records, and much else that would once have been destroyed as unimportant, they rarely cast much light on individuals. In Mr Johnson's case, his father's business or his own farm might appear in a trade directory, his wage payments might appear in a farmer's account book, or he might appear in a membership list of a friendly society, but none of this is certain and it tells us nothing about him as a person. It is not likely that anyone can drop through the net of documentary records today with such finality as a medieval peasant, but what does anyone who is not a part of it really know of the lives of hill-farming families, of shipyard workers, or of women in slum districts? Or of all the other categories of individuals that make up society and yet are not open to inspection? Or the intimate, behind-the-scenes detail of lives that seem open but are only partially recorded in documents? How will the people of the future, living in a changed society, be able to understand the variety of life now from purely documentary sources?

All too often, ordinary people still appear only in fleeting glimpses in records compiled by others for their own reasons. It is remarkable what can be done with slight clues, but it is surely much better that Mr Johnson's own voice is preserved, giving his version of his own life. A comparison can be made with the recent realisation of the value of old photographs, which are now prized, after decades of neglect and destruction. It is hard to conceive now how anyone could ever have ignored the value of pictures such as Plate 1.2 as keys to the past, but it is only because glass plate negatives can survive years of appalling treatment that we have been able to recover large numbers of images of Victorian and Edwardian times. It illustrates beautifully Mr Johnson's memories, yet it was saved from destruction more or less by chance in the 1960s after the original owner died, for the pictures were about to be thrown on a fire when Mr Walker asked if he could have them. The threat to memories is rarely so clear cut and it is not so easy to save them from oblivion, for we have to act before a crisis by actively seeking out and recording them. Record offices are increasingly finding room on their shelves for tapes, for oral history has been a growth industry for the past two decades, but there is still room for any number of people to collect reminiscences without fear of duplicating each other's work.

Without oral recording, large tracts of human experience simply

Plate 1.2 This and the other photographs I collected from Mr Walker add up to a remarkably complete picture of farmwork at Manor Farm, Thixendale, between York and Driffield in the 1890s. I copied 29 them, and most of the rest appear in my book Amongst Farm Horses. They may well be the work of the farmer himself since they span several years. Dr Colin Hayfield discovered the series independently after me and did a considerable amount of research into them among the residents of Thixendale. This boy is probably fourteen or so, and is taking his horses out to the fields. They are harnessed for ploughing.

vanish. Whole industries can disappear in this time of technological change, leaving behind only a few enigmatic fossils in the form of old tools whose use we hardly know. Dialects, and even languages, are lost and communities can be uprooted and scattered. Perhaps the rapid rate of change and its wholesale nature have contributed to the importance oral history has assumed in the last few decades, for previously the high profile events with which history traditionally concerned itself seemed to move in front of a backdrop of ordinary existence that could be taken for granted. Change did occur in ordinary people's lives, and locally it could be rapid and far reaching, but on the whole it was organic and steady, so there was a lack of awareness of the processes involved and few records were kept of what was vanishing. Folklore, for instance, was never more than a minority interest and it was always a source of wonder to me when researching rural life that agriculture figured so little in local histories of country districts – presumably because it was seen as common to all. Even where it was mentioned, the workers would almost certainly be ignored, for people looked through farmworkers rather than at them, literally taking them for granted. The recent surge of interest in the environment is a comparable phenomenon, I feel, for after assuming for time out of mind that nothing humans could do could have more than a local effect, we are now forced to realise that for decades we have actually been damaging our own life-support system and may now face serious consequences. Concern for oral recording can be seen as a response to similar fears about what we are doing to our social environment and the institutions that have been its basis, such as the family and the community.

The sheer quantity and diversity of documentary records now kept can be just as effective a block to real understanding as their destruction. They may swamp us with information which still does scant justice to ordinary people. Leah Leneman researched the government's creation of smallholdings for Scottish crofters out of large existing farms after the First World War. Her book *Fit for Heroes* (1989) says very little about how such settlements worked in the long run, however, because paradoxically, 'for state-owned farms the sheer volume of files makes it almost impossible to build up a coherent picture.'[5] She chose the 16,000 acre farm of Shinness in Sutherland as her main case study, in fact, because the landlord was the Sutherland estate, and kept *fewer* records than the state-owned projects, but even so it was oral history that fleshed out a comprehensible and balanced view of the community. The bulk of her book concerns the administrative processes behind the creation of the farms, the classic terrain of documentary history. Even here, however, oral history has something to offer, for crofters pressing for land in their native communities saw matters very differently from the officials who had the thankless task of finding it for them in the teeth of almost universal opposition from landlords, and yet, on the whole, only the official view survives in writing. To use oral testimony alongside, not instead of, other material is not to propose anything truly radical, merely to extend the range of history, and the onus is really on those who disapprove to say why huge sections of human experience are not fit subjects for study.

In the past, it has been the perception of verifiability which has ensured the primacy of written evidence. Regardless of how much truth it really embodies, the fact that a written document can be checked by others places a limit on the possibility of distorting history. It does not rule it out: people can distort even the most solid evidence, and many a footnote in an academic book will go unchallenged because no-one has the time or the inclination to find out that it is wrong or misleading, intentionally or unintentionally. It simply means that anyone who does distort is running a risk of being found out. Moreover, virtually all historians use ephemeral sources such as letters, diaries, and working notes made by the participants in significant events. This helps them comprehend the real process of decision making (which is often obscured in formal records by the need to present a publicly acceptable face) as well as enlivening history with a human touch. A letter or diary, however, is only the expression of an individual opinion and even a private diary may be written in the knowledge that it may be published. Oral evidence offers much the same possibilities, with the advantage that contributors can be asked to expand on what they have said, or challenged if it seems dubious. In all walks of life its use naturally pre-dates written evidence, for speech pre-dates writing, and our judicial system still relies largely on oral testimony given directly in court, precisely because it can then be challenged. The only thing that can explain the reluctance of modern historians to use oral sources is that there was no way for a reader to check them until recently.

Even a seemingly verbatim transcript of speech reproduced in a book could be completely fraudulent, and matters are even more complicated when we get a case like the early example of an oral history book, *The British Workman Past and Present,* by the Reverend Marmaduke Morris. He was an active folklorist and collector of traditions from the East Riding in the late nineteenth and early twentieth centuries and one man he met, William Blades, born in 1839 and the son of a farmworker, fascinated him so much that he made

> a long series of visits.... He was possessed of a surprisingly retentive memory; indeed for accuracy in minute details connected with events long past I cannot remember ever to have met any one to equal him; so that in the course of time I gained from him a vast amount of interesting information connected with his early life and work.... As he unfolded to me by degrees the story of his career, I was able to make mental and other notes of his observations, and I had frequent and abundant proof of the strict accuracy of his statements.[6]

The book based on these sessions is fascinating, carrying us back three quarters of a century before Mr Johnson, and there is so much agreement between their accounts that there is no room for doubting the general truth that underlies the book. Moreover, as Rev. Morris implies, William Blades lived in an oral culture where written documents were not normally used, so people's memories had to be reliable. Even in the 1930s, farm servants' contracts were entirely oral, with no documentary record kept at all, and yet I never heard of a farmer trying to pay less than the agreed sum at the year's end. I would therefore place great reliance on the original testimony, but even if others agree with me on this, there is no way of knowing if the final text really is what was said, and still less if it represents what was intended, as in the following:

> I once asked William Blades if he still continued to drink beer, which in his younger days he found so refreshing and sustaining. He replied that he did not; adding that the beer of the present day did not agree with him. To one who had been accustomed to drink good home-brewed ale, this result was not surprising. To whatever cause or causes it may be attributed, there can be no question that the habits of the people generally are more temperate now than they were a generation or two ago; and I am convinced that if all beer was made of nothing but good malt and hops there would be even less intemperance than there is at the present time.[7]

This is so much a composite of phrases from William Blades and opinions that seem to be entirely Rev. Morris's that no real value can be placed on it. For much of the book, the author remains more in the background, but he is always there as a commentator and always prone to interweave himself into the reminiscences. If anyone doubts whether I have misrepresented Mr Johnson, there are tapes of our talks, but real records of these conversations do not seem to have ever existed. Tape recorders have, therefore, transformed the reliability of oral evidence and also given historical records a new dimension. A good recording has a quality that bears no comparison with any other historical source except film. To be able to hear someone's actual voice, with all the subtleties of speech that sometimes contribute as much as the words themselves, with the original accent, and delivered exactly as they said it, is something very special, even though it does not put oral material beyond question, any more than a written document can be seen as tamper-proof, or above suspicion as a forgery. It is also worth stating that it is not the recorder that gives value to the reminiscences, which may be reliable or unreliable, interesting or dull, significant or worthless. Tape recorders have simply created more of a level playing field, and in doing so they have become the symbol of oral history.

Oral history has, in fact, acquired a misleading air of high-tech wizardry by its use of equipment that associates it with television and radio. Since the media rely on the extensive use of interviews for the content of many factual and news programmes, this reinforces the connections, and it has also accustomed all of us to seeing oral evidence taken seriously, even if we do not realise it consciously. I do not believe it is accidental that the technology that has threatened and destroyed so much of traditional culture, through the creation of the mass media, is also the technology that gives us the chance to save something from the wreckage. It is important to stress right from the start, however, that the tape recorder is a tool, a means to an end, and that an oral historian has no need for a knowledge of electronics. It should be a means of opening up history by involving people who would not feel capable of using an archive, but it can become a barrier, deterring people from ever trying to record for themselves. Alternatively, it can become a dead-end, involving users in endless agonies over the different machines, tapes, and methods of working.

Do not confuse the medium with the product, for the words of William Blades show that oral history existed before tape recorders and there is no need to produce a perfect tape to make it worth recording someone. As long as their words are audible, even audible with effort, then their memories have been preserved and made accessible to others. One of my own recordings, made on the old reel tape, was nearly inaudible because a strip of silver foil on the leading edge of the tape got stuck in front of the machine's recording head, giving the same effect as putting a pillow over the microphone. As I had travelled for the best part of a day on trains and buses to make the recording I was devastated, but with the machine at top volume and with much hard labour, I managed to reconstruct the vast majority of what had been said. I could never expect anyone to get anything from listening to it in a normal manner, but Mr Harper's words are on record and can be validated. As an instance, Mr Harper and another lad once took their waggons out on a winter's day and when they returned they were met by the *wag,* short for *waggoner,* the head horselad all farms with more than one or two farm servants. He had heard that one of the married farm labourers, who lived in cottages in the village, was being evicted and had nowhere to go.

> 'Don't *lowse* your horses out of [your waggon],' wag says, 'we'll go down to Warter, fetch t'labourer's furniture under cover.' Well, t'parson o' Warter parish took pity on him. He gave him two rooms to live in and we put all his furniture in t'outbuildings. But his beds was absolutely ruined. When he landed back all his stuff was turned out into t'street. And it was snowing and blowing heavens high that day. We all went back and what we couldn't get on t'load, we carried with our hands.

> *What had he done to get evicted?*

> Nobody knowed what he'd done. And he'd been on that estate

eighteen years. But we never knew from that day to this what [her ladyship] turned him out for. And best on it was,... there was a sergeant, a police sergeant, and a constable come from Pocklington, and when they were [inaudible], this here young policeman..., he started laughing. His sergeant said, 'What are you laughing at?'
He said, 'Having all this lot to carry out into t'street.'
He said, 'Lookstha, my lad..., thoo's single yet,' he says, 'I'm in a tied house same as this chap's been,' he says. 'If I ever did anything wrong in t'police force and I was found out guilty,' he says, 'I could be turned out into t'street.' He said, 'Bear in mind this my lad,' he says, 'tha's thy life to come on yet, tha might be turned out...thyself. Look, it's no laughing matter,' he said. 'This is a job I don't like, but,' he says, 'you've got to do it if time comes.'
And he was in t'parson's two rooms six months before he could get another cottage in Londesbrough. And when he got a cottage in Londesbrough, we went to t'two rooms and shifted all his stuff out o't'vicarage to Londesbrough.... And he had five *bairns*. Two lads and three lasses. (Tape 17/1)

This sort of scene is often overlooked in nostalgic accounts of rural life in estate villages. Conventional documents are not likely to do justice to such an event, if they survive at all, for the cottage's owner has no interest in recording the distress caused, or the reaction of bystanders and others such as these policemen, and usually they would want to play the whole thing down. On the other hand, documents might record the reason for the eviction, which is lost here. Put them both together and we have a fuller picture than either could give alone, and this is only possible because of my recording, even if it is nearly inaudible.

The act of collection is what makes oral history decisively different from other ways of working – autobiographies apart – for the collector has an active role to play in the creation of the primary source material. This is not merely a matter of selection from surviving evidence as when using pre-existing documents, for these are by definition capable of yielding only what was put into them, and the decision on that was taken many years ago. My questions were a part of the final version of Mr Harper's retelling of this incident, and without them it might have been left at the first paragraph. Collectors and contributors together determine what is put on record and an oral recording session can range over a whole lifetime of experience, attitudes, skills, and philosophy. No-one could ever do more than retrieve a very partial sampling of all this. Thus, one collector may concentrate on work methods and skills in a purely technical way that excludes a sense of the contributor as an individual within a society. Another may do the reverse, giving the social and political matrix centre stage, so that at

times we forget that the contributor is a farmer, a weaver, or whatever.
Neither is wrong unless the collector is determined to pursue their line
against the wishes of the contributor.

In *Ask the Fellows who Cut the Hay*, one of several books about
Blaxhall in Suffolk, George Ewart Evans deals in some detail with
Lionel (Liney) Richardson, a noted nineteenth-century shepherd. He
was widely known and a contemporary artist and naturalist, George
Rope, 1846–1929, left this description of him:

> Much of his time was spent with his flock on the heath; with certain
> parts of which his presence came to be so intimately connected that
> they still bear his name.... [He] was about middle height. He had
> good regular and rather refined features. His gait, like that of many
> whose work is entirely restricted to the tending of sheep, was quite
> free from the swaying, rolling movements so often acquired by those
> who have long been accustomed to follow the plough. With his
> shepherd's *slop* or smock flowing gracefully behind him; with crook
> on shoulder and dog at heel he would sail grandly in front of his
> sheep at a steady, even pace, his body leaning slightly forward and
> head thrown back – a picturesque figure in the landscape; but also a
> personage of some importance in the district: the consulting surgeon
> and physician of the parish in all cases of injury to sheep....
> It is impossible in writing to give any idea of his fine rendering of the
> pure Suffolk dialect; or the true pronunciation of certain vowels and
> diphthongs. Liney had the courteous and respectful but dignified
> manner often notable in the elder shepherds and farm labourers of his
> time.[8]

The tone is admiring and respectful, yet it concentrates firmly on
Liney as a respectable *character* who knew his place within a
traditional, deferential community. A girl who grew up in his
household became the mother of one of George Ewart Evans'
contributors, and he passed on facets of Liney's life that alter our
picture of him remarkably, even though they complement rather than
contradict, and this shows how easy it is to see only what we want to
see, as Rope did. Robert Savage passed on memories of

> almost constant poverty, if not actual want. There were, however,
> two ways of relieving this poverty: poaching and smuggling. Both
> were unlawful; but at that time, in spite of heavy penalties, they were
> both so commonly practised as to be hardly thought of as crimes at
> all. Liney's way of relieving the poverty of his family was by
> smuggling. The sheep walks extended right down to an inlet in the
> coast where cargoes of contraband goods were regularly landed on
> dark nights. Liney was in league with the smugglers, and his job was
> to help them to put away the cargoes in a safe place before the
> morning; he also kept them well informed about the movements of
> the 'preventive men'....

Old Liney's chief task on the night when a cargo was being *run* was to keep his eyes open and to turn his flock of sheep from the fold and quickly cover up the tracks of any wagon when it returned full.... It was a clever excise man who could trace exactly the route of the wagon after Liney's sheep had been walking down the road.

The story comes down that Liney's wife knew well when a cargo was being run. And on these occasions it was her practice to gather all her children round her and sit by the kitchen fire; and not one of them dared move or utter a word until their father returned safely. Many people from this area had suffered transportation for life, ending their days in the penal settlements of Australia for smuggling offences.[9]

Liney was never caught, but the stress put on the family by the smuggling is deliberately emphasised to prevent one stereotype, of 'the peaceful, rather idyllic shepherd of George Rope's word-picture'[10], as George Ewart Evans puts it, being replaced with another, of the daring, artful smuggler running effortless rings around an ineffectual enforcement system. Liney emerges not as a character from a romantic past, and not as an instinctive rebel, but as a human being, doing his best for his family when even his universally respected skills with sheep would not bring in a living wage. Only by capturing the whole human being can we really understand the functioning of the communities of which they were part, and so often accounts from the past make no attempt to do this. As collectors we must be aware of the risk of doing the same, and we usually have to take responsibility for weighing the evidence of testimony when we come to construct history from it. Not all testimony is equally usable, and it is especially important to remember that direct experience is worth far more than hearsay, though in a community with an active oral tradition, this qualification is not as strong. What I know I can vouch for, what someone else tells me, I can pass on with a comment on their reliability, but what I hear from someone who heard it from someone else really is just a rumour.

In addition, there is safety in numbers, for memory can be unreliable, as the police know only too well. Witnesses can flatly contradict each other on virtually every detail of a robbery, for instance, even when interviewed very soon after the event. Decades on, it may be that some event was etched so deeply in people's minds that every detail is correct, but the presumption has to be the reverse until checks have been made. This is not to belittle the contribution that oral testimony can make to any investigation or even to assert the primacy of documents. It is a matter of judging which is the best in any particular situation, as in the case of Mr Harper's eviction story. Details of everyday life are worn into the brain by constant repetition

21

and are not subject to anything like the same uncertainty as memories of unusual events. Incidents like that eviction which relate closely to the normal pattern are likely to be remembered accurately because they fit into the existing framework, where really extraordinary events do not. They may seem mundane, but they are what life was made up of for the vast majority, and it is the typical rather than the exceptional that should normally interest a historian.

Thus, a museum curator may seem to have much in common with an antiques collector, but the latter usually seeks rarities to make a collection special, where a curator should reject them because they do not show an accurate picture of the past. It has always irritated me to see displays about childhood in museums which focus on the nursery and on elaborate displays of toys. Childhood looms large in oral history, as we shall see, and the picture that is painted rarely includes anything of this sort. Only a tiny fraction of the population ever had a nursery for their children, and though more had toys, for the vast majority they were few and usually homemade, notably whips and tops, crude dolls, and hoops to roll. Ordinary children played outside in groups, and the real relics of their childhood are the rules of the games they played and the chants and songs they used. Nursery displays rarely even include a statement that what they show is atypical: they blithely talk of *children* when what they mean is *the children of the rich*. Documentary sources rarely provide any means of authenticating this sort of detail, but it usually verifies itself through cross-checking with other oral testimony, because many people will cover the same ground automatically. I have given introductory talks on oral history to college students very recently where, as an exercise, I have asked them to interview each other and suggested using childhood games as a subject where they are all likely to have something to contribute. They grew up in the 1970s, and yet they discovered that, names apart, they share a solid core of common experience. The games they are recalling are not learned from books, television, or adults: they are passed on by a continuing oral tradition dispersed over the whole country.

A broad sample of contributors further allows us to discover common strands that run through all, or nearly all, versions and to identify and, if necessary, eliminate purely personal attitudes and beliefs. This results in a blend of personal and communal experience which gives history an unrivalled human face, and it is this type of approach which is most relevant to the work of the local historian. Used correctly, the strong links between historian and contributor are a positive element that brings history to life, for when it is well done,

Plate 1.3 This was taken at Fryston, West Yorkshire, shortly after the Second World War, but it is so representative of previous decades that it is extremely hard to date from internal evidence. The men would be coal miners. A local person commented, 'Men would think nothing of playing games with kids in the street. It could be a real laugh; hordes of us playing circle games with the younger men or someone's dad in the centre.' *(World Famous Round Here: The Photographs of Jack Hulme* (1990)) Few, if any, of these children would have many toys and they spent a considerable part of their lives playing like this outside their houses rather than inside.

listening to a recording is like sitting in on the past. Special care has to be taken, however, where we are dealing with people who are used to managing interviews, for it encourages us to be uncritical, and even a desire to avoid causing offence can make bad history. If there is something which cannot be said, and there very rarely is, we must not bend the truth so as to be able to use a more acceptable version.

The collector's role is crucial from the very start because it is the collector who normally brings together the contributors, finding and selecting them, unless, of course, a group is doing its own oral history. As well as taking responsibility for organising and running sessions, the collector has to develop personal relationships with contributors. This introduces an element into historical research that most historians do not encounter, but it is really only a version of normal social skills and it does not require an ability to strike up instant, deep friendships with every person recorded. Most of my contributors, though by no means all, were elderly, like Mr Harper and Mr Johnson, and this is

often the case. This has both advantages and drawbacks, but the collector should always remember that some contributors find the experience of sharing their recollections a very positive one. Although far from senile, many may be having difficulties adjusting to retirement or coping with extreme old age. They grew up in a world quite different from the one in which they now find themselves, and as children they were expected to give way to the elderly and respect their experience. Now their turn has come to be treated with deference, however, they are rejected and told that the parade has gone by. Many find it hard to come to terms with this devaluation of the experience they have acquired over the years. Their advice seems of little value because their experience seems to younger people to have no bearing on present problems.

Old farmworkers, for instance, were often very dubious about the long-term impact of changes in agriculture over the past few decades. Mr Johnson never made any doom-laden predictions to me about the consequences of using chemical fertilisers and weedkillers to replace the careful working of the soil that the extensive ploughing of the past had achieved, but he did feel there had been a value in the old approach and that it had simply been ignored. The increasing awareness of the fragility of the environment has now made us more willing to listen and to see the value of a system that did not cause widespread pollution or lead to the wastefulness typified by the straw burning of recent times. He and others acknowledged the higher crop yields of today and never suggested that a simple return to old methods would be a good thing, yet until very recently, even such mild reservations seemed like an obstinate refusal to follow a profitable course of action that had been fully endorsed by scientists and governments. It is still far from clear if agriculture really is set on a non-sustainable course, and it is certain that farming could not have stood still if our steadily growing number of mouths was to be fed, but we should not just cast aside the elderly as being, by definition, out-of-date and irrelevant.

Few ordinary people of any age, in fact, believe that their knowledge is of any relevance to others and they rarely feel they could set it down properly if they decided to try. Yet when shown examples of oral history, they are usually very interested in it. This was summed up for me by a Sutherland crofter in the 1940s, excited by reading a book, *Highland Journey*, or *Sul Air Ais*, by Colin MacDonald about his area and its people. He said, 'It's a *grand* book! – there's nothing in it! – *anyone* could *write* a book like yon! – if he could *write* it!'[11] When they were collecting oral material in 1987 the Yorkshire Art Circus was

repeatedly told that 'nothing interesting ever happened to me' and so they used this as the title of a book they put together from what they had been given by ordinary people of two Halifax council estates, the 'fascinating, intriguing, funny, sometimes sad events and memories from their own lives – but all of them [were] invariably interesting'[12]. Approaching someone to record them shows that their life is of value and significance in itself, quite apart from any history which may result and the respect implicit in this can be of tremendous importance to a wide range of people. It can be of positive therapeutic benefit to some who may seem to be sliding relentlessly into senility. Oral history is a two-way process, giving something to a contributor as well as the researcher, and requiring something from the collector as well as the contributor.

There is a definite place for the historian, then, especially because oral history is in many ways still in the pioneer stage and most projects are still setting off into relatively uncharted territory. This can be compared to the European mapping of Africa in the nineteenth century. Explorers of unknown parts startled audiences back home with announcements of tremendous discoveries, many of them made by chance and all of them due to the use of African porters and guides. They already knew all about their own territory and without them the explorers could not have survived. The explorers' distinctive contribution was to create a general map of Africa out of the fragmentary knowledge that existed before. This proved to be the precursor of conquest, however, and Europeans soon owned what they had been shown, whereupon they set about exploiting it for their own ends. Revelations through oral history are also totally dependent on pre-existing knowledge, recorded before death rubs the slate clean. After that, no amount of intrepid exploration can recreate more than a shadow of the original. Hopefully, oral historians will not also seek to colonise the history they uncover, but this is always a danger. The tape recorder should not be used to set oral historians apart as a group with special skills, and so promote the process of takeover. If they act as friends and enablers they can help the possessors of the original knowledge to realise the significance of their own wealth and help prevent these vast new historical territories becoming the exclusive possessions and empires of remote scholars. The fitting of local knowledge and experience into a general framework is a worthy task that has to be conducted at many different levels and using many different skills. Some things undoubtedly require the special skills of trained historians, but there is plenty of work to be done that does not need all, or any, of these skills and one of oral history's greatest attractions to me is its democratic possibilities. Anyone can contribute to oral history, and the more who do, the better for everyone.

NOTES AND REFERENCES

1. J.F.C. Harrison, 1984, *The Common People*, Fontana, p.73.
2. A.S.P. Woodhouse, 1938, *Puritanism and Liberty: Being the Army Debates 1647–1649 from the Clarke MSS*, Dent, p.53.
3. K. Brownlow, 1968, *The Parade's Gone By* . . . Abacus, p.1.
4. *Ibid.*, p.410.
5. L. Leneman, 1989, *Fit for Heroes*, Aberdeen University Press, p.67.
6. M.F.C Morris, 1928. *The British Workman Past and Present*, Oxford University Press, p.2.
7. *Ibid.*, p. 141.
8. G.E. Evans, 1956, *Ask the Fellows Who Cut the Hay*, Faber, pp. 29–30.
9. *Ibid.*, p.31–2.
10. *Ibid.*, p. 53.
11. C. Macdonald, 1943, *Highland Journey*, The Moray Press, pp. 12–13.
12. Yorkshire Art Circus and Calderdale Libraries (eds), 1987, *Nothing Interesting Ever Happened to Me: a Proto-book by the Community of Illingworth and Mixenden*, Yorkshire Art Circus, foreword.

CHAPTER TWO

People and Places

The next five chapters show a range of methods of using oral material, each one covering one approach, or a cluster of closely related approaches, starting with those requiring least intervention by the collector. Approaches that seem more complex are not necessarily superior, however, for the important thing is to select the right approach, appropriate both for the task and the temperament of the collector. In practice, a good many people start recording with no clear aim, perhaps simply feeling that the reminiscences of elderly neighbours ought to be preserved, and, since no-one else seems likely to do it, they try themselves. This can lead to a lack of focus, producing desultory chats that seem to have little historical relevance. The most obvious way of giving a point to a session is to work within the framework of the contributor's life. Reminiscences have a natural tendency towards autobiography, and the *life story* or *life history* is a powerful way of structuring taping sessions. Life story work is different from conventional autobiographies, and also from the use of a recorder as part of the research for a conventional biography, though this is a perfectly legitimate way to work in itself.

A life story concentrates on an ordinary person's life seen through their own eyes, and is very much a personal statement, despite the collector's involvement. The quote from Mr Johnson that began Chapter one is a perfect example of this type of material, which need not be complete, but may just cover childhood, or employment, or any other section of a life. Direct reminiscences often have a narrative power that transcends the subject matter and local speech forms are seen in their correct setting, so working-class contributors can reveal a fluency that would never have been possible for them in written English. Local interest is what sustains the majority of individual life stories that have been published, as typical lives well told, but they can have a much wider interest, for in being so typical they stand for the experiences of large numbers. As such, these stories form a recognised tool of sociologists, who use them to examine life at a level of detail that would be quite impossible to achieve for whole populations, but which is essential for understanding the complex web of forces that make up all societies. The strength of life stories lies in dealing with those who are normally overlooked, and since conventional autobiographies deal with such a tiny percentage of the population, this need not mean searching for groups that are obvious outsiders. Even middle and upper-class women, for example, are rarely seen in their own terms, and can be good subjects even though their fathers or husbands might not. Moreover, life stories have a cumulative value when linked together, for in bringing out common factors they come to be far more than the sum of their parts. Jean McCrindle and Sheila Rowbotham produced a book called *Dutiful Daughters*, a collection of women's reminiscences that came from all classes, for instance, and they commented:

> We chose this group of women from amongst our friends, our friends' mothers and contacts we have made through the women's movement. They are not supposed to be typical or representative, but simply individual women talking about their lives – how they see themselves, what they remember, what significance they give to personal and public events....
>
> A series of oral testimonies does not make a history. History is worked over more consciously; different sources open up various ways of looking at what happened. These interviews are fragments, as an individual life is a fragment and as an individual caught for a moment presents a fragment of a fragment. The personal oral account can be a source not for knowing that something was so, but for wondering about questions that are not often considered. So this should be seen not as a book with historical or sociological conclusions but as a stimulus to further investigation.[1]

Those who want to widen the definition of what is acceptable as history may find themselves throwing open doors into areas within human experience that were known only to closed groups, but often what is found is more tragic: secrets which were actually shared unknowingly by large numbers, each of whom is left isolated and often guilty. Most of the older women in *Dutiful Daughters* 'mention the shock, ignorance and guilt they experienced at the onset of puberty. Unable to talk freely with anyone because of the silence that surrounded women's sexuality, many of them hid the blood of menstruation rather than mention it to their mothers'.[2] Maggie Fuller came from Leith, the daughter of a disabled docker. He died while Maggie was in her teens and her mother brought up on her own the seven children who survived:

> I had a period before my sister, you see, and I dutifully tried to wash these things. Anyway, I had an awful good aunt, you see. I got a hold of my aunt and I said to her, 'Do you know, I don't know what I am going to do.' Well, she said, 'You've told your mother?' 'No,' I said, 'I am frightened.' 'Oh,' she said, 'You'll have to tell her.' I never said anything more, she told her for me. She gets me into this room, and I'll never forget it, and she said to me, 'When you're like that,' she said, 'you just keep away from men.' I think now it's an awful horrible thing she done; then I don't know what I thought. She got a bairn's nappy and she showed me how to put it on! [Laughs.] And do you know what I used to do when I was like that? When I saw a man I used to run like hell – I did! Do you know, I've never forgiven my mother for those things that she's done, it was all wrong. 'Well you keep away from men,' that's all she said, and when I saw a man I used to run.
>
> Do you know when the running stopped? I met my sister one day, I was going like the hammers, you know, and I was getting on, I must be about fourteen at the time, and she said, 'Good God, Maggie! Why are you running like that?' 'Well,' I said, 'I've got yon in,' I said, 'I've got –' So she says, 'What? Oh!' She says, 'Come on, I am going to see Aunt Ella about this.' And Aunt Ella says, 'Did your mother no tell you anything? Well,' she says, 'she should have done.'... Somewhere my sister Annie managed to learn – oh well she worked in a factory, you see, she may have got it there. Aunt Ella said, 'Well I'll see your mother about it.' She didn't tell me anything. It was all whispered. It's wrong! I always said if God spared me to have a girl she would know from a very young age, and it wouldn't be a shock to her. I mean, they talk about girls no being right – how the hang do they know how to be? Imagine a mother telling you, 'Keep away from him.' Well, naturally, you got to your bloody feet and you ran, didn't you? [Laughs.][3]

Since women are normally a majority of the population, something so basic to their lives might, in theory, seem inevitably to be a unifying experience, but it clearly was exactly the opposite. In all classes and even in families that were more open than that one, most were brought up to keep their experiences to themselves, despite the evident and natural networks for sharing that existed everywhere. Peggy Wood was born into a Protestant, Northern Irish family, with a mother who was middle class by origin and a father who had acquired middle class status through working in insurance. Interestingly, this stands out to me as a more stilted, less spontaneous and dramatic piece than most because it is from someone essentially trained to speak a written form of the language:

My parents left books lying around the house. They told me a bit –
my mother told me about sex, but told me in a slightly mawkish way
too young, and embarrassed me very much by telling me very early
on when I was in the bath, and I felt conscious of being naked in front
of my mother. It was an odd thing, must have been before I had the
curse, because I think I had that at the age of about thirteen, because
it was theoretically supposed to be fourteen in those days.... I had far
too much pain and trouble about it, and it was a kind of – well, must
be sensible about it, but, er, you know, you couldn't be expected to
play games of the same order when you had the curse. Quite the
reverse from what came up from our elder daughter when she was
that age – you know, you must play games like mad, exercise is
good....

My mother would talk about sex in a poetical way and I despised
her for this when I grew up. But later on I understood more, because
you cannot talk about your sex life to your child, it's difficult, and I
don't want my children envisaging my sex life. I mean, we can have
better sex when they're not in the house. It's a sort of limiting factor.
There must be a terrible taboo somewhere, I don't know. Oh God,
bloody Oedipus. The man is so. . .. I get so bloody mad at Freud
anyway, you know, I want to be a bit suspicious of that. But anyway
there's a taboo that I must be involved in, and therefore don't find so
unacceptable in my mother as I did at the time. But sex was
something my father could not have spoken to – to his daughters,
who were so sort of – you know, it must have been rather wonderful
to him, he'd created these two marvellous characters who were way
out of the life he'd lived. There we were, we could play piano and we
went to church on Sundays and we wore nice clothes and we spoke
nicely. And this must have been a marvellous satisfaction for him,
knowing the struggle he had to raise himself in the way he did....

So she didn't tell me enough, but she realized the limitation of it
and she left sort of ooey-gooey books around and medical books
around and also . . .. Oh, there was one awful book about, er, I can't
remember now, it was sort of vaguely religious, and it was all about
the birds and the bees, but in a soupy kind of way, and then it ended
up with the birth of a baby and about how this baby grew under the
mother's heart, and I thought, now, your heart's here . . .. I can see
now as a parent how difficult it is to get the thing across.[4]

In a life story it is the contributor who is setting both the agenda and
the tone, and only when we know what it was that people considered
important are we really in a position to fit their lives into a grander
pattern. Where a local audience can involve itself in the minutiae of the
story and is familiar with the places described, there is seemingly
unlimited scope for publishing such material, but it may well be that
there will come a time when greater selectivity will be called for to
reach a wider audience. Thus, even though rural life is still far from
fully explored, enough work has been done to make some things

over-familiar. I recently had to review a book that was a collection of fragmentary rural recollections from all across the country, with no other unifying factor, and while there were points of interest, nothing was developed very far. Forty years ago it would have been new, but today it is necessary to present a fuller picture, more firmly rooted in a particular locality if anything is to be added to what is already known.

All God's Dangers: the Life of Nate Shaw is probably as good an example as will ever be found of what the life story can be. Theodore Rosengarten contacted Nate Shaw in 1969 while researching the Alabama Sharecroppers' Union of the 1930s. Shaw was so articulate, and had such a story to tell about what it was like to be black in rural Alabama in the first half of this century, that on its own his testimony produced a six-hundred page book. He was an ordinary man of his race and class by birth and upbringing, but his ambitions and abilities meant that he was never able to accept the subservient role allotted to black farmers by the white men who ran Alabama. He was not a natural rebel: his aim was simply to do well for his family, but the way farms were let to black farmers was designed primarily to prevent them achieving this. Most were illiterate and poor, and they were kept permanently in debt to their landlords by sharecropping and by the system of annually advancing them money for the purchase of seed and tools, to be repaid out of the coming crop. The landlords actually took most of every crop, creating perpetual debt, and they could distrain their tenants' property at any time.

Shaw's farming skills enabled him to get free of debt, to buy cars and to begin to buy a farm, but it became clear that, as a success, he was a threat to the system that could not be tolerated. He found that he was to be sold up, using faked evidence of debt. He preferred to fight rather than submit quietly to having his property taken from him, and this was when he turned to the sharecroppers' union:

> I recommended it thoroughly to particular ones I knowed – some of em was too scared to join and some of em was too scared not to join; they didn't want to be left alone when push come to shove. I recommended it to my brother Peter, but he never did join it. He was livin [farming] on Mr. Watson's individual place at that time, about a mile and a half from me on the Crane's Ford road toward Apafalya. He got along with Mr. Watson by giving him what he made – Mr. Watson got it all, that's the truth of it. My brother Peter was easy and high-mouthed and he just settled down to that. He made up his mind that he weren't goin to have anything, and after that, why, nothin could hurt him. He's my own dear brother – he said he was discouraged of this organization but I knowed he was afraid....

In a few weeks' time it come off, it come off. Mr. Watson sent the deputy sheriff to Virgil Jones' to attach his stock and bring it away from there. Virgil had got word of the plot and he come to warn me and several other men of the organization. I knowed I was goin to be next because my name was ringing in it as loud as Virgil Jones' was. Virgil come and told me about it on a Saturday evenin. That next Monday mornin I fixed myself up and walked over there, bout a mile from where I was livin.... Got there and good God I run into a crowd, and Virgil Logan, deputy sheriff, was there fixin to attach up everything. I just walked up like somebody walkin about, that's the way I played it. Several of us met there too, but we had no plan strictly about what we was goin to do. Leroy Roberts and two or three more of em come there early and left before I got there. Well, the devil started his work that mornin. I asked Mr. Logan ... kindly, talkin to all of em, 'What's the matter here? What's all this about?'

The deputy said, 'I'm goin to take all old Virgil Jones got this mornin.'....

I begged him not to do it, begged him. 'You'll dispossess him of bein able to feed his family.... Go back to the ones that gived you orders to do this and tell em the circumstances. He aint able to support his family. Aint got a dime to support his family.'

He said, 'I got orders to take it and I'll be damned if I aint goin to take it.'

Well that brought up a whole lot of hard words then. I just politely told him he weren't goin to do it, he weren't going to do it. 'Well, if you take it, I'll be damned if you don't take it over my dead body. Go ahead and take it.'

He got hot. After a while I seed Cecil Pickett go in the lot with bridles in his hands to catch Virgil Jones' mules. That was a colored fellow had no sense; white folks could get him to do anything they wanted him to do....

I said, 'Go ahead and catch em, if you that game. I'll be damned if you won't ever bring them out of that gate.'

Somebody got to stand up. If we don't we niggers in this country are easy prey. Nigger had anything a white man wanted, the white man took it; made no difference how the cut might have come, he took it.

Mr. Logan seed I meant it – I was crowin so strong and I was fixin to start a shootin frolic then.

'Come out, Cece,' Logan said, 'Come on back, Cece. Let em alone. Come out.'

Then the deputy walked up to me and said, 'You done said enough already for me to be done killed you.'[5]

The deputy retired, but came back with more men, and by then everyone but Nate Shaw had fled. Shots were fired, and again the deputies gave up, but now that he had fired on them he was a marked man. He surrendered several days later and served twelve years in jail, while a friend who tried to escape was shot down.

Nate Shaw's intimate knowledge of this oppressive system, as only those that are oppressed can know it, offers unique insights into the US Deep South. The overwhelming message of the book is that, in the last resort, Alabama society was geared entirely to maintaining white supremacy, and that the full force of the law could be co-opted to that end because all those in power were white. Right and wrong counted when big issues were not at stake, but in a situation like this, black farmers had to be shown that they could not win. This means that the documentary evidence to which historians normally look for objective evidence has no real claim to that status here. Documents were created as part of the system of oppression, for mortgages, agreements, court proceedings, and judgements were all part of the bonds that tied down the black people, and to use them as they would normally be used by historians is to join the conspiracy. Doubtless, there are aspects of Nate Shaw's story with which which others would disagree, for it remains a personal statement, but the overall picture has an undeniable ring of truth. It is worth noting how little support he got from his sons, for instance, who saw the whole thing as a hopeless gesture that put him in prison, ruined the family, and left them to rebuild it. This is a magnificent book in itself and the insight it provides into a system that could almost have been designed to deceive outsiders makes it invaluable as history.

Community history thus grows naturally out of life stories. Ingenious use of what archival material there is has produced some worthwhile and convincing results, of which the most accessible and readable for the pre-industrial period are probably Peter Laslett's *The World We Have Lost: Further Explored* (1983) and David Hey's reworking of Richard Gough's *History of Myddle* (1981). These are worth reading – if only for the constant reminders they provide that everyday life, though taken utterly for granted at the time, becomes strange, and sometimes incomprehensible, after time elapses. It then becomes difficult for us to rediscover – 'you don't miss your water till your well runs dry,' is a proverb quoted by Nate Shaw and by George Ewart Evans. All the men I talked from the East Riding had taken it for granted that they would leave home to lodge on farms on finishing school, but to anyone growing up only a few decades later, this seems like something from the middle ages. For communities that still exist, or from which there are survivors, oral history allows the direct collection of information from those whose knowledge is first-hand, rather than waiting decades before attempting to build up a picture of the way they worked:

In November 1971 one of the best known and longest established factories in the west end of Newcastle [upon Tyne] finally closed down its trading operations. Known locally as Richardson's Leather Works, it had by that time become a small and relatively insignificant part of a large multinational company.

Several years later, at a discussion session held by the Elswick Local History Group, stories about the factory and its closure began to emerge from a number of the redundant workers. It soon became apparent that they not only had an interesting story to tell, but also that they could help us understand something about changes in industrial practice over the years, about the vitality of social life in a tight-knit working class community, and they could also give us some knowledge of those factors which control the working lives of local people, and which have helped to create so much unemployment in the west end. So it was that at two subsequent meetings of the History Group the ex-workers recounted their experiences to fellow-members...:

The total workforce employed there in the early years was approximately one hundred and eighty.... The workers came mostly from Shumac Street, Water Street and Crucible Place which were adjacent to the factory. There were generations of families – grandfathers, fathers and some of their women folk worked in the factory. It was a closed shop. That is, you were unlikely to get a job there unless you knew someone that worked there. Nearly everyone who lived in the houses, which were owned by Richardsons, also worked in the factory.

When you had your tea breaks, one in the morning and one in the afternoon.... if you lived in the factory houses you were free to go home for your teabreak....

You saw people come and go but the majority worked there quite a number of years.... I have not known anyone leaving to work elsewhere till after the second world war. In 1954 those who had thirty years or more service got a gold watch given, presented by the directors, one of the Richardsons. I'd been there 34 years then and there were about thirty five people roughly got a gold watch.[6]

Richardson's Leather Works: The Workers' Story portrays a harmonious community, but it would be wrong to build up a romantic picture on such evidence instead of finding out what life was really like. The paternalism that went with family firms was not always welcomed by employees, at least some of whom felt that a gold watch was a poor compensation for the interference in day-to-day life that it often involved. Studying a community should not begin with the assumption that all the old-style ones were good or that they were all similar, sharing values that are now offered up as stereotypes in innumerable novels and television programmes. Elswick people remembered that:

Strangers used to come and complain about the smell and some used to be sick but we never noticed it. You got used to it. The only time you seemed to notice it was if you had been on holiday or off for a day or two and you came back and then you could smell it....

At night time, before I went home I used to set two cages for rats which caught them alive. They got in and they couldn't get out. I've seen six in a cage. Mr John Richardson used to bring his fox terrier into work and he would take the cages down to where there was an empty pit in the factory. He'd put the plug in the bung hole and he would put his terrier in. Then he would put the rats in and he would see how many rats the dog could kill in a certain time....

Anthrax was a very bad thing... there was one fatal case that I know of – a man called Corless and he was in the lime department. Some of the hides used to come from the Middle and Far East. They were dried out in the sun and they were the most dangerous ones because the edges of the skins were quite hard and horny and you could get a cut in your skin and the dust was a hazard. Now this chap they didn't know what he had until quite a few days when he was in hospital, and it was too late, and apparently it had affected his stomach and he'd been breathing the dust of the hair because the hair was still on them.[7]

The last study is a short one that grew naturally out of its own locality, but the most ambitious projects of this type can end up as thick books and attract national attention. Ronald Blythe's *Akenfield: Portrait of an English Village* (1969), to take one obvious example, made the story of a Suffolk village into a national best seller. Ronald Blythe presented it as a straightforward oral history, though with all names changed. In the introduction he produced a potted history complete with quotations from Domesday Book, together with quite elaborate modern statistics to show the nature of its farming. The main bulk of the book consists of statements from named people, varying from less than a page to ten pages or so. The memories of Horry Rose, the village saddler, are typical:

I lost my father when I was nine, so I had to think about work. In those days families didn't have money and boys hurried to work as early as they could so they could earn something. I thought I would be a harness-maker. There was this saddler's shop, you see, right in front of our cottage and a new plate glass window had been fixed over the small panes of the old window, so you saw the saddlers at work in the lamplight behind the double window. The scene took my eye. I used to long to be inside the window and working away there with the men. It all looked so peaceful and secure. When I was 12½ I forced myself to go inside and talk to the owner, Mr Peterson – Knacker Peterson was what this gentleman was called – and I told him how I had watched him at work and how I would like to be like him. He listened and then said, 'Very well, I'll take you on. I will give you sixpence a week.'

I wasn't a bound apprentice. I worked a four-year apprenticeship and then one year as an improver. I worked from seven till seven

Plate 2.1 Marsall Wilkinson, a saddler of Gomersal, in the Spen Valley in West Yorkshire, at work in the interwar years. He did a certain amount of trade with farmers, most of it repair work on decrepit harness, but this was a textile area and a considerable number of horses were kept by the mills. He also got a lot of work repairing the belting that drove the machinery in the mills, for his aim was to make a living, and not to conform to rural stereotypes of craftwork. This drawing was done by Jeff Heald, of Heckmondwike, while working on a museum exhibition as part of the Spen Valley Local History Survey in 1983–4, an employment scheme funded by the Manpower Services Commission. It was done on the basis of descriptions by Mr Wilkinson of his workshop, which was then just a shell, and he was delighted by the result.

each day and after I became fourteen I got 1s. a week. The war had just started and there was a lot to do, and soon the old gentleman was giving me eighteen-pence a week. Two saddlers were called up and that left only the foreman and myself, which meant I had to do man's work. So my wages rose to 5s. – which wasn't man's money. My mother said, 'Well you can't help it; you've got to honour the arrangement and put up with it.' It was never a very highly paid job for anybody. A journeyman got £1 a week and the foreman a shilling extra. The old gentleman didn't die a rich man, but he had his satisfactions. After you had got a job you thought less about what you were paid for it than you did in perfecting what you had to do. No matter how many times a young craftsman did his work badly, his boss could afford to say, 'Do that again.' Time was money but such small money made no difference. We had to 'honour bargains' – it was a religious law amongst the tradesmen.... We had our customers for life. I will say this for the Suffolk farmers, that if you gave them a good deal, they'd stay by you for always. We lived by loyalty.[8]

A quotation from *The Guardian* soon appeared opposite the contents page: 'A hundred years from now, anyone wanting to know how things were on the land in 1969 will turn more profitably to *Akenfield*... than to a sheaf of anaemically professional social surveys.'[9] The writer evidently believed Ronald Blythe's role was only that of collector and organiser, but doubts were soon expressed about the strict authenticity of the extracts, and even about the existence of the village itself. It turned out to be a composite of several communities, and that extracts had been reworked rather than edited. This is not to say that the end result may not be a solid portrait of an average village near Ipswich, but it is not the oral history it purported to be. As long as this is borne in mind, it remains an enjoyable, worthwhile read that can cast a great deal of light on the functioning of a real economic system as well as 'a way of life'. Horry Rose's testimony, for instance, covers attitudes to work, ways of selecting careers, the structure of traditional businesses, the apprenticeship system and more besides and there is no reason to doubt its accuracy.

It must be remembered that saddlers made no money out of being quaint or old-fashioned for the sake of it, and they supplied a vital service to farmers and to the wider rural community. The way they operated had evolved as the most practical way of earning a living in this situation. It was not an unchanging trade, either, for an ever-increasing use of horses had been a crucial part of enormous increases in farming productivity over the two centuries before this saddler's time, and the harness that enabled them to work effectively was subject to continuous development. Such memories help to unravel how trades that had apparently not been revolutionised by the factory system could still contribute to change, rather than simply drag out an existence as relics. Saddlery is, however, a good example of learning not to jump to conclusions about lack of factory methods, for the village craftsman actually relied totally on the supply of the wood and metal parts necessary to his craft from factories in Walsall. We can still agree that *The Guardian's* future researcher will find that *Akenfield* puts the humanity into the study of the early twentieth-century countryside, but it must be used in conjunction with more verifiable, even if more anaemic, material.

In contrast to this, Melvyn Bragg says unequivocally of *Speak for England*, that 'everything quoted in this book is directly quoted and, as far as is humanly possible, accurately quoted from the person stated. No lines are switched from one person to another for effect. No lines

are added by me'.[10] This is a study of his home town, Wigton, in Cumbria today but part of Cumberland before 1974. If it did not achieve the same fame, and notoriety, as *Akenfield,* it is arguably a better example of what can be achieved in oral history terms. He believes that it can tell us about more than one community:

> If we want a new start we must look to the past. The present is too occupied, the future too obscure.
> I believe this to be true, both for countries and for individuals. When my first wife died I found one of the courses of action I eventually took was to bring our daughter back to the place where I was born.... While we were there I began working on this book which reaches back in order to go forward as I did. I began to interview people, make notes, find out about life this century as experienced by the people of that district. As the number of interviews grew over the next two or three years I saw that the material was not so much a cross-section of local history as a representative record of English life during this century.[11]

Parallels to the Elswick study are clear, though its scale was much smaller, for it aimed to show ordinary people that their own area had a history, and one that was worth telling, something that conventional history teaching never conveyed until quite recently. In these times of massive redundancies and the wholesale scrapping of skills that once provided secure livelihoods for hundreds or thousands of families, there is a real risk that communities and towns can lose faith in themselves because the outside world values them so little and rejects them so continuously. Places like Elswick formed the backbone of the manufacturing economy before the war, but they are not beautiful, and their inhabitants are well used to the hostile, uninterested, or condescending attitudes of outsiders. As long as the saying that 'muck means brass' held true, they could cope with such attitudes, but when all that is left is the muck, it is hard to retain your pride. The destruction of town centres over the last few decades seems to me a symptom of this loss of faith in past certainties, with no real alternative

---

Plate 2.2 The Clarence Works of Hampson and Scott, wholesale saddlery manufacturers of Walsall, established 1794, as they proudly boasted on the trade catalogue from which this illustration comes. It is undated, but internal evidence suggests an Edwardian date. The scenes here are a graphic reminder that saddlers like Horry Rose were just one part of a complex industry and not isolated and self-sufficient, as they are usually portrayed. He would have relied on a firm of this sort, perhaps even used a copy of this catalogue, to supply his tools, the metal fittings for the harness, and even the wooden structures onto which saddles were built.

taking its place, just a desire to seek renewal through the generally accepted version of modernity that property developers were offering. There is no need to romanticise towns that were often shabby and in desperate need of some redevelopment to see that the course chosen has all too frequently thrown out the baby with the bathwater. Local pride is essential to making the most of what a locality has to offer, and the return of interest in local building styles, even in town centres, is a very hopeful sign. Oral history can record how people felt about their towns, villages, and neighbourhoods, and search for the things that made them more human places, despite all the obvious disadvantages that had to be remedied. It can show an interest and thereby help to reinstate a feeling that development should be organic, building on the past rather than bulldozing it out of existence.

Melvyn Bragg's claim that Wigton's history had more than a local significance rests on the same basis as the use of 'typical' life stories, for it had an uninterrupted history as a country market town, yet it also had industry. It was large enough to have real urban characteristics, it had people living in it from every layer of the class system, and the farming round about was mixed in its nature, so he believed that it could indeed 'speak for England'. Whether any one place can really span enough of our great regional divergences to stand for all of them is highly debatable, but Wigton can probably do the job as well as any, as Elizabeth Armstrong illustrated when she recalled her own family:

> We were really part country and part town. We knew about the farming as well as mining. My brothers went into farm service first and finished up mining when they got married. They went into farm service first because there was no room at home for sleeping accommodation and such as that, and I think it was the easiest way to get into any job and a bed. Same as myself when I left school at fourteen I had to get away. I was fourteen one week and I was in service the next week. Three pounds for the half year. I went to a little place called East End at Hayton, the other side of Aspatria....
>
> I had quite a nice room at my first place. I've never really had a bad bedroom. It's been fairly decent and of course cold in winter and red hot in summer. There was just one farmer that we didn't have our meals with, and they sat at one end of the kitchen and we sat at the other. I sat with the farm lads and they sat up at the other end, and that was when I was at Westfield House.[12]

Joseph Graham's reminiscences of the street-life of his childhood in the 1940s show its urban institutions and habits:

> In those days homes were so small you had to sort of get outside or your mother would chuck you out anyway and say, Oh away and play. Or you wanted to be out of the way in case you got a job.... My

mother would say to me, Go to the Co-operative for the rations. You went once a week – everything was once a week in those days – you didn't go in for dribs and drabs. You were organised. You would stand in the Co-operative from maybe nine o'clock and not come out till half past twelve, with two big bags full of groceries. And all the grown-ups that came in, mainly women, they would get served before you....

We used to play games like 'You can't cross the golden river'. Now hoppie was another game – that was a popular game, hopscotch, as they called it in Scotland.... But I think the most popular game with us was chessy. One boy chasing all the others: had to touch them to catch them and enrol them. Tiggy was a good game but chessy... it's one, two, three on the head. You would be a big gang of lads and you would all stand in a line and you would have a dip, as all games did, to find out who was it.... But chessy was a game where you could run and use a bit of craft, slyness, because you would set off maybe twenty or thirty kids. They would disappear and muggins would be left counting; they all got away... hiding his face and counting up to a hundred. You'd be all round the streets – you know what the streets were like in Wigton; Church Street, Market Hill, Water Street; there were all sorts of twisty lanes and cul de sacs....

We used to run plays in the old houses in Water Street that were condemned and empty. We used to put plays on and things like that.... We had a heck of a time in those old houses.[13]

To integrate the personal side of oral history with the conclusions it supports, chapters alternate between one person's testimony and wider themes, showing how Wigton has changed and developed, literally within living memory. Combining autobiographical pieces makes them more than personal views, yet keeps the intimacy that is their great strength. Life stories do not need to be complete, nor to stand alone, and as the most direct way to work with reminiscences, they have much to recommend them. The life story is not a soft option and some oral historians feel it is the most genuine form, precisely because there has been so little interference.

NOTES AND REFERENCES

1. J. McCrindle and S. Rowbotham, 1977, *Dutiful Daughters*, Allen Lane, p.1.
2. *Ibid.*, p.1.
3. *Ibid.*, pp.119–20.
4. *Ibid.*, pp. 165–6.
5. T. Rosengarten, 1974, *All God's Dangers*, Avon, pp. 320–3.
6. Elswick Local History Group, 1985, *Richardson's Leather Works:*

The Worker's Story, Elswick Local History Group, Newcastle, p.1.

7. *Ibid.,* p.18.

8. R. Blythe, 1969, *Akenfield: Portrait of an English Village,* Allen Lane, pp. 158–9.

9. *Ibid.,* opposite title page.

10. M. Bragg, 1976, *Speak for England,* Secker and Warburg, p. 4.

11. *Ibid.,* p. 1.

12. *Ibid.,* p. 40.

13. *Ibid.,* pp. 462–3.

CHAPTER THREE

Lifestyles and Language

Perhaps the oldest strand in oral history in this country is the study of the social bonds that tie people together in traditional communities and contribute to their sense of identity, that is, folklore or popular culture. Collectors often need a wider scale than a village or locality can provide, and some study just one aspect, such as folk dance, over a very wide area. This began in a serious manner in the late nineteenth century, when most counties were the subject of at least one volume such as Mrs Elizabeth Gutch's *Examples of Printed Folk-lore Concerning the East Riding of Yorkshire* (1911). They concentrate on the collection and preservation of material such as proverbs and sayings, folk songs, legends and folk tales, and public performances and festivals. Such work sprang out of a conviction that, by talking to old country folk, it was possible to practise the cultural equivalent of archaeology. Contact with Africa and Asia had aroused awareness of the huge variety that existed in human culture, and evolutionary theory had provided a framework whereby these could be seen as more or less advanced rather than just different. 'Primitive' societies could therefore provide information on the stages most others had left behind, and especially on the evolution of religious belief. This was applied at home as well, for it was widely believed by the educated that cultural innovations always began in the higher echelons of society, and spread slowly down through emulation. The poor therefore preserved the remnants of a culture that the others had discarded, but were only of interest as unwitting conduits for information from the past. They were not felt to have the ability to play an active role in understanding what they passed on. Folk songs, folk tales, customs, and beliefs were all collected on this basis.

Such attitudes have now largely vanished and there is still an active interest in this type of work, especially in the Celtic countries, where it has always had strong claims to support as a defence against an English cultural hegemony to match political control. In England it exists today largely for its own sake, for as an academic field of study it survives in only a handful of places, and this comes through in works like *The National Trust Guide to the Traditional Customs of Britain* (1985), edited by Brian Shuel. The interest lies in customs and beliefs that clearly stand out as archaic, especially the visible ones such as processions and dances. It is worth looking back at the Victorian and, Edwardian folklore surveys of your area. These vary in quality and though some are extremely valuable as the only records of popular culture that exist, most show how limited this approach is in understanding the societies that generated such activities, for they are essentially lists of events and beliefs, with no real context. The largest compilation of this type is *British Calendar Customs (1936–41),* which, as the name implies, covers those aspects of popular tradition linked to specific dates or seasons. Mere collection is like seeing archaeology as being about the accumulation of things dug up out of the ground, whereas archaeologists have long since learned that any find must be meticulously mapped before removal to show how it lay in relation to everything else on the site, and which time layer it was in. Similarly, a custom stripped of its place in society is more or less meaningless to anyone but the finder. In so far as customs carry us back to the past, it is the villagers' own, and we should also be asking what function that survival plays today. As with archaeology, those interested in folklore have had to move on and develop their methods.

George Ewart Evans stands out as an oral historian who has promoted a sensible and yet still fascinating approach to folklore studies in recent times. His most obviously folkloristic find related to the skills of farm horsemen in East Anglia, and was first revealed in *The Horse in the Furrow*:

> The management of his horses was a skill in which most of the old horsemen took a great pride.... The ability to control a horse undoubtedly ran in families, and involved – as well as the handing down of secrets – the careful schooling of the son by the father, both by means of precept and direct example.... Yet in the folklore of the countryside it is not the straight-forward methods of training that are most noteworthy but the semi-magical control over horses said to have been possessed by a class of men known in many areas – but not, as far as is known, in Suffolk – as the 'whisperers'. They are so called from their alleged practice of whispering a few ritual and magic words to the horse they wish to control....
> There was a class of horse charmers known in the Ely and

Peterborough districts ... as *Toadmen*. A *toadman* was accounted a kind of witch.... [and] to obtain the power of the frog's bone one had to perform the following ritual: 'You get a frog and take it to a running stream at midnight, but before this you have killed it and pounded it up. You throw it into the water and some of it will flow downstream, but a part of it – a bone – will float upstream. This is the part you have to keep.'... Possession of the frog's bone was believed to give a horseman absolute power over the most intractable horse that came into his care.[1]

A horseman pointed out that 'the frog's boon was the same shape as the frog in a horse's hoof.'[2] The *frog* is a fleshy pad on the horse's sole that is pressed on the ground as the horse puts its foot down. It acts as a pump to assist the circulation of blood back up its long legs, so damage to the frog can cripple the horse. Similarity of shape is held to give the frog's bone an affinity to the frog, and hence to affect the horse's ability to move about. The control of one thing by another that is similar in shape is a familiar principle in folk beliefs, and the principle that 'like controls like' underlies homeopathy today. We seem therefore to be firmly in a world of strange rituals and magical powers at this point, and the mystery of the powers of these masterful horsemen could be explained as just a matter of the extra confidence they derived from their belief in their charm, especially as 'it is said that no animal can sense better than a horse any nervous tension in a person who is approaching him. Nervous tension is rightly interpreted as fear by the horse; and fear begets fear and trouble is bound to follow'.[3]

Simple reinforcement of the horseman's confidence could not, however, explain everything and he was convinced that 'there was very much more to the frog's bone than this – at least as it was used by horsemen, certain horsemen, here in Suffolk.'[4] A farmer told him, for instance, 'I seen one of 'em put a stick up in a field in front of his pair of horses, and they wouldn't budge from where they were for anybody. The horseman could go off to Ipswich and they'd still be there when he came back'.[5] Another man suggested that this kind of skill had practical uses besides showing off, given the precariousness of employment on Suffolk farms before the Second World War, when his contributors were working:

They had about a hundred horses at ... Hall the time I'm telling you about. A man who was working there got wrong with 'em over something or other – I don't know what happened. Anyhow he got the sack. But thet night he went and did something to the horses. Next day not one on 'em would go near the harness. No one could do anything with 'em. In the end they had to fetch that man back for him to put it right. No one ever knew how he did it. He went in and locked the stable doors. But not long afterwards they harnessed the

> horses and they came out as if nothing had happened....
> I reckon the fellow who got the sack didn't do anything to the horses. He put something on the harness, you ma' depend.[6]

The horsemen involved, in other words, were not just using a magical amulet, but also substances that could be smeared on sticks, door frames, or harness. Many horsemen believed that horses were extremely sensitive to smell – far more so than most people realised – and it seemed likely that something was being applied which horses found intolerable, even though people could not detect anything. They would not wear the tainted harness or pass through a treated door. The folkloric elements acted as distractions to draw attention away from the real basis of what the horsemen were doing. We do not have to say that the horsemen themselves saw the frog's bone as a stage magician's prop, for they probably believed that every part of the ritual was essential for success. The magical suggestions undoubtedly served both to stop outsiders from looking for a more material explanation, and made the horsemen feel special, which made them more confident horsemen.

This interweaving of many different functions is very typical of the complexity of folk cultures, and how we as collectors disentangle the beliefs that underlie discoveries like these is what separates out good practice from bad. Such analysis is not separate from collecting, but determines the course an investigation takes, for had Evans merely been seeking to make a list of curious practices, he would have stopped with the frog's bone. He stressed, in fact, his belief that 'it is almost useless for a folklorist to ask the direct question – at least in a cold and purely 'informative' atmosphere. The real information comes of its own accord, is nourished by a kind of involuntary flow between the questioner and the questioned; and when the time is ripe it comes unannounced'.[7] The real discoveries lie in establishing what made and makes people value and maintain particular customs or beliefs. We should fit them into a framework of attitudes and general beliefs, for however quaint they may appear now, however out of touch with the realities of ordinary life, customs only evolved because they once did a job that the community felt was worth doing. This job may have changed with the years, and a custom may end up valued as a link back to a previous era when its original reason for existence is all but forgotten, but even this tells us something about the way that society looks on itself. It implies a dissatisfaction with the present that is worth investigating seriously.

Quaintness is a very dangerous standard to use for selecting themes to follow up. Not all horsemen sought control of horses through magic, for instance, and Thomas Davidson has showed that an exclusive and secretive society of horsemen seems to have existed nationally in 'The Horseman's Word', *Gwerin,* 1 (1956–7). They served an elite who developed their abilities by mutual assistance. This could stand quite apart from the authentic folk traditions concerning the control of horses like those Evans uncovered, or it could be mixed up with them. I was told about it by Mr Orr from Kirkcudbrightshire and he saw it as a specialised friendly society, with no folkloristic overtones. However, the men involved still used their skills to baffle outsiders. He recalled one occasion when a member, Bob Jack, was asked to lead a stallion at Crieff in the annual parade held to display the animals to farmers. It was notorious and had run amok the year before, but:

> they reckoned this horse come out onto the street at Crieff and ... he was just like a gentleman. And there was some old farmer that knew this Jack, 'By,' he says, 'You've made a good job of him,' he says, 'what did you do to him?'
>
> He says, 'I've done nothing to him.' He says, 'I just whispered in his ear this morning to be a good fellow'.... He was a, well, he was the best – there were two that I knew but he was the best of the two. I remember and all he was leading [stallions for] Montgomery this year and he was leading in Fife and he'd gotten trampled on, and by God he had a bad foot – he was off about three weeks and.... Montgomery sent me up to Fife to go with this horse until he got better. So I was up, I was up very near a month and Bob came back to work and you know in Fife they were very, very big farms, arable farms, three and four and five and six pair of horses working on them.... Before I went home, this farm we were staying at, I think there was seven pair on it and you know, at night, after you'd finished, there was a seat along outside the stable in the summertime and a lot of young lads that was working the horses they were all sitting telling such yarns, what they could do with this horse and what they could do – and I was just sitting listening, like. Bob Jack was sitting. Oh, it went on for a good bit.
>
> 'By,' he said, 'you fellers can tell some yarns, but,' he says, 'I'm gonna let you see something.' And this yard was in a square and you'd just the one entrance out and his horse was in a box there and he went out across and he opened the door and let his horse out wi' nothing on. No bridle. And he had him walking around the *brechan.* And he made him lie down. And he sat on him. Then told him to get up and get back into the box. I was like the rest of the fellers, I went to this entrance out, I thought the horse was going to go out the entrance , but, mind, I was like the rest of the lads, I was standing with my mouth wide open. I was wondering what was going to happen. But he was a *sworn-in* horseman, by, he was clever.
>
> *It was a bit of a secret society wasn't it?*
>
> It was, yes, it was. Oh, they wouldn't tell you anything.... They

reckoned that if one of these sworn-in horsemen like, if they tackle a horse and the horse gets the better of them, they reckon there's no other body need have a go at them. (Beamish Tape 2/1)

The only men I met from East Yorkshire who claimed these kinds of skills made no mention of either society or folklore. This may be because there were actually very few career horsemen in the county. The head horseman was the foreman, who had a general responsibility not only for the horses and the horselads, but also for the married farm labourers who did all the jobs that did not involve horses. On a normal day the foreman had too much to do as a supervisor to get personally involved with the horses, and his skills showed mostly in abnormal times, such as when a horse was ill, or when a mare was due to foal, and in the training of young horses. I discovered no folk beliefs surrounding the care of the horses, and I soon ceased asking about it. Farm horselads were proud of their skills in a straightforward practical way and rarely shared them with others, but there was no mystique about the tricks they used. Perhaps, unlike George Ewart Evans, I was unable to create the right atmosphere for this sort of recollection to surface, but it is suggestive that Mrs Gutch noted similar difficulties in her folklore volume on the county in the Edwardian period. This does not mean that the county had no traditional culture of its own, for its farm servant system is clear proof to the contrary. The county's farming was up to date, however, and hiring was still an integral part of a county-wide and evidently practical way of organising work on farms before the 1930s. It was therefore deemed not to be part of folklore, except for a handful of customs and events associated with it.

Hiring servants caused farmers many inconveniences that could have been avoided had they all been treated as labourers, and since their wage was fixed whatever happened during the year, there was a risk that the farmers might not get sufficient work out of them to justify it. The system survived not because it was customary but because farmers still found it useful to have a pool of reliable and fully-committed labour to perform the essential routine horsework. Servants were also hired in Scotland, but Bob Jack was a stallion leader, not a horselad or foreman, so he had an incentive to join a society. Horselads could not be sacked unless they broke their year's contract, but he could, and the horses with which he was dealing regularly went out in public as well as being the most difficult of all to handle. The Scottish Lowlands were like the East Riding in that a relative labour shortage encouraged both the hiring of farm servants and high farm wages, and we must always be wary of ascribing something that seems unique to local factors when in fact it is part of a more general pattern. When we look at several versions of the servant system together, we have a better chance of understanding what were its essential elements, despite the differences between individual examples. In Suffolk, where servants had not been needed or hired since the early nineteenth century, there is no question that surrounding their abilities with mystery served a real purpose for horsemen: 'the set-up on some of the farms during these years... was anything but idyllic; and the description that they gave of the rivalry, back-biting and sometimes open malice that existed, even among the men themselves, should be taken into account when there is any impulse to depict the countryside under the old order as a haven of peace and rural contentment.'[8]

By the twentieth century most of the inhabitants of villages had lost all possibility of making their own living from the land, or even of contributing to it. They had to have wages and they became no more than a pool of labour from which the large farmers could draw as needed, not fellow members of a community. The separation between employers and employees was greatest in the south of England where there were consistently far too many men for the work that needed to be done. As the century progressed, the oversupply of labour lessened, but never to the point where farmers there really had to look on labour as most industrial employers did – as an expensive commodity on which to economise. Wages remained extremely low, even for skilled men, such as shepherds like Liney Riches whom we looked at earlier, and whereas a farm labourer in the East Riding in 1902 received 19s 2d per week, in Suffolk the figure was only 15s 6d. There was no longer any perceived need among employers to maintain the old social obligations that had tied communities together. Those that survived were mostly just reminders of the past, quaint and overtly functionless, while some were artificially recreated to tie the new society together in a mould seen as more suited to the new realities. James Obelkevitch's account of how the modern harvest festival evolved in Lincolnshire in the nineteenth century accords very well with the descriptions I was given from the East Riding, and his whole book *Religion and Rural Society: South Lindsey, 1825–75* is well worth reading as an account of the rebuilding of a culture in this period and as a cautionary note on the real antiquity of customs and beliefs. He drew heavily on folklore for this book and it shows the value that this material has when sensitively handled.

Everyone is a part of some culture, and, when we look more closely, all regional or national cultures turn out to be composed of smaller sub-cultures when we look more closely. There is no such thing as a real cultural boundary cutting off neighbours from each other. One aspect of a region's culture may seem unique, another will clearly ally it with one set of neighbours, while another will tie it just as clearly to those on the opposite side. They may even suggest links with distant areas, missing out neighbours. Thus, even though farm servants were hired throughout the north of England, most of it was given over to pasture and small farms, and so had no need for the large groups of servants who characterised the East Riding. Lowland Scotland, on the other hand, was economically similar and this finds echoes in its use of servants. Such links are more important than differences, for cultures are like rainbow colours, identifiable but not distinct. They shade off into each other in all directions, and they also change, no matter how static they may seem to us today. Suffolk horsemen did not invent the story of the frog's bone because the East Anglian labour market was overstocked, but it was, and this was a clear result of the earlier collapse of the local textile industry, which had provided so much employment in the seventeenth and early eighteenth centuries before industrialisation removed it to northern textile mills. Horsemen as a group constantly and unconsciously reworked existing beliefs into a new form suited to the society of the day.

Towns were generally regarded by the early folklorists as unproductive places in which to collect, because this was where change was concentrated. The gathering together of migrants from many districts, or even countries, seemed bound to produce a mixture of cultures that rendered the archaeological approach to collecting pointless, and there was no interest in the new cultural patterns that were growing up. Distrust and fear of this process of change was often, in fact, the root of the desire to preserve the ways of the countryside. Marmaduke Morris' life of William Blades shows perfectly this harking back to a purer, better life that is about to vanish forever:

> All nervous complaints appear to be much more prevalent than they were in early Victorian days; this no doubt is due to the high pressure under which we now live; rapid motion and excitement of all kinds.... Village life in the middle of the last century was very different from what it is at this day when so many of our countryfolk are attracted to the towns....
>
> Farm life sixty years ago was anything but monotonous. It was infinitely varied – in fact no two days were alike; and what saved the men and lads from any feeling of dullness was the fact that they all took a vast deal more interest in their work than is the case at this day [1928]. Now all work is done in a more perfunctory manner, simply as a means for earning, with as little trouble as possible, so much money, most of which is quickly spent. At the end of each day the

lads get on their bicycles and hurry off to the nearest town, where
they spend their time and their money in amusements of various
kinds.[9]

It is not my purpose to poke fun, hence my use of a quotation rather
than paraphrasing and possibly misrepresenting his words. It was
certainly true that farm servants were changing their lives as he
indicates, but there was no need to associate this change with moral
decay. In 1928 the East Riding farm servant system was under strain,
since it threatened to trap lads of the rural areas in an anachronistic
lifestyle that few shared or even understood, and its survival depended
on adaptation to keep the system acceptable, not on the rejection of
change. Bicycles did bring mobility, and even the limited attractions of
East Riding country market towns did lead to changes in leisure habits.
Indeed, it is not going too far to say that they were part of a realisation
that leisure could exist on workdays, instead of being separated out
into special times set apart from work, as it traditionally had been. But
most lads still worked much longer hours than any normal job required
and they remained closely involved with their work by any
contemporary standards. Outside influences could not have been kept
out, and if that generation had really broken entirely with the past, I
could not have achieved what I did, for this was the generation to
whom I talked most. From the perspective of today, the changes that
had occurred by 1928 seem slight.

G.K. Nelson recently remarked in the introduction to his book *To
be a Farmer's Boy,* which consists of recollections of the countryside
between the wars, that 'my grandfather had more in common with a
British peasant at the time of the Roman occupation than with a
farmworker of the present day. The inter-war period was the last
period in which it was possible to experience a truly rural style of life in
England, a period in which machines were still marginal and most
work was carried out by hand or with the assistance of horses.'[10] There
is an immediacy about such statements that appeals to our sense of
living through rapid change, but any glance at the rural society of
Roman Britain will show that technology, cropping, methods of
working, and the nature of rural society itself were really so different
that this is simply ludicrous. This concept of irretrievable loss is
expressed in every generation throughout history, for the changes of
our time stand in stark relief, whereas all others shade off into the
distance and are assumed to be unimportant by contrast. The interest
we feel in other cultures, or in variants of our own, should stem from a
desire to understand them in their own right, taken on their own terms.

This means being prepared to look in unorthodox places, such as the children's customs and games from Wigton recalled by Joseph Graham. Children are seen as the future, not the past, and they are continually changing their interests and their behaviour as they grow up, so a more unlikely population than city school children would be hard to imagine as a source for folklore. In fact, Iona and Peter Opie stated in 1959 in the preface to their monumental study *The Lore and Language of Schoolchildren* that,

> The curious lore passing between children aged about 6–14, which today holds in its spell some 7 million inhabitants of this island, continues to be almost unnoticed by the other six-sevenths of the population.... The generally held opinion, both inside and outside academic circles, was that children no longer cherished their traditional lore. We were told that the young had lost the power of entertaining themselves; that the cinema, the wireless, and the television had become the focus of their attention; and that we had started our investigation fifty years too late.
>
> The study which comes the nearest to being a predecessor to the present work is Norman Douglas's 'breathless catalogue' of *London Street Games* published in 1916.... The reason he made his catalogue, he said, was to see whether the next lot of children knew even the names of the street sports he recorded. So it may be as well to report straight away that, of the 137 child-chants and fragments of chants which Norman Douglas heard in the streets the other side of two world wars, more than 78% (108 verses to be precise) are still being chanted by youngsters today....
>
> The modern schoolchild, when out of sight and on his own, appears to be rich in language, well-versed in custom, a respecter of the details of his own code, and a practising authority on traditional self-amusements.[11]

The Opies collected in every type of state school in every part of mainland Britain and Ireland, and the results have been fascinating scholars and ordinary people ever since. It could be taken as a catalogue of curiosities, but play is now widely recognised as having an educational purpose. Children are learning to socialise with each other and learning roles that they will play later in life, most notably those of male and female. They copy adult behaviour, and fairness, rules, and power structures are concepts with which all children rapidly become familiar, whether they accept them or reject them:

> The children frequently mention spoil-sports as being the people they most dislike. 'When playing games', says a 9-year-old in Dovenby, Cumberland, 'if one of the girls falls out we shout sulky puss or spoil sport or Baby baby bunting Daddy's gone a hunting for a rabbit skin to lap the baby in or Water works'....
>
> To a moaner who keeps whining 'Oh dear me!' Forfar children put the question, 'Fat's dear aboot you and dirt sae chaip?' A peevish

Plate 3.1   The school children of Thixendale in the East Riding of Yorkshire in ther late 1890s. Although we would initially think of such a group as too young to have acquired the sort of knowledge in which an oral historian would be interested, they would, in fact, have an enormous repertoire of traditional games, songs, chants, and so on, and would be actively involved in passing them down from the eldest to the youngest, selecting and adapting where something no longer seemed appropriate.

person is referred to as a Cross-patch, Old Grousey or Grumpy, Misery, Mardy-baby, Peevy, Sourpuss, or Sulky Sue....

One who blabs to a teacher or to a senior is a 'blabber-mouth', 'rotten sneak', 'dirty tell tale tit'. Young children, in particular, will hound him (as we have witnessed) until he is almost pulp, a quivering sobbing heap having to bear the double agony of blows and reiterated refrain:
'Tell tale tit,
Your Tongue shall be slit,
And all the dogs in the town
Shall have a little bit,'

A threat which has been stinging in the ears of blabbers for more than 200 years....

In Ecclesfield an abusive term for a bully is 'Ichabod'. In Enfield.... the following account [shows] how to deal with a bully....

'The victim [ie the bully] is captured and tied to an object consisting of two ashen poles. The bully is then dragged up a very bumpy hill to shake him about. He is then untied and hung upside down from a tree by his feet for a few minutes until he begs for mercy. The captors then hoist him down and fight him until he says will leave us alone. This is done to every bully in our village.'[12]

Oral History

It is no accident that the first classic folk-tale collections, by Andersen and the Grimms, are seen by the general public as children's stories, for children often inherit fragments of adult culture from times gone by. The survival of particular nursery rhymes is heavily influenced by adults, but the bulk of childhood culture is the children's own affair and nothing can stop an irrelevant game or chant being discarded, as many are. Change and survival are two sides of the same coin. The Opies followed up *Lore and Language* in the 1960s with a comparable survey of games and play which was published as *Children's Games in Street and Playground*. It would be well worthwhile adding to these now, three decades on, to see what changes have occurred since, as streets have become too full of traffic to play in as of old, and video games have added another rival for children's attention. If, however, it did turn out that change is speeding up, it would be important not to equate this purely with loss. Children are being prepared, and are preparing themselves, for a different world, and therefore must do some things differently.

Another seeming paradox in folklore collection is that the best preservers of culture in the frozen state that was taken as normal are often not those who stay at home but migrants to foreign parts. There are many immigrant communities in America that preserve cultural traditions and even whole dialects lost in the homeland, such as the Amish of Lancaster County, Pennsylvania, who have recently become a favourite setting for film makers. Originally from Germany, they emigrated to follow a communal religious life and they reject all modern machinery, persevering as (highly successful) horse farmers. One of my contributors had had little contact with East Riding farming for decades before talking to me, but this meant that his memories were not influenced by later events, and provided a check on those of people who had lived through the decline of the system. In this country, Lancashire and London both retain clear regional accents despite massive nineteenth-century migratory flows, when thousands of Irish people in particular were drawn in: according to family tradition, my own great-grandmother could not speak English on her arrival. Lancashire shows the tenacity of a native culture when we consider how rapidly it became urbanised in this period, and it is already clear that more recent black additions to regional populations learn their English with a local accent. This does not necessarily mean assimilation, as we saw above, and it can produce something new. In Liverpool, many of the nineteenth-century changes were at their fiercest, and it now has an instantly recognisable accent of its own, unlike that of the surrounding towns, and an immensely strong culture.

The dynamics of how two or more traditions come together is itself a field of study with immense interest and importance today.

Accents and dialects inevitably attract attention in any oral project, and are an endless source of fascination. They have been studied on many levels, but linguistic technicalities are really only for experts and I would not venture to try my hand here. Where anyone can do useful work is in collecting words and expressions, and in the study of the way language is used. It is easy, however, to make this patronising in the extreme by refusing to see it as part of the real world. To praise a way of speaking as wonderful to hear, but to reject it as unacceptable in normal life, is to reduce those who speak that way to a sideshow. People are sensitive about the image they present and it should not be assumed that a contributor will naturally use a broad accent, or if they do not, that this means that they never speak in one. They often take their tone from the collector, and I soon realised that when I was being told a story that involved recalling a conversation, the words put in as speech commonly switched to dialect or became more heavily accented than the main body of the reminiscence. It must have seemed to contributors appropriate to slip into dialect at that point, whereas their own words to me were automatically closer to Standard English. The same is true of swearing: all my contributors clearly saw it as inappropriate for our sessions and so never used more than the mildest exclamations, even in remembered speech. Throughout my interviews I actually recorded very little strong dialect, or even strong accents. This description of corn harvesting from Mr Harper is a fair sample of the speech of those who had not moved outside the county:

> Well then, five or six of you. Three of you were one line, opening out by hand, right round a forty acre field or whatever acreage it was. And, I remember once, it was a real hot Saturday ... and me and t'box lad were tying up behind t'old labourer what was mowing, so I says to him, 'Let me have a go, Joe, to spell you'. 'Thoo can't mow'. Real blunt, you know ... When we gets ... our *ratch* finished, Tommy Owt was starting afront on us. He says, 'Let lad have a go, Joe, to ease you'.
> 'He can't mow'.
> He says, 'Let him have a go'.
> 'Well, all right'.
> I says, 'Sharpen her up, sharpen scythe up'. 'Cause two of you can't sharp alike. No. Not with a scythe nor any implement that has to be sharped with a whetstone or a *bullstone*. So he sharped her up. And I just did it for badness, I set off and I left 'em standing, I left 'em about sixty yards behind .... T'other chaps was on front and foreman feller ... he just says to his man what was behind him, waggoner and third lad, he says, 'Look at that bloody lad. By God', he says, 'can't he go'. (Tape 16/2)

This account contains many points of interest, even though no outsider should have much difficulty with it. There is the use of *thou* in its East Riding form as *thoo,* and the northern form of *the,* where it is sounded as *t'* or turned into a catch in the throat known as a glottal stop. There are also words like *ratch* and *bullstone,* and many grammatical variations from Standard English. The piece should not be considered in isolation, however: it is a description of something that was already archaic. The horse-drawn reaper or the reaper-binder had taken over most of the harvesting of corn in the early years of this century, but taking the first cut round the field, which is what *opening out* was, remained a problem. If a reaper had merely been pulled along, with the blade working behind the horses, they would have trampled the standing corn before the cutting blade reached it, so the blade was mounted to project out to one side. The horses could then walk over the cleared ground where the corn had already been cut. Lads still learned to use the scythe to cut the first swathe in a field to give the horses somewhere to walk. This included tying a sheaf up in the traditional manner, as Mr Johnson described: 'One man on t'scythe, another man went behind with ... a gathering rake and gathered it up, and then there was maybe a lad or two tying up behind'. (Tape 15/2) Mr Harper's account shows how opening out preserved the implement, the associated working methods, the smaller skills like proper sharpening, and the terminology of the job.

In the depression years between the wars, farmers decided that it was cheaper to trample the first swathe and come back to it at the end with the machine to get what they could. The scythe was then restricted to gardens and smallholdings, and the words associated with it are bound to vanish when the scythe finally goes out of use. Much dialect vocabulary was similarly technical, and only parts of it could be adapted to new operations. The dialect associated with horses coped with a gradual influx of new methods and tools, but the tractor was different because it came with its own ready-made vocabulary, much of it invented by the motor industry. The extent of vocabulary change will vary even in such situations, however, for in an industry where new recruits are taught their skills entirely by old hands, these will naturally adapt and pass along as many familiar terms as possible and youngsters will have no reason to reject them. Where tuition comes from educational institutions or books, it is outside terms that will predominate. While at university, I worked for several summers for our local council on a grass-cutting gang, and experience from farms on harvesting techniques like Mr Harper's was being handed down from men near retirement to teenagers even in this unlikely setting. One

Plate 3.2 Two men loading hay onto a waggon with pitchforks at Kilham, East Yorkshire, in the 1930s. The load is overhanging so far that the waggon sides are invisible, but done with skill, such a load will be perfectly stable. If it was simply heaped up much of it would slide off as soon as the waggon moved. Such skills are still useful today in farming and horticulture, though their importance has diminished a great deal.

small example was that an ordinary garden fork was commonly referred to as a *pikle,* which is the Lancashire dialect name for a pitchfork, the function for which we used them for. I learned how to use the fork to move astonishing quantities of cut grass, how to heap it neatly and securely, and how to make a load of grass in a trailer or waggon which would rise way above the sides, and overhang them, without toppling over when it was moved.

My area had many micro-dialects, which were noticeably much stronger among the nearby coal-mining communities that were then still plentiful than in the towns and villages that earned their living in some other way. Despite tremendous changes in technology and a high degree of formal instruction now given to new starters, most trainers in the coal industry are miners and because mining is so unlike other jobs, Standard English has made surprisingly little headway here. There was also a high degree of regional differentiation between dialects, due to the separateness of the individual coalfields, though with the collapse of mining employment and the mixing of miners from many areas into the few remaining pits, it will be interesting to see how much of linguistic distinctiveness is lost in the future. Dave Douglass, himself a miner, and himself decanted from the declining Durham coalfield into the then-thriving Yorkshire coalfield in the 1960s, wrote 'Pit Talk in County Durham', which appears in *Miners, Quarrymen and Saltworkers* based upon his own experiences. It is a striking piece of work in the way it shows language not as an isolated aspect of life but one that is fully integrated into it, with work terms entering the vocabulary of the wider community. Particularly interesting is the stress on development, not stasis:

> I had thought that the Durham pitman of the 1970s would have used much the same terminology as the Durham pitman of the 1840s; after all they were still down the same dark holes in the ground doing in essence the same filthy work. In effect many of the terms are the same, but their meanings have altered with changes underground, and the new mining methods. What has in fact changed in many cases is not the terms but the objects which they describe. They say a Durham pitman is a man of few words. If this is really so, it is not surprising that he was not prepared to let a perfectly good word go out of existence when there was a new object that needed a name.[13]

The very nature of dialect is much misunderstood, as well as the distinction between dialects and accents. Few people are free of preconceived ideas about this, and all there is space to do here is to raise some issues for consideration. An accent is a way of pronouncing words, whether dialect or standard, and as long as it is not extreme, it should be no real barrier to mutual understanding. It can be regional, ethnic, or class-based. Dialects are genuinely varying forms of a language with their own vocabulary and grammatical rules. The differences may be small, but they have to be there to justify calling a way of speaking a dialect and strength of accent has nothing to do with whether a particular area has a dialect of its own. All the words a dialect speaker uses are part of the dialect, not just those that vary from the standard, so individual dialects are not distinct ways of speaking but more or less overlapping ones. English has never been a unified language and this is why it is quite wrong to see any version as less correct than others: it is precisely the possession of rules of its own that makes a dialect worth studying.

Variant forms of any living language are constantly separating off, as American English has from British English, and others are simultaneously coalescing, as our own regional dialects mostly are at the moment. Changes in pronunciation and usage have been occurring as far back as the language can be traced, and while all have doubtless been deplored by some contemporaries, they are only accepted into

Plate 3.3 A carnival procession in Fryston, West Yorkshire in the 1950s with Fryston Colliery looming over the terraced houses. The village was isolated by rail lines and the river Aire, and its only reason for existing was the colliery. Today the mine has shut and most of the houses have been demolished. Such tight-knit communities often preserve distinctive accents, dialects, and cultures. They are tremendously productive places for anyone interested in popular culture to work, belying the idea that only in rural backwaters is there anything for folklorists to concern themselves with.

the language on a permanent basis if they fill a widespread need. Language is a tool we use to promote communication, and it responds constantly to our changing needs, so slang can be viewed as a sort of language laboratory where a never-ending series of experiments is run with new words. It is only necessary to think back over the past decade or so to see how few slang words really take root. How many of the wave of 1960s words, that we were then told were threatening the language, are in common use today? Even those that seem to sweep all before them for months or years mostly fall by the wayside in the long term because the majority of people never accept them, or tire of them.

In linguistic terms, all forms of English are dialects on an equal footing, including those that are socially preferred. A particular dialect will often flourish or decline according to how large and far-flung the group is within which good mutual understanding is necessary. In the mid-nineteenth century an East Riding farmworker lived most of his life within a circle of people who shared his strong local dialect, so that it did not inconvenience him to lack skills in the language of the upper classes. In so far as he met such people as an employee or in passing, a careful choice of the numerous words they had in common sufficed. Only rare closer contacts brought out the gulf between them. Mary Simpson, for instance, the daughter of the rector of Carnaby in the East Riding in the mid-nineteenth century, took it as her life's work to educate farm lads, as part of her efforts to convert them from Methodism to Anglicanism. She set up a night school, and sent off to London for teaching materials from the Society for the Propagation of Christian Knowledge. When they came they proved incomprehensible, as they probably would be to many today, for they used a very Latin-influenced English that many educated people admired at the time, but which has since largely been abandoned.

Neither the lads nor the written material were using 'correct' English, and the surprise of Mary Simpson at how wide the gulf was between the two shows how unaware most people were of it. It may be that the lads exaggerated their difficulties to get out of reading books that sound as dull as ditchwater, but Mary knew them well and would not have been easy to fool. Today it is much harder to maintain widely differing strands of a common language alongside each other, for there are now few places or jobs where there is no need for contact with the wider world. The history of Scots English is a good illustration of this. The Scottish Lowlands were conquered and settled by Anglo-Saxon invaders in the same way that England was and it is anachronistic to view Scottish English as fundamentally different from English English, or as a recent importation. As long as Scotland was independent, its own dialect, or at least the dialect of the capital, was the natural language of government, but after the union this became less and less true. Scottish English is, however, the one dialect of the family of English languages on these islands that has historically been accepted more as a rival to than a variant from Standard English, with its own literature and international acceptance. No-one could deny the standing of Robert Burns, whereas most dialect literature is for local consumption only.

The clear association of particular ways of speaking with social class has also intensified the pressure on accents and dialect over the last century in this country, yet the aristocracy traditionally has spoken with pronounced accents, dropping its aitches and going in for huntin', shootin' and fishin'. The Received Pronunciation that passes for the norm for all other forms of British English is largely a modern middle-class creation, and yet it is widely assumed to be the correct form of English from which all others have fallen away. On the whole, accents seem to be enjoying a revival of esteem since the Second World War and are now much more accepted than they were, but the Edwardians were intensely conscious of them. 'You got a lot of people who were beginning to make a lot of money; we used to call them the 'parvenus'. They'd no breeding, but plenty of money... and you might find quite a poor person who came from a wonderful family, very well bred. Definitely class distinction was there; usually when they opened their mouth, that was the real criterion,'[14] said Grace Fulford, an upper-middle-class woman who is quoted in Paul Thompson's *The Edwardians: The Remaking of British Society*. Lower down the scale, but still within the middle class, where awareness of this type of thing was at its most intense, Sidney Ford said,

> You were taught that there were families who came of very high breeding and people who were well off and could afford nice things and had had better education were social superiors..., people who spoke very nicely and used correct English, and one tried to copy them, sometimes with very poor results, really, you got the grammar all wrong, but still...[15]

I have made no attempt here to deal with languages other than English, because I do not have the knowledge to do them justice, but everything said above applies to Welsh and to Scottish and Irish Gaelic as much as to English. They all have dialects and local accents and they all undergo change over time. For speakers of these languages, however, there is the added complication of the pressure to learn and use English in preference to their native tongue. It still suffices for most of the needs of many people in their own areas, but few business organisations would promote a non-English speaker to managerial posts and most of the media-borne entertainment that is so important today is available only in English. Even goods bought in shops have the instructions written in English, so the scope for living a full, modern life in Welsh alone, say, is clearly limited, despite successes in promoting bi-lingual official signs and securing a Welsh language television channel. Ethnic communities with their own mother tongues feel the same pressures, but much more intensely, as the communities are smaller and less capable of satisfying all the needs of their members without recourse to English. All dialects, including Scots, have become similarly isolated today, and the solution for those brought up in them is the same as for many Welsh speakers: they become bi-lingual, or multi-lingual.

An interesting study of this among the Afro-Caribbean black community in Britain today is David Sutcliffe's *British Black English*. Although about Black English, it is illuminating for anyone interested in making real sense of the function and use of any dialect or pronounced accent. He stresses that it is quite wrong to see people as speaking only one particular dialect, for in today's world this is not possible. Instead, there is a continuous range of possibilities between the most extreme form of dialect known to any speaker, and Standard English. The way they speak in any situation depends on how they feel, which fits perfectly with my earlier point that, as a collector, I was likely to hear a very toned-down version of East Riding speech. I am aware of modifying my speech and doing this myself all the time, since I do not speak as I write, and I am conscious that my accent may cause difficulties or create certain impressions in some settings. Most people are less happy with Standard English, and so make more mistakes when using it, but what look like grammatical errors in many people's speech and writing may well be the mixing of several different grammars. This was clearly, if unconsciously, stated by Sidney Ford above. It is not only deference that determines speech forms, however. People may also want to stress their separateness when they feel threatened, as many black youths continually do, reviving West Indian forms of speech that might otherwise die out.

Far more dialect therefore survives than can be heard by outsiders. The extent to which both strong accents and dialects emerged at work was truly surprising to me in my grass-cutting days, even though my family was working class and I was working around my home town. Swearing was both accepted and, to a degree, expected, and it was here that I realised fully that most people do not swear randomly, as some non-swearers seem to believe, but in very clearly defined situations which vary according to the group involved. *Thee* and *thou* were extensively used, and northern England has many communities where they still survive, but are only used between friends and acquaintances. This may well be the case in other areas too, and the total numbers of speakers involved would probably astonish if there were any way to work it out. *Aye* is still commonly used alongside *yes* well beyond the Scottish border and seems to be coming more out into the open, being heard regularly on the television on programmes like 'Coronation Street'. Moreover, enclosed communities like mining villages often retain dialects that baffle those from even a mile or two away, yet their inhabitants know how to cope in the wider world.

If folklore is seen as the study of communities, their values, and their histories, and if the study of the language of the people is part of that, it should be given the dignity of being taken seriously. Scholars today frequently shy away from the very name as a result of its image in the past, but this does not change the thing that they are studying.

Customary beliefs were never just amusing fancies, but real and effective bodies of knowledge and thought. That they were the property of groups outside the elite, and were often despised by the elite, does not make them unworthy of serious consideration, but it does make them very hard to study by any means other than oral history. Far more people lived by and under such codes than were active in elite societies, so to ignore them is to write off the experience of most people who have ever lived, and to assert that all real change and progress has been the product of those elite groups. This seems to me self-evidently ridiculous and the success of museums and the heritage industry over the last two decades can be taken as proof that people do want history to include more than it used to: they are prepared to pay money for it.

The type of history they want is less clear, however. The easy option is to leave them with a warm glow about a better, more integrated past, so that they will come back and tell their friends to come in their turn. In any institution that claims to be educational, this is absurd and yet it is spreading. Many pamphlets or books do the same thing, and oral historians who collude in the sanitizing of the past are not opening up history but closing it down, as some early folklore studies did. Flann O'Brien satirised an extreme form of this attitude in Ireland in *The Poor Mouth,* when he wrote a tongue-in-cheek account of the study of Gaelic culture and its identification with poverty-stricken rural areas:

> There was a man in this townland at one time and he was named Sitric O'Sanassa…. I can never remember him during my time possessing the least thing, even the quantity of little potatoes needful to keep body and soul joined together. In Corkadoragha, where every human being was sunk in poverty, we always regarded him as a recipient of alms and compassion. The gentlemen from Dublin who came in motors to inspect the paupers praised him for his Gaelic poverty and stated that they never saw anyone who appeared so truly Gaelic. One of the gentlemen broke a little bottle of water which Sitric had, because, said he, it spoiled the effect. There was no one in Ireland comparable to O'Sanassa in the excellence of his poverty; the amount of famine delineated in his person. He had neither pig nor cup nor any household goods. In the depths of winter I often saw him on the hillside fighting and competing with a stray dog, both contending for a narrow hard bone…. He had no cabin either, nor any acquaintance with shelter or kitchen heat. He had excavated a hole with his two hands in the middle of the countryside and over its mouth he had placed old sacks and branches of trees as well as any useful object that might provide shelter.[16]

It is part of respecting contributors not to make them look like curiosities or to play up circumstances of their lives which they would gladly have changed. Life was harder in the past for the vast majority and many occupations were dangerous, with insufficient precautions taken against accidents and exposure to substances that maimed and killed in the long term. In this country, most people's lives are now materially better than their parents' and grandparents' were. Even though they disliked some aspects of change, no ex-horselad ever expressed a wish to me to give up the comforts and farming technology of today to return to the old ways, however positive their views of their experiences. What they did want was to show that those experiences had been positive, and that the things they had done and learned still had value. Genuine respect for the old communities and their customs lies in putting them in a clear and real context, not in portraying history as a long theatrical pageant of happy people. Respecting the power of customs to hold a society together does not mean automatic approval of the goals and aims of that society. Nationalism is once again showing the dangers of glorification of any culture or ethnic heritage, and the fact that groups could be left satisfied with a grossly unequal share of the available wealth of a society, or even brought to acquiesce in their own exploitation, does not mean that we should condone or romanticise inequality or exploitation.

NOTES AND REFERENCES

1. G.E. Evans, 1960, *The Horse in the Furrow*, Faber, pp. 238–40, 246–7.
2. *Ibid.*, p. 248.
3. *Ibid.*, pp. 249–50.
4. *Ibid.*, p. 250.
5. *Ibid.*, p. 254.
6. *Ibid.*, p. 254.
7. *Ibid.*, p. 261.
8. *Ibid.*, p. 258.
9. M.C.F. Morris, 1928, *The British Workman Past and Present*, Oxford University Press, pp. 14, 42–3.
10. G.K. Nelson, 1991, *To be a Farmer's Boy,* Alan Sutton, p. xxi.
11. I. and P. Opie, 1959, *The Lore and Language of Schoolchildren*, Oxford University Press, pp. v–ix.
12. *Ibid.*, p. 176–92.
13. D. Douglass, 'Pit Talk in County Durham' in R. Samuel (ed),

1977, *Miners, Quarrymen and Saltworkers,* Routledge & Kegan Paul, pp. 299–300.
14. P. Thompson, 1975, *The Edwardians: The Remaking of British Society,* Weidenfield & Nicholson, p. 93.
15. *Ibid.,* p.106.
16. F. O'Brien, 1973, *The Poor Mouth,* Hart-Davis, MacGibbon, pp. 88–9.

CHAPTER FOUR
Alternative History

Extending the range of history must involve taking risks and tackling subjects that are uncomfortable to deal with, as well as those that are likely to have wide appeal, or else we distort the past. Everyone has aspects of their life they are not proud of, and so does every society. We all do things whose consequences we do not foresee, and facing up to responsibility is very difficult. The historian who tries to make a society do so can expect to arouse great hostility, but admitting responsibility promotes maturity and helps to cut down on mistakes in the future. Most European states find it hard to be honest about what happened in the Second World War, for instance, especially those which were occupied. When liberation came, the people who had been in charge were tainted with collaboration, but the need to keep things running usually prevented wholesale change. Scapegoats were prosecuted, even persecuted, and the rest, often the senior figures, were tacitly purged of guilt. A good deal of oral history on the continent has been concerned with the war in an effort to see behind this facade, but this example may seem like a poor choice for a book mostly dealing with Britain.

The last decade has shown that this is just as true of the Channel Islands as it is of France or the Netherlands, however. It is only recently that it has been possible to talk openly about the details of their occupation, and it is still impossible to investigate fully. It has not been easy to admit that some British governmental officials also collaborated or that some British businessmen grew rich while their fellows literally starved. Only a few days after writing this, by a strange coincidence, *The Guardian* of May 4th 1992 ran as its main story a piece concerning the activities of the SS on Alderney, one of the Channel Islands, where they established a work camp to build fortifications. Most inmates were Russian, but there were other nationalities as well, including some British.

> A Nazi commander implicated in the biggest mass murder on British soil this century, for which he has never faced trial, is alive in Germany.... This provides the most compelling evidence yet that the Government tried to cover up the scale of atrocities committed during the German occupation of the Channel Islands – possibly to avoid revealing the extent of islanders' collaboration – by ensuring there were no war crimes trials.... Only one man appears to have been prosecuted for crimes on Alderney, and he was hanged in East Germany in 1963....
>
> Many papers relating to the wartime history of the Channel Islands – including a British military intelligence (MI19) Report into the Alderney death camps – are classified until 2045 under Whitehall's tightest secrecy rules. Not even the War Crimes Inquiry has had access.
>
> Any cover-up must have been ordered at the highest level to prevent the emergence in court of humiliating details of Nazi death camps on British soil.... Old wounds about the extent of collaboration were reopened early this year after the theft of Jersey's entire wartime archives, when the documents were hawked round pubs and antique shops.[1]

Questions were asked in Parliament as a result, but it was soon clear that the government was simply seeking to defend what had been done in the past. The purpose in raising this is not to imply that the islanders acted any differently, or any worse, than any group of people in such circumstances, rather to show that this is still a live issue and that the general British assumption that such things could not happen here is quite unwarranted. It also shows that unless we can face the facts about the way people cope with the pressures of life, we may allow the vilest of crimes to go unpunished so as to be able to ignore lesser but more general wrongdoing. This is a particularly clear case, but the principle is relevant to all areas of historical study. If nostalgia-driven rural history crowds out the need to face the reality of our collective past, the historian is doing active harm.

Traditional communities, for instance, often seem to allocate roles to members at birth, which can cut down, or even remove entirely, many sources of friction between individuals. Their strength lies in common action and hence they evolve mechanisms that promote this and encourage individuals to accept clear rules as to what constitutes normal behaviour. This destroys individuality, however, and some roles may be limiting or even actively objectionable. The most obvious example of this is the testimony of Nate Shaw: black people were allocated a place in the Deep South of the USA that few, if any, can

have enjoyed, and yet, on any given day, there would have been no outward sign in most towns that they felt this way. Their relations with individual whites were often cordial and they could not show their true feelings because the price of doing so was too high. Stability can mean social peace and a chance to get on with your life, but it can also mean the preservation of great inequality and overt or covert oppression. If community means looking after your own, the reverse of this can all too easily be a hatred of outsiders, or of those like Southern blacks and Jews in Europe who live among a community that denies them real membership.

In this country, this most obviously means looking at the experience of immigrants and their children, perhaps, but the very linkage of racial issues to immigration, and usually to black immigration, betrays our stereotyped thinking. In some localities there are ethnic groups who are completely overlooked except by those intimately involved with them, most notably those from Eastern Europe who arrived during and after the Second World War. Their presence is often visible only in the signs outside Polish Ex-Servicemen's Clubs and the like, but they provided a vital boost to the labour force in strategic industries, and especially coal mining, in the immediate post-war years. *Something in Common* is one of the *Lifetimes* series of booklets published in 1975 and 1976 by Manchester Polytechnic and the bulk of it is devoted to a British woman, Dolly and her husband, Frank, who actually began life as Ivan, a farmer's son in southern Russia in the years immediately after the Russian Revolution:

> I was brought up on my grandfather's farm in Rostow Nadanov, west of the Volga. The farm was part of a village called Lobow, after my grandfather's family. There were about 30 households, or 200 people in a community that was almost self-sufficient. It was far off the beaten track, in open rolling country, criss-crossed by rivers. We had corn, meat, poultry, cheese, sheep, cattle, camels, vegetables and orchards. The only things that had to be bought in were things like salt and frying pans.[2]

Plate 4.1 This photograph, from the Bradford Heritage Recording Unit exhibition *Ukraine's Forbidden History*, shows an elderly Ukrainian-born man extinguishing candles at the end of a church service in Eccleshill, Bradford, 1991. Its caption was an oral history extract: 'Another Christmas will be coming and in the Ukraine there is an old tradition that on Christmas Eve at the Holy Supper a vacant seat is left at the table and a candle is lit and placed in the window. It is to light the way for a missing member of the family to come safely home. Then perhaps there will also be a vacant place and a lit candle for me, if someone still remembers.'

The cultural dislocation involved in adjusting to life in Britain could be severe with a background like this, and such accounts can lead to valuable insights into the nature of our own society, as well as describing the diverse origins of the populations of many of our cities, like Manchester. John Best was born in Barbados in 1929 and he had been in Britain for about twenty years when his memories were published as *Once There Was a Way* in the same series. He was asked what view he had had of white people as a child:

> JOHN Great. [My boss's] son was a good friend of mine, we used to spar together, call each other 'black bastard', 'white bastard' and all that. And there was this other chap, I got to know him through my brother, the tailor, when he was being measured up for a suit. And I met him seven or eight months later at the sugar-cane factory. He was an overseer or a foreman and he says 'Bloody hell, isn't it a small world? Tell you what, you'll never be the same as your kid. He's the best tailor in the world.' This bloke was possibly 26 or 27, very friendly and talkative. It wasn't as though 'you're white and I'm black.'
> In fact you don't see as much of that there as you do here. You've got these exclusive clubs in the West Indies, but it's not a colour bar so much as financial. They keep you away because you don't have the money.... I've talked to other people who've come from Barbados and they don't understand why it's like it is here....
> GREG You still paint a fairly rosy picture. Was there nothing that really upset or worried you?
> JOHN I don't think so.... I think my youngsters now have got more fears now than I had. They live on their nerves more than I did. They're not free, they're captives. In the West Indies I could just go under a tree and lie down. The only poisonous thing you had was something you ate which didn't agree with you. There were no lions or snakes. You could go under any tree, you could say 'I'm fed up with this area, I'm fed up with you lot,' you could just get yourself lost.... You could lie on your back and look into that sky.... My youngsters are trapped, they have only to leave here and the police have got them.... With us back home I think people were honest because they knew what people were up to.... I feel that our little village had a lot on other places, because we could trust each other, because we felt that sooner or later 'I'm going to need you and if you can't trust me, I can't trust you. And if you can't trust me, you're going to say "Now buggar off" when I really need you.'
> The thing about 'community' is that its a posh name, like 'sociology'. And I feel that people, if they are living together, no matter if they are running naked or hanging by their tails, as long as these people understand each other and relate to each other, never mind the word 'community'.[3]

Parallel statements could be taken from virtually all immigrant communities, but they would diverge sharply when talking about their

Plate 4.2 This was one of a vast collection of studio portraits taken of Asians in Bradford at the Belle Vue Studio. They were often sent to relatives as a way of maintaining links with the homeland, and a selection were displayed at the Bradford Heritage Recording Unit as part of *Destination Bradford* in 1987. This one was linked to the following oral history extract: 'In Pakistan it was ironic that they thought we who were in England were living the "life of Reilly". They didn't realise that we were actually working-class people, we weren't living it up. Yes, we were always provided for, but it was not upper-class living how they imagined. Those photos we sent home probably reinforced those ideas.'

countries of origin and their views of society. The main thing most ethnic groups have in common is their status as outsiders, and, if this is taken away, we start to see them as individuals and as part of distinctive cultures.

The children of immigrants may assimilate almost entirely if they are white, and there are now thousands of young people with Eastern European surnames who have grown up very much as British children would, especially where their mother was British. For black people born here, it is not so easy, and for those who wish to hold on to their traditional culture in their new home, there may be great tensions in trying to reconcile this with the normal desire to fit in. In many of our cities there are long-established communities from all parts of the world, members of which can trace roots back in that place further than their white neighbours. Some retain a clear sense of separation, most obviously the Orthodox Jews and the Chinese, but even for those groups which seem to have assimilated most completely, this rarely means surrender of their own past and blind acceptance of the traditions of a new home, as the Irish community has proved in many urban areas. They frequently remain a distinct group, but not a separate group. Racism is too large a topic to tackle here in detail, but the personal experiences of those who have been through it are literally the only way that we will ever know its true nature. Most incidents go unreported, and even when they are reported many of the overtones that make them so frightening to their victims will be lost. Nate Shaw's testimony is ample proof of this for the USA, and while he was suffering under a more pervasive and organised system than prevails in Britain, the example of the Channel Islands shows that an automatic reaction that it cannot happen here is not good enough.

Women's experiences may seem more accessible, but women rarely appear in conventional history as anything but the support of men. Working-class history is often no better than elite history, for attention focuses on work outside the home, trade union activity, and politics, all of which are dominated by men. The women stay at home and keep the family together, and the work involved in this is largely taken for granted. Again, this is an enormous subject that a fragment of a chapter cannot hope to cover, but *Oral History* has devoted two issues to women's history, one in 1977 and one in 1982, and they show the wide range of subjects that can be linked together in this common strand. While factors like class, race, and wealth divide women, as they do all people, studying how far gender overrides such things is very rewarding. It is almost inevitable that much of any oral history done with ordinary women will centre on the home, and it is easy to seem to support and justify a very unequal arrangement of society, so we should consider whether domesticity is natural or imposed. We have already seen in the extracts on puberty in Chapter 2, that shared experiences do not guarantee solidarity or mutual support, so does the identification with the home that occurs in all classes unite or fragment women? It is important to remember, moreover, that most women worked for wages at some stage in their lives, and even those who describe themselves as full-time housewives may well have part-time jobs.

Two articles from the 1977 issue illustrate very well the difficulties inherent in giving a fair and accurate picture of women's lives. They concern separate but neighbouring areas of Lancashire around the turn of this century, and both authors are feminists, so the wide disparity that is evident in their findings is not due to their different beliefs. Jill Liddington based her collecting on the textile towns of the Pennines north of Manchester, while Elizabeth Roberts concentrated on Barrow and Lancaster where, as in most of Edwardian England, paid full-time work after marriage was not normal for women. This did not mean a life of idleness, for looking after a family was an onerous task involving hard, physical work that went on even longer than the factory. A typical routine is described by Elizabeth Roberts in 'Working Class Women in the North West':

> Washing day was a full day's heavy manual work – clothes were boiled, pounded in the dolly tub, rinsed, starched, blued, mangled and ironed. Baths were tin tubs which had to be filled and emptied by hand. Heating the house and cooking required buckets of coal to be carried in and buckets of ash to be carried out. Floors and staircases were scrubbed, as were front steps, and even pavements. Ranges were black leaded and fire irons polished every week; stones of flour were kneaded into bread; in fact all aspects of housework required a lot of time and even more energy.... The Victorian work ethic is a recurring theme in almost every aspect of working class life. Victorians and Edwardians believed that salvation lay through work and damnation through idleness. One respondent's mother used to say rather pithily, 'Don't waste what you can't make and you can't make time.' Thus social pressures from neighbours ensured that much time was spent in cleaning windows and washing and donkey-stoning the front door step. A dirty exterior to a house was equated with moral laxity.[4]

A wife was not just a skivvy, however, for she almost always handled the family's finances:

> They were schemers and providers in them days but I'm sticking up for the woman. The provider had a little wage and it was the women who were the schemers. There was always something on our table and they always had a supper.
> I think in those days that the man passed over the money, much more than he does today. I mean today they sit down and talk it out and there's so much for him and so much for the house. But in those days the wages were so poor that really the man didn't get a lot out of it.... It was handed over and the women did the allotting where it went.... I mean some of these that were always drunk must have got a lot back. I think they perhaps didn't treat their wives fairly. I mean I can remember when I was smaller when my father was at Williamsons in the Warehouse Office he got a shilling a week to spend, and he only smoked half an ounce of twist, but it was fourpence. And of course he never went to work on a bus or anything, he walked both ways....[5]

Drunken, bullying husbands existed, but of eighteen marriages on

Plate 4.3 While others stand to have their photographs taken, a woman goes on scrubbing her doorstep in Fryston in the 1930s. Maintaining its appearance was vitally important in the struggle for respectability in working-class communities until very recently, even though hardly anyone used the front door in the normal course of events. It was hard, manual work that was no sooner done that it would be spoiled, and the whole pavement that fronted the house was also kept up to a lesser degree.

which she had details, 'there was only one case of a husband completely failing in his role as provider and ill-treating his wife because of heavy drinking. His wife died aged thirty-two, and he was banished from the family, being denied shelter, food and access to his children by his mother-in-law'[6]. Only in such families was the man dominant in every sphere, ruling through fear. They frequently ended up in court over their ill-treatment and the wife invariably won such cases. In fact women showed a good deal of solidarity against such men, with neighbours turning on them and at least one landlady refusing them drink. It was not Elizabeth Roberts' expectation that she would find such a high acceptance of domesticity among the women she spoke to, but the evidence was overwhelming that they saw life as a struggle that could only be successful if they and their husbands worked together in their respective spheres.

Jill Liddington's article, 'Working Class Women in the North West II', however, undermines any suggestion of inevitability about women's domestic role:

> Over a quarter of a million Lancashire women went out to work each day in the cotton mills. This tradition had continued through the

nineteenth century (even in the face of the widely-held view that an adult man should earn a 'family wage' sufficient to maintain his wife and children), and was particularly strong in the northern weaving towns – notably Preston, Blackburn and Burnley.... In communities like these, the majority of the workers were women; there were 152,000 women weavers compared to only 60,000 men – and in Blackburn alone no fewer than 16,000 women went to work in the local weaving sheds....

As many as a third of married women worked. In Blackburn the proportions were the highest in the country with 77% of unmarried women and 38% of married women working. Particularly remarkable was the large numbers of married women of child-bearing age who worked: 66% of 20–25 year old and 54% of 25–35 year olds.... Their jobs gave them a valuable status and respectability, [and] their wages were important to their family's well-being.... A respondent from Nelson, just north of Burnley, whose mother, Selina Cooper, worked as a winder (preparing the yarn for the weavers) in one of the neighbouring mills, explained:

'We're near the mills – they used to come and get the kids' breakfast and then go back again. They used to be running with sandwiches, and – bacon sandwiches and chip butties and – but they kept a certain respectability, you know what I mean. And that going out to work made it. They wouldn't have been able to but for that. No. They just couldn't stop at home. Oh no.'[7]

Wages in the mills were high for women, but apart from a few elite groups, the men earned much less than the national average. Women's wages therefore formed an essential part of a family's income, and employers depended on wives being willing to work. One Blackburn woman described the attitudes prevalent when her mother, born in 1879, was old enough to start work:

That was a big thing they used to talk about, the cotton workers, 'You've a *trade* in your hands, a wonderful trade, a weaver. A trade in your hands if you learned to weave.' So (her elder brothers and sisters) said, 'Well, she ought to go in and learn to weave, she'd always have something in her hands.'[8]

We will return to this topic later, but it should be clear already that we need to work towards a history of women judged by the kind of achievements that women themselves valued, by the kind of things that were important to women and possible for women, and the best people to do this are women working through oral history. We need to appreciate the true value of all that unpaid and underpaid work. It is clear that throughout the western world at the very least, even the nuclear family, seen by many as the fundamental unit of our society in the past, is finding it hard to survive the pressures of modern life. It may come to be a curiosity like farm service if current trends persist.

Since it cannot be assumed that women today take on the traditional role within a relationship that they always did, tape recordings of 'ordinary' lives from very recent times could acquire a rarity value unthinkable only a short time ago. Future generations would want to know how traditional family structures operated, warts and all, without romanticising or propagating a restrictive view of women, and there must be no question of endorsing a patronising special status. Even farm servants had more choice about their careers than women ever had in modern times and the socialising of both sexes around such a fundamental dichotomy as there was between male and female roles, together with the effects this had on individuals, deserves full investigation.

Similarly, any oral historian gets used to disparaging comments about the 'rough' sort of people who do not succeed in reaching 'normal' standards of behaviour. The reason is usually economic, either due to a general lack of jobs in the area that pay a real living wage, or to a family disaster such as a drunken father or a dead parent. To view the working class as monolithic is quite indefensible: from above it may look like a mass of poor people, but from the inside there are endless ramifications of status and income differentials that separate off districts, streets, and families from each other. By definition, the really rough were rarely envied except by romantics who did not understand the hardships of chaotic lifestyles. Although often seen as a menace to society, many of the most poor were so dependent on charity and casual work for their 'betters' that they were often more socially conservative than those in regular work. Every village had its rough families, every town had its rough district or street, every county had its rough settlements, and, if we want to portray past life accurately, they must be recorded like everything else and accorded due weight in the overall scheme. Disapproval must not push them out, and romanticism must not exaggerate either their numbers or their role.

Thea Thompson made a conscious effort to do this in *Edwardian Childhoods,* which consists of a series of reminiscences of individual childhoods. Tommy Morgan's stood for those at the bottom of the heap:

> I was born the third of August 1892 – number 5 King's Bench Street, Pocock Street, Blackfriars Road, [London].... We nearly always had one room, she used to have a sheet on the line to separate one room – make two of it. Us children slept one side and father and mother the other side. I can only remember once my mother having two rooms – 'course they was never long in one place you see. Always got

chucked out or turned out or something.... Many a time I've gone home, come home from school as a child until about seven – six, seven and eight – I've come home from school with all the other boys and girls and find the furniture outside the door in the street....

I've seen my mother sitting about brooding – where's she going to get this and where's she going to get that. And I used to say, 'Mother – got a ha'penny?'

'Get out of it, get out – I've got enough troubles now. I've got the rent. I've got to find this – I've got to find that,' she said, 'I've nothing to pawn – get out of it'.... They were known as the two biggest drunkards in Waterloo and Blackfriars. My father could get drunk three times a day. He was a coal heaver.... My father was a ganger. And they earned five shillings to empty a bargeload of coal sixty to eighty ton. That was a day's wages [for five men].... If there wasn't a barge in they used to go into the tap room [of a nearby pub] and there was a pail of beer. They'd sit down and finish that pail of beer. Of course they got drunk. Home. Get up. Go in the pub. Get drunk again. 'Course they was open from five till twelve o'clock at night then.

And my mother was a big drinker. When I was a child she worked in Covent Garden shelling peas, peeling potatoes for the Savoy Hotel.... About a dozen women, and when they pick their money up, about eighteen pence, something like that, they used to go down Wellington Street. Some went straight home but the others went into that pub next to the Lyceum Theatre... and got drunk on what they'd earned....

Always had a regular meal on a Sunday.... [because] Saturday... we used to all have a place to go to buy food. I used to go to Jermyn Street for two pennorth of giblets.... Another one had to go to the Strand for stale bread. Another one used to have to go to [the butchers near closing time for] ... five or six pounds of good meat. 'Course they didn't have no fridges in them days.... it was either sell it or give it away or throw it away you see....

Clothes – always secondhand. Off the barrow down the market place.... She used to buy scenery out the ... Opera House in Waterloo Road. Used to buy the old scenery – fetch it home, put it in a bath in the yard and let it soak for about a week. And when that was done two or three times we had a bedsheet. You could never tear 'em. My mother never used to buy new sheets because the old man, in his drink, he used to flop on the bed in his coal clothes and everything see. So what was the good of sheets?....

'Course my mother and father used to get for drunkenness, they used to go and do like seven days or fourteen days [in jail] and me, or whoever was at home at the time, used to go round to a sister or brother who was old enough to take us in till they came out.... My father went and chopped up wood many a time to get relief.... well my mother used to go down mostly, 'Look he ain't been home for three days – we've got nothing to eat – I've got – you know – two or three children. They're hungry!' Right. Used to get a loaf, butter or something like that – not much. 'When your husband comes home you'll tell him he's got to come straight down here'. Well when he did come home my mother'd say. 'You've got to go down to the Guardian – Relieving Officer'. Well he used to go down. Right. He didn't used to come home. My mother used to go down to him, 'He ain't home – he ain't come back again'. He said, 'No. He's in the casual ward. He's in for three days chopping up wood for the food you've had'.

Having the run of the streets like that in those days, there was always a clique of us – about twenty – none of their mothers and fathers looked after 'em, like me, see. And we had the run of the streets, fetched ourselves up in the best way we could. Well, as I said, we used to all get together, play up at the court or the street, or the roadway where we lived, and we'd be playing up there twelve o'clock, half past twelve, one o'clock in the morning, see. And I can remember an occasion when we had all stopped out, slept in some buildings underneath – some in the lavatory, some under the sink – Westminster Bridge Road.... And we got a hiding for that....

She didn't hit us hard you know with the flat of her hand, but always had a cane up on the line – ha'penny cane.... I can never remember my father hitting me or any of my brothers or sisters. He was very cruel to her. He used to hit her like he'd hit a man, although my mother's a big strong woman.... The only time he was in he'd come home and get sober – then go out again and get drunk. I've seen 'em stand up – I can remember several times – stand in the middle of the room. He get hold of her, punch her. She'd punch him back and they'd finish up on the floor both of them punching at one another....

He was a big gambler, very big gambler he was.... He'd come home, he'd say, 'What's those on here?'

'Three and sixpence.'

'What's that?'

'Mother told me to pay the rent with that.'

'Oh all right – pay two next week.' He'd take the three and sixpence and go out and gamble with that three and sixpence, see....

I had two brothers – five sisters. But there was several died in between you see. 'Course they had no control over me 'cause I was the only one left. I was the last one of thirteen.... One sister was sent to a truant school... for stealing a haddock underneath a stall at the Elephant and Castle, in London Road, more for, you know, like larking about than anything. They sent her to a truant school. After she came out at fourteen they sent her to Wales as a servant on a farm. That's the last one that died. I had one decent sister, she was a nurse at Romford hospital, but my mother's sister adopted her and her husband was a big sea captain. Of course he had plenty of money. He could afford to have her sent to college. But all the others they all left home before they were twelve year old, somebody took 'em in. I left home about thirteen when they sent me to charity school. So they all found a place – lived with different people, neighbours mostly. Well most of them started work for about twelve years old. Now and again one used to come back for about a week, but they soon went

again, 'cause of the rows and fights with him and her you see. I had
nowhere else to go. Nobody didn't want me being a cripple you see.
That was the trouble.[9]

No-one would envy Tommy this life: there is not a thing in his
reminiscences that suggests that the hardships of his life were
compensated for by other satisfactions. Most parents would have done
anything to look after their families better than this, and, in this sense,
the desire for respectability that is such a feature of so many working-
class communities is wholly admirable. On the other hand, where it led
to sacrifices the family could not afford in order to keep curtains at the
window, to unnecessary labour to impress others, and to being ruled
by the fear of comments from neighbours, it warped and twisted many
lives. Some people and families were unrespectable only in that they
defied conventions, most notably in villages which required deference
to be paid to the squire, the parson, and the rest of the better-off. They
had too much self-respect to join in something they personally found
degrading and hypocritical. Clifford Hills recalled an experience
shared by many in this extract, also taken from Thea Thompson's
book:

> One thing as a boy I didn't like, and it sticks in my mind today. I
> came to the conclusion that church-goers were something like the
> railway carriages were at one time – first, second and third class. You
> see my mother was a person of the lower class, she was a poor
> woman, and she and her friends were all poor, but they were great
> church goers, regular church goers, kindly gentle people. But they
> had to sit in ... the back pews. In the middle of the church were the
> local shopkeepers and people who were considered to be a little bit
> superior to the others, better educated perhaps. And right at the top
> of the church, behind where the choir used to sit, were the local
> farmers, the local bigwigs, you see, posh people. And when people
> left the church, although as I said he was a nice kindly vicar, he didn't
> seem to have any time for the lower classes. Mother and her friends
> would pass out the church door, the vicar would stand near the
> church door, and he would just nod and smile, perhaps not that even.
> But when the higher class people came out he would shake hands
> and beam to everyone of them as if they were far superior to my
> mother and her friends, the poor, the very poor. And I didn't like
> that. I thought my mother was worth a handshake as well as the rich.
> There was Captain Peele and other local farmers who were
> considered to be rich in those days, they were select. They had
> chosen seats, reserved seats. My mother's seat wasn't reserved. If
> there was something important on and the church was full of people,
> it wouldn't matter to anyone whether she got in the church or not,
> although she went so regular. They did most of the work. They did all
> the cleaning. They did all the decorating I remember. I must have
> been perhaps twelve when it used to strike me. Yes, it did because I

used to discuss this sort of thing with my mother, the other brothers never talked about it. I said it wasn't right, it wasn't proper. I said she shouldn't go to church. She said, 'Nothing will ever stop me from going to my church.'.... I think she said once or twice, she said, 'We can't all be rich. It wouldn't be right that we should, no one would do the work if we were all rich.'[10]

Thea Thompson points out that it was a similar incident that set Joseph Arch on his road to founding the first national farmworkers' trade union in the 1870s. Mr Hills' father lived, like Arch, by taking skilled work on farms on a piecework basis rather than holding a steady job, which left him his own master, even though it also meant spells without any work. He supplemented his income by poaching, but he was basically a contented man and this was the limit of his rebellion: his son had to put up with things as they were. Those who, like Arch, found the deference expected of them really intolerable threatened the status quo even though they were few in numbers. No randomly gathered group can be expected to fit a pre-ordained pattern, however, and though years of training from infancy lessened the chance of open rebellion, there would always be people who could not be brought wholly into line. They could be coerced, of course, or removed, forcibly if need be, but the very act of coercion is itself destructive of the harmony that real communities must have. It is far more effective to persuade the dissatisfied to meet the community halfway in such cases. Moreover, while individualism was not at all encouraged in a general way, it was relished for its entertainment value in those few determined enough to cope with a general image as a *character*, and it was thereby contained. They received a limited licence to misbehave, especially as they also provided an awful example to the next generation when they were felt to be in danger of kicking over the traces. In the East Riding, for instance, the general shortage of farm labour at peak times left farmers willing to hire almost anyone at harvest time, or when other labour-intensive tasks had to be performed, which made the county something of a haven for tramps. Mr Johnson recalled that one job no-one on a farm wanted was spreading soot:

They used to use it on wheat, fertilize wheat: soot. That was to buy.
But that was a rotten job, that was, working among soot: oh Lord....
And they used to let sowing that soot to.... casual men, you know.
They would have had a job to persuade the regular men to take it on.
'Cause ... once [a bag] dropped, I mean, it used to fly about, you had to be careful. Well now, this man, when he went to sow that field with soot, he'd wear some old clothes and he never went home till he finished it. He slept in his clothes in the barn or anywhere, and they'd give him his grub at the farmhouse. (Tape 15/2)

Plate 4.4   Percy Grundell, from Batley, West Yorkshire, who was universally known as 'Doc' and died of a heart attack in 1965 while on his rag-collecting rounds. The Grundells had been known as characters for several generations and they figure in many local stories. He occasionally had to take work in the local textile mills, but he much preferred to be his own boss out on the streets with his beloved pony, 'Captain'.

His grandfather began the medical tradition by selling herbal remedies, telling potential customers how, 'as I look out the window of my house over the beautiful countryside, I see all these herbs...'. In fact he lived in a slum where the view must have been anything but picturesque! Doc's father hawked anything he could get hold of round the streets, from bananas to kippers, all sold from wicker baskets. Although plenty of tales about Doc are still current in Batley, the fact that there are still many relatives living made it hard to get anyone to tell them once it was known that they might be published, a clear example of how working in a tight community can create difficulties as well as opportunities for the historian.

Mr Baines said, 'They never used to get washed while they'd finished.... They were tinkers and really – you know, black-bright, smothered in it. They just used to wipe their mouth over for their food and drink' (Tape 9/1). Mr Playforth, talking to Mr Rispin, recalled that this could be awkward for the horselads, who used to raid the farm outhouses in their spare time, in search of forbidden delicacies for their horses:

> Mr P: When I was at Harpham we used to have a place... to keep such as chaff in there, and there was some steps used to go up to a granary. Well, we always used to keep all chicken corn and all such as

that up there. And every tramp that came to t'door, the man said, 'Why, go into there,' he said, 'and don't set nowt afire but you can stop t'night'.... We used to be up at half past five in a morning and I used to go up there for some barley or summat of that and go up first steps and tumble over summat and it used to be such a shock – it was a tramp in a bag!.... He used to be frightened and I did and all! You couldn't have a light, like if you went with a light they'd have known what you were doing, you see, when you got in there, you see....

Mr R: Oh aye, you used to have a lot of tramps come round at harvest time, men on t'roads, you know... come begging.... Used to give them summat to eat and used to take 'em up – they always locked 'em up, always locked 'em up... They would give them some bags and they would make themselves sort of a bed, why, they got into a bag, didn't they. Why, I had one go to one house I was in and next morning, like, I went and opened door, he was all right when I opened door, and we went for our breakfasts, goes to work. However,.... tells missus, I have to have, he had to have his breakfast! She believed him! She believed him! Aye.

Mrs R: I said, 'What did you send that chap round for his breakfast for?' He says, 'I never did'. I says, 'That's what he said: "Foreman says I have to have my breakfast."'

Mr P: Shows the sort of characters you were dealing with like, you know: you were.... You don't get owt o' that today.

Mrs R: I know one night we had six in. (Tape 22/1)

Talking to old people almost inevitably brings out a story of this sort, with this rider that such people no longer exist. The character was actually filling a role every bit as much as the more overtly conventional people around them, and like many such roles, in most places it has no function today. It did then, for such behaviour was no serious threat to anyone and it livened things up a little. The farm lads, isolated for a year on outlying farms and with no access to entertainment in most cases, appreciated seeing a fresh face from time to time, and hearing some news from other parts of the county. Angela Antrim was fascinated by these tramps from childhood and she has written a book, *The Yorkshire Wold Rangers* (Driffield 1981), about them, using as her title the nickname by which they were generally known. She is a member of the Sykes family of Sledmere, the largest landowners in the county in 1914, and one with a particularly strong conception of its own place in the county community. They refused down the generations to take a title commensurate with their wealth, and Sir Tatton Sykes, 1772–1863, might be the archetypal rich eccentric to set alongside the tramps at the other end of the social scale, though high rank meant he could be much more outrageous without suffering the consequences. He preferred speaking broad Yorkshire to anything else and could often be found in ordinary clothes, mixing with roadmenders and others around his estate. He was passionate about horses and performed several feats of horsemanship that were so foolhardy that they were talked about long after his death. He hung a bell by the back door of Sledmere House and gave instructions that anyone who rang it was to be fed, something that became a family tradition even away from Sledmere. This was how Angela Antrim came into friendly contact with people of whom she would normally be expected to be in complete ignorance.

Most of the material had to be collected orally, of course, even though there are few direct quotations. The Rangers had regular meeting places, and some social structures of their own, but it is clear that many would today be classed as mentally ill. There were women as well as men, and some had skills that would normally have kept them in some style. One had been an accountant and he regularly and expertly handled farmers' accounts, for instance, but he could not cope with this as a routine. Their numbers increased when there was a depression, and one or two were still to be found in the late 1970s. The mental hospitals of the time had little to offer in the way of treatment and were forbidding, sometimes terrifying places. It is clear that the Wold Rangers themselves preferred their way of life to institutional help, for they had their independence and usually enough money to live on, but arguments like this can easily become a patronising and self-serving justification for turning a blind eye to real distress. People can become trapped in a stereotyped role, especially that of the village idiot.

Communities could be tolerant and caring to people in this position, and even seeming cruelty could still provide a sense of belonging that no institution could ever provide. A man with whom I worked, who must have been born around the time of the First World War, and who had lived all his life in a County Durham pit village with a strong community sense, once recounted a story of such a man, a little younger than he, who was often the butt of practical jokes. When he died in an accident, the entire village turned out at the funeral, giving him a better send-off than anyone else in living memory. Would he have been better served by a hospital or institution? Community care is currently being touted as the way to move people out of mental hospitals that are widely felt to have failed many of those placed in them. However, the results seem all too often to involve many ex-patients being thrust to the margins of society because they are part of no community, so these are issues that have a real relevance. I certainly have no answers, but further investigation by oral historians could make a real contribution to this current debate.

This was brought home to me recently by a television series based entirely on oral history, *Out of Sight,* which was put together by Stephen Humphries, a well known oral historian who specialises in this sort of investigation. The testimony of disabled people growing up, and not just in the distant past, is a horrifying catalogue of prejudice, fear, bureaucratic maltreatment and lack of any real attempt to address their problems. Even something as simple as deafness was likely to lead to years of needless suffering. Whole lifetimes were wasted as a result, and if parents and communities come out badly, the official services do no better. Anyone studying the provision of special schools and centres through conventional sources would be compelled to base their account on the records of the service providers, and would doubtless be impressed by the steady increase in money spent and places provided, even if they had reservations about the inevitably old-fashioned approaches of past decades. The oral evidence destroys all this. Those who were supposed to be being helped were in fact being forced into a mould that had little or no relation to their requirements. Many felt they were harmed not helped by what was done to them.

This is an appropriate note on which to close. A lot of people who worked in such services will no doubt be disturbed and upset by such conclusions. They have their own story to tell as well, and it should be collected and listened to, but priority must go to those who at whom the services were aimed. If the things they have to say make us uncomfortable, that is all the more reason for listening closely and trying to set things right for the future. The same is true for all those groups whose complaints are not usually heard, who all too often are persuaded that they have no right to complain. Just because there is no audible dissent we cannot assume that everything is proceeding smoothly. If we are to understand the way our society works, we must look at its victims and at those required to make sacrifices as well as at those who do well.

NOTES AND REFERENCES

1. *The Guardian*, 4th May 1992.
2. *Lifetimes: Something in Common.* 1975–6, Manchester Polytechnic Institute of Advanced Studies, p. 3.
3. *Lifetimes: Once There was a Way,* 1975–6, Manchester Polytechnic Institute of Advanced Studies, pp. 14–16.
4. E. Roberts. 'Working Women in the North West', *Oral History*, Vol 5, no 2, 1977, p. 10.

5. *Ibid.*, pp. 12–13.
6. *Ibid.*, p. 13.
7. J. Liddington, *'Working Women in the North West: II'*, *Oral History*, Vol 5, no 2, 1977, pp. 31–2.
8. *Ibid.*, p. 33.
9. T. Thompson, 1981, *Edwardian Childhoods*, Routledge & Kegan Paul, pp. 13–25.
10. *Ibid.*, pp. 51–2.

CHAPTER FIVE
Contemporary Themes

It is, of course, quite impossible to treat most of the themes raised in the last chapter purely as historical subjects, with a termination point after which they cease to matter. They all continue to be sources of tension and dispute, and sometimes of overt conflict. History unfolds around us constantly; what is happening now is part of a process that stretches back into the past without a break, and extrapolation from what we know of the past helps us shape the future. For people who have come to this country as immigrants, the experience of being in a land different from that of their birth only ends with death or return, and even if their children have never seen their parents' country, they inherit at least part of its culture. Ivan, who described his home village in Russia in the last chapter, came to this country after the war, and in the mid-1970s he had established a new life in Manchester as Frank, married to Dolly:

> Frank now works in a Co-op margarine factory across the Ship Canal from Partington, and Dolly is one four local workers in the Partington People's Rights Office. He attends union branch meetings, she keeps house for him, their two grown-up children, her mother and her brother.... Frank works shifts, operating various machines. He does overtime to make up low wages and spends a couple of hours each day travelling: the Co-op works is only a couple of miles as the crow flies, but there's no proper bridge across the Canal, nor a bus to take him the long way round.[1]

Frank had no involvement with politics in Russia, but both he and Dolly became involved in a rent strike and struggles for a better deal for their community. A lot of space in the study is devoted to this contemporary material, and many issues are raised alongside the obvious discussion of events. One, for instance, concerns the attitude of Frank's fellow workers to someone who is clearly not British-born, but who argues for radical political change in his adopted country:

> ERIC   Frank, do you still get this thing – these handicapped [prejudiced] people saying 'Get back to Russia,' and all that?
> FRANK   Not from officials [of the union], but I did get that many times from workmates.... Practically everyday, ... you know, when a conversation develops and it's not to their liking, that's the first thing they throw in your face. It can start from anything – you know, the present crisis, unemployment and so on. If I point out that unemployment is un-necessary – they realise we're talking politics then, but it's not their politics....
> GREG   What do you actually do at work?
> FRANK   At present very little, because at this place where I am now it's like dynamite to open your mouth.... You're a great guy provided you don't open your mouth....
> ERIC   Frank, what I was asking, though, is do you come across prejudice?
> FRANK   Not personally, no. Only when I'm saying something that's not to their liking.... I generally just sit there, try to mind my own business. But when they start attacking themselves – that's what they're doing in a way through their own back door. Because when these other workers [who are demanding higher wages] are defeated, it'll be their pay packets that are cut down at the same time.... They throw that at me as well 'You only read one Communist paper, and you don't know anything else.' And I say 'I can talk just the same way whether I read it or not, I'm only informed because I read the Daily Mirror and the other papers as well. I read the other side and you only read the one.' But since I started at the margarine, I don't really involve myself, I leave the discussion to them....
> RON   How long have you been there, Frank?
> FRANK   About eighteen months. Because people who come from a different land, with a different accent, who lecture them... This is simply not accepted.[2]

This group session is now nearly twenty years in the past, and the world is a very different place from the one with which Frank and Dolly were struggling. If Frank is still alive, he will be retired and this activism in the workplace is now a part of his history, just as his days in Russia were then. His political views cannot be the same now as then, if only because of the events in Russia. It seems obvious that collecting material in this way, while it is fresh in everyone's mind, is a very appropriate use of oral history. Why wait for memory to fade, and risk key contributors dying or moving away? Why wait until the only memories available are those of people who were just children or adolescents at the time? There is a clear case for recording events either as they happen, or shortly after – long before they would normally be considered as history. Christine Mahoney of Armthorpe, for instance, was asked about her involvement in the miners' strike of 1984–85 while it was still in progress:

> I've assisted the strike in every way. Collecting, picketing, fund raising, dinners, I've been on everything that's going, all of it. You're that busy you don't think about what stands out most. I've been one of about six women who've organised the food in the kitchen, getting it ready, putting it out, then you've got all the washing up and clearing up to do. It's not easy, you're doing more, a hell of a lot more, than before the strike, in fact I don't know what we're going to do when it's all over. It's going to be very quiet compared to what it is now.
>
> When the strike first started I was chief fund raiser, so I got a raffle going every week. I've seen me be out till 11 o'clock at night, it's been one or two in the morning before I got to bed. I got a group of women and we'd do the whole village. As long as I saw money coming in I didn't mind. My daughter does her whack and my eldest son's done his bit, young'un gives papers out, everyone's involved, the whole family, we're all in this.
>
> Why am I doing it? It's not just for mine, we're all in this together, it's not like you've just got one husband, you look after everybody, and that's how it should be in a village. In a mining village everyone sticks together. I've found it has made a difference to the community in Armthorpe. I can remember when I was little, it was a mining village, then all of a sudden you got your hoity-toitys coming in and it sort of split. Well now everybody's back where they should be, there's no fences in village now. In my view that's some good come out of the strike, that's the only thing I'm really pleased about, everybody's back together the way they should be. Now, I've hundreds of friends round here, five of us may share one bag of flour, they're friends, but I've lost previous so-called friends through strike. I've got no one to thank when this is over. My husband's family, not one's come forward to help, only my own mother, but she's worse off than us, my stepfather's a miner, they're on their own, so they get nothing. But best memory I'll have is way strike's brought everyone together and new friends I've made in the community.
>
> Sacrifices, God, there's more than I can say. No coal for a start, no clothes, no shoes. I've got a whacking great big dog, he's on half food but I won't get rid of him.... In my view, when all this is over, many attitudes will have been changed. I've been on picket lines with the other women and those women are never going to go back to the way they used to be. A lot of the men don't like it, and think a woman's place is in the home but most of the women who had that old-fashioned attitude have changed now. Also I think it's going to take a lot of years to get over the experiences we've had with the police. When all's said and done, they've got to live in this village and I don't think it will ever be the same again. My son was arrested a fortnight ago, he's not a miner but he's been helping out, and police came for him. I nearly got taken away with him. My worst memory of the strike will be when they fetched the riot squad into village in August.

Sometimes we get fed up with the strike, but we're all in the same boat, we have to help each other out of the depressions. We sit down and talk it over with someone else. It's gone on a long time and it does cause tensions at home. We split up three weeks ago, but only for a few days, we've had twenty-one years and it's not first strike I've had. I mean we've argued before.

It's Christmas in a few days and the kids know it won't be the same. I can only get them one present each, they realise that, but as big as they are it still hurts. Still, we'll have our Christmas when they go back, they know that. They're not bothered, they haven't done that bad. We'll have some'at on the table to eat.[3]

These are aspects of the strike that received little attention in the mass media while it was on, and so it cannot be assumed that future historians will ever be able to recover them from conventional sources. Christine Mahoney spontaneously raises issues like the nature of communities, the way they function, and attitudes to family roles, all things we have seen in other contexts, and which are easily overlooked in conventional analyses of events like this. They have a wider relevance as well, showing how close-knit communities adapt to and conflict with today's individualist world. *The Enemy Within*, edited by Raphael Samuel, Barbara Bloomfield and Guy Boanas, will therefore be a godsend for future historians, and the tapes from which it was made even more so. If there is a real and proven problem with oral testimony collected many years after the event, it is that memories of particular events such as this strike do become confused, not just through forgetting, but also because they merge with other similar events like the two previous strikes of the 1970s, and because they become mythologised. This is not pure loss, because the way that such memories are reshaped is itself valuable information on the way a community like this sees its own past, but it does mean a lot of work in cross-checking facts and there is always a residual doubt.

By collecting at the time, we do not eliminate distortion, for contributors may be honestly mistaken, they may worry about the repercussions of telling the truth, such as prosecution for criminal offences, and they may wish to put a good face on something they find discreditable in their hearts. This is true of any testimony, however, and it provides us with the perfect counterpart for oral material collected decades later. When we put them together, we see the way perception has changed, we can see the process of legend-creation in operation. This has been traced for the Second World War Blitz in Tom Harrisson's *Living Through the Blitz*. This is not based on oral history, but written reports and diaries compiled by ordinary people for the Mass Observation organisation as the blitz happened. Since no-one was collecting contemporary impressions on tape, it is the nearest thing we are going to get. In a short chapter, *Down Memory Lane,* Tom Harrisson contrasts many of the attitudes people came to believe they had taken at the time, and their memories of events, with the versions that were prevalent in the 1970s. It is quite clear that extensive – if unconscious – rewriting has taken place, and he uses this as the basis for an attack on oral history in general. In fact, this is unfair given the nature of this event, which has received constant public attention since it happened and which has been mythologised on a national scale as well as a local one. In addition, the modern material he uses frequently comes from a few people, who are often not those to whom an oral historian would turn. His basic point about the adapting of memory is indisputable, however, but is only provable so clearly because of the availability of contemporary accounts.

If there is a sequence of collecting, we can inject a truly dynamic element into the evidence and it becomes the equivalent of cine-film rather than snapshots. Normally, we ask people about distant events, the conclusion of which is known, and their memory of how they felt as things developed cannot help but be influenced by their knowledge of the outcome. Taping the same people at intervals gives a much more complete picture of highs and lows, misunderstandings, and the reasons why particular decisions are being taken. As an instance, consider the views of Iris Preston in April 1986 on the aftermath of the miners' strike:

> The morale is low... for quite a lot... because this year has cost them their homes... it's cost men prison, jobs, their homes, their wives, and what they've got in this next coming two years is work, more work and more work to cover that year. When I say to my son, 'Would you go on strike again?', he says, 'If it was a fight for the communities and a fight for a better standard, I would fight again and so would many others.' But it doesn't alter the fact that they've got several years of just sheer hard work to try and repair, to make homes, bring themselves to any sort of living, so, the men are despondent.... Sometimes we're down to as low as eight – this is the Sheffield women's group – and why? because the women can't get out because the men are working over....

> *During the strike, people said that everything would be changed afterwards, that the women in the villages would never be the same. Is that true?*

> For some aspects of it, it's not true, such as men involving women in the Union. The women fought one whole long year alongside the men, but Union business is still a closed shop to the men....

Give an example.

> Oh when the Bevercotes came out on strike, Lance said to me,
> 'Bevercotes are out'. I said, 'Have you had a Union meeting?',
> 'Yes','What was said?', 'Oh, we're back up in the action.' 'Yeah, but
> how do you mean, do you mean strike action?' 'Well, mother, it's
> Union business.' I could ha' kicked him in the teeth. It's not only
> Union business, it's all our business. We made it our business....
> Well, they *let* us make it our business when they accepted us on the
> picket lines and accepted the help that we were more than willing to
> give. If there was Union meetings during the strike, every word
> would come home and the wife would sit there and hang on every
> word, and discuss it, but now I think a lot of the men are wanting
> their women back into the sink, no matter what lip service they give.
> I think a lot of them are afraid of their new women, as if they feel
> that we've metamorphosed too much.
>   A lot of the women's groups has folded. Some of them just
> collapsed when the strike collapsed. Some of the women wanted to go
> back to living normal... they wanted to forget the strike. For some of
> them it was very traumatic, and for others it was the greatest thing
> that ever happened to them.[4]

It would be very instructive to have more follow-up since then,
particularly now that the worst nightmares of the strikers have been far
exceeded by events. Any project like this should be as comprehensive
as possible, but some things are impossible: the police would never
give open access to anyone during an event like the miners' strike, any
more than the National Union of Mineworkers' leadership would have
allowed collectors carte blanche to record everything it was doing and
deciding. *The Enemy Within* is undoubtedly partisan, but it does
include a few of the memories of miners who worked on during the
strike, and those who were affected by or involved in the creation of
the Union of Democratic Mineworkers, like Colin Bottomore, Branch
Secretary of Bentinck Colliery in Nottinghamshire:

> At the beginning I was for the strike because before the strike
> obviously myself and the rest of the union committee were trying to
> influence any strike ballot that might take place. I mean in favour of
> the strike.... But when we had the meeting the mood from that
> meeting was obvious that the men didn't wish to support a strike. Of
> the 500-600 men who attended the meeting, I didn't hear anyone at
> that meeting, there was no-one from that audience spoke in favour of
> the strike.... and then of course the attitude hardened against the
> striking miners because of the violent picketing that took place from
> the very first day they entered into Nottinghamshire. On the first shift
> that they came to Bentinck I spoke to about twenty to thirty pickets
> and came in the canteen and I personally bought them all a cup of
> tea, we were that close in friendship. And then... about half past
> ten... the pub just up the road turned about fifty to sixty pickets out

and violence started immediately they came out, violence towards men walking to work, running men across fields, chasing men in groups, chasing individuals through the gate and shoving them onto the road. And from that moment I said I would have nothing to do with them....

How did you react to the obvious hardship cases that you must have heard about among the strikers?

We didn't hear of any hardship cases among striking miners, we heard exactly the opposite because obviously the tales that were fed back to me were from people that were working and their attitude was to harden my attitude, see? And I know for a fact that every evening they were in the public house and every dinner so they couldn't have been that hard up for money, them particular strikers we had. It hardened me against them in some respect because of the violence that was used against my wife, because someone stopped my wife in the town and spat all over her and pushed her against a bus stop and some women had to come and help her out....

What do you think is going to happen at the ballot [to form the Union of Democratic Mineworkers] this week?

It can only be a matter of conjecture to me or anyone else. The support will come from Nottinghamshire in my opinion. My own view is a contradiction of terms I would think. I would have said six months ago that I would have nothing to do with the breakaway union. But now I'm going to vote for it. Pride plays a large part. I've always thought I had a right to a say in my union.[5]

The historian has to acknowledge the conflicts both of evidence and of interpretation that this point of view creates when put beside the others, reconcile them where possible, and explain them where it is not, not merely brush them aside. Oral testimony from both sides of an argument is essential if we are to understand what it was about, though circumstances may lead us to give more weight to one side or the other according to what they stand to gain or lose by what they say. It is worth reiterating here that oral testimony is not truth, just evidence. Conflict is particularly clear in an event like the miners' strike, but even less controversial issues that seem more likely to concern the average local historian are still bound to include differences of viewpoint. Recording any decision-making process as it happens, such as a campaign for a community centre, would illustrate the many strands of opinion that affect the actual outcome even of seemingly simple issues. As long as there was a promise of complete confidentiality while negotiations were proceeding, so as not to endanger the chances of reaching a normal solution, and as long as the recordings were treated sensitively afterwards, this would be worth trying, and even if some officials refused to participate, it would still be worth proceeding on a partial basis. It would also be truly enlightening to follow through important business decisions, but it would be a rare firm indeed that was willing to risk this.

This type of work can, of course, lead in unforeseen directions if things do not go as expected, and this is often when the result is most illuminating. Eamon Dunphy undertook to keep a comprehensive taped diary of his experiences as a professional footballer with Millwall in the 1973–74 season. The club confidently expected promotion to the First Division on the strength of a strong team and a good previous season, so his account was expected to be celebratory, a recording of success. From the start, however, nothing went right for Millwall. In a sport that normally tries to hide from honest examination of internal tensions, the resulting book is excruciatingly honest as a personal view, and it has a ring of truth that sets it apart from the innumerable ghosted football autobiographies. Eamon Dunphy says in his introduction:

> I was ... delighted, when talking to some of the Scunthorpe players recently, to find that they had read and identified with some of the extracts in the *Guardian*. That they had identified with it, and that individually each player picked on a different passage as his favourite, was enormously reassuring.
>
> The emotions displayed are often raw. I wrote it as I felt it, without benefit of hindsight. It is in part uncompromising and irrational. But such is the nature of our life that to have allowed myself the luxury of rationality would have obscured the very thing I was trying to explore.
>
> Looking back through the pages now, two years on, I find much that is embarrassing. Is that snide bigoted little man really rational, open-minded, tolerant me?[6]

The tone of the entries changes rapidly from the initial calm confidence as it becomes clear that something is seriously wrong, and near panic sets in when they have to accept that the team is not just going through a bad patch. Dunphy himself was playing badly and was dropped:

> 4 October
> Sheffield Wednesday 3 Millwall 2
> So we went up to Sheffield. I wasn't on the bench, I went as thirteenth man. You go into the dressing room before the game, and you smile and say 'All the best, lads.' What does that mean? If they do well you stay out. And when they get beaten, as we did last night, what do you do? You act. Because you can't come in with a big smile all over your face saying 'Great. Now you've been beaten I can get back in.' Everybody else is sick. But you aren't. You are pleased. So you come in and make faces; pretend that you are sick like the rest of them. But everyone knows that you are acting.

I sat in the stand with John Sissons, who is injured. I was sitting among some Millwall supporters too. They were all saying 'Cor, you not in, Eamon? What a liberty! He should have dropped someone else.' You can't say anything. And they say the same to everyone when they are dropped. Some of them mean it, some don't.

The game was a shambles. Terrible. First half was diabolical. Kingy kept like a clown, gave away two goals. And he was being watched by Manchester City. Their scout left before the end. But while they are out there what am I to do? I'm sitting in the stand wanting them to lose, but unable to show it. Because there are people around, I've got to pretend to want them to win. I can't jump up in the air when Sheffield score. Which I want to do. And when Millwall score I'm sick, but I have to jump in the air....

I went to the dressing-room afterwards. People were throwing their boots off disconsolately, swearing a lot. I looked at Dennis. He shrugged his shoulders. He wasn't surprised. He looked as if he was past caring. Another confirmation for him of what he thinks about Millwall. I couldn't look at Alan. He is my closest friend, but I couldn't go to him. Because I was still isolated. I had not been part of the defeat.... The lads who played and Benny [the manager] are sharing the gloom, just as it would be their joy to share if they had done well. So I kept quiet. I sat down and read the programme for the fiftieth time, and tried to grab half a cup of tea. There was me, Benny and Jack while the lads were having their baths. Benny was walking around shaking his head. There was nothing he wanted to say to me; and nothing I wanted to say to him.[7]

On November 28th Dunphy was transferred to Charlton Athletic, a move down into the Third Division which cut short the diary after only four months, but it is probably more revealing than if everything had gone according to plan and Dunphy had covered the entire season. If all the team, and the manager, had kept similar diaries, the results would have been even better because the different views would eliminate discrepancies and purely personal outlooks. Even so this transcends the apparent limitations of being a sport book, for Dunphy's closing comments apply to any activity that depends on working with other people:

I hope that Charlton will be different, that it will be somewhere where the set-up is right. Because that is the most important thing. It is like a rose. In good soil they bloom; on stony ground they don't. And footballers are the same. At Millwall we had the players, the character, the desire and the skill. But the set-up was wrong.[8]

This undertaking is reminiscent of the Mass Observation Blitz project, though the fact that it was a taped diary makes it more clearly linked to oral history. It would be possible to argue that its subject is irrelevant to history, but football is the country's leading spectator sport and it has formed a large part of the leisure culture of millions of young people in this century, as well as many older ones. It is an enormous business, but one run on completely unbusinesslike lines, and the fate of individual clubs often has a great impact on the communities whose names they bear. Just as Kevin Brownlow found that the history of the cinema had been discounted, so too has that of sport except for a huge number of exploitative and unreliable 'inside stories'. With the birth of the Premier League, and the clear message this has sent that football is to be openly dominated by the big money clubs, the Football League in which Eamon Dunphy played is already a memory. If this seems to be outside the normal definition of history, then to me it confirms that our usual definition of history is too narrow.

While much contemporary collecting is radical in tone, projects such as this show that it does not have to be. That so much of it is simply reflects the fact that it is controversial events which are most likely to fire a collector up to do some recording, and it would be interesting to see more projects undertaken purely for their own sake, giving a more balanced coverage. This is particularly appropriate for a local history group, but it will only occur when collectors feel it is worth setting aside more obviously historical work for a while. This, in turn, is likeliest where official records or the media are clearly going to form an inadequate account of events about which a collector cares deeply. It is worth stressing that anything we do with the testimony we gather is likely to date fast, for we cannot look on our own times as people will in the future.

All these points are illustrated by Jill Liddington's account of the women's peace camp at Greenham Common, *The Long Road to Greenham: Feminism and Anti-Militarism in Britain since 1820*. This is a subject that arouses strong feelings, but so did the suffragettes in their day, for example. When the campaign was at its height and women were being force-fed in jails, there would have been no more chance of a bi-partisan account than there is today about Greenham. On the other hand, few people today would feel it a good thing if all friendly recording of the suffragette cause had been suppressed, but that is the risk if controversial subjects are regarded as too hot to handle. Given the government's overwhelming hostility to the camp at Greenham, the similar attitude of much of the media, and the camp's own deliberate policy of having no central organising body that could create the kind of bureaucratic minutes on which historians mostly rely, Jill Liddington's oral material is perhaps the only direct source showing what the participants hoped to achieve and what their participation meant to them. If the balance of opinion nationally should end up against the camp, it still played a significant part in the last stages of the Cold War and it deserves recording. The actuality that this book preserves is in stark contrast to the image of the Greenham Common women as harpies, who were at least half-mad, which so much of the press put about.

The original march to Greenham to protest about the use of the base for American cruise missiles – the 'Women for Life on Earth Peace March' of 1981 – began as an idea, not a plan, which gradually took shape through the enthusiasm it generated in a few individuals. The initial inspiration came from Wales, so a nuclear weapons factory in Cardiff was chosen as the starting point for the trek, and though it was to be led by women, men were not excluded. About forty participants gathered and Ann Pettit, who had done much of the organising, recalled:

> And the amazing thing was, when we all talked afterwards about the feelings we brought to [Cardiff].... Everybody had gone there feeling sure that what they would *find* would be female experts of some variety or other – women who were either all young and single and very politically astute, or who were all cleverer than them, or who all had done this kind of thing before.... Everybody thought that everybody else would be very intimidating.
>
> And it was such a revelation. We were such a revelation to each other. Because we all looked around and my first thought was, 'Oh, my God, they really do all look so ordinary'. Quite a lot of them were quite old. And then I just got – got talking to them.... And all these young single politicoes that I'd expected to come on it... I don't think there was anyone in that category at all.[9]

Denise Aaron joined the march later:

> I suddenly realized with horror [that I was] going somewhere ALONE for the first time since I'd been married thirteen years previously. It felt extraordinarily good... Confidence and exhilaration evaporated instantly... when I saw marching towards me over the Severn Bridge a ragged, motley little – very little – band of women, dressed in all sorts of odd garments, carrying what was already a very faded banner proclaiming them to be Women for Life on Earth... The oddness of their appearance was explicable after half a day's marching in the intense heat. Clothes had to be shed but heads and backs protected. Feet were blistered. We took it in turns to push pushchairs... and carry the banner.[10]

Odd though they looked, newspapers were not interested in them and the idea evolved that, when they arrived at Greenham, four of them should chain themselves to the fence to provoke some coverage. A lot of expressions of support followed, and some rather hostile news coverage, but no public discussion of the issues they wanted to air, so, she continued:

By day, we deliberated over our fire about how to spread our news. By night we took it in turns to sleep chained to the fence [and] lay insomniac with fear and excitement under the early morning stars. The American soldiers jeered and wondered at us.

And then it became, well, we had to stay . . ... And people in the Newbury [Campaign Against Cruise] group came along... and lent us camping equipment, because we didn't have any... and kept saying 'You really ought to stay here, you know'. And of course it was very difficult for those of us with children... So what happened was that a group of older women and some of the younger women, the ones with less commitments, said to those of us who were rather chafing to get home – or those who had jobs to go back to – 'It's all right, because we can stay on'.[11]

Enough people wanted to stay to make the idea workable, and, Jill Liddington writes, 'according to legend, this was the moment they emerged from the tent to discover a double rainbow arched over the common.'[12] Those who went home put all possible effort into spreading the news about the camp, which at this point was 'a fragile flame of defiance: a dozen people and a few tents'.[13]

The decision to become a women-only camp, changes in personnel and in the whole peace movement are all recorded in the words of participants. The book ends with the agreement to scrap the missiles as part of US/Soviet disarmament negotiations, and this is the perfect illustration of the need to accept that yours is not the final word if you aim to publish quickly. Far from proceeding on any foreseeable line from that point, disarmament has become a process driven by forces no-one would have dared to predict, most obviously the collapse of the Soviet Union.

We cannot evaluate accurately what is going on when we are so close to events, and it is worse if we are actually part of them. We have to do what seems correct to us, but a few bits and pieces on many unrelated things with nothing substantial on any of them is not what future researchers will be looking for. The sheer scale of contemporary human experience can be overwhelming, especially for a historian, who is used to a role as a victim of other people's decisions about what records to preserve. We must try to look at contemporary society with a historian's eye, remembering that it is often not the issues contemporaries are most aware of that prove to be of lasting importance. However, dithering and procrastinating because we cannot be sure which subjects most need recording is not the same thing as avoiding bad choices. Look for topics where oral material will be particularly effective, for it is pointless putting a lot of effort into anything that is adequately served by the public record. In addition to reminiscences, it is also worth collecting other types of material that

Plate 5.1 Beer bottle labels from the old Yorkshire Clubs' Brewery at Huntington, near York, which was demolished in 1977. It had been a co-operative venture established in 1923 by some of the Yorkshire Workingmen's Clubs as a logical extension of their highly successful activities that had cut out publicans and brewers from the retailing of beer in many working-class communities. At its peak, fifteen to twenty people worked there, but it shared the fate of most small breweries in the 1960s and 70s. It was not unique, and the much larger Federation Brewery in Newcastle-upon-Tyne still flourishes, undergoing thorough modernisation at roughly the same time as the Huntington brewery was foundering.

I was given a tour of the building after it had closed, recording an account of the brewing process as it had been practised there as we went round. The labels had simply been left lying around, and now they add an extra dimension to the story of an enterprise that is just a distant memory. The Lancashire Clubs' Brewery commemorated here in the two centre labels, had already closed, but some of its ales had been produced in Huntington for a few years afterwards.

you are almost certain to come across in passing like photographs, notices, posters, leaflets, mementoes, and even documents that no-one wants to keep, so as to put your recording in context.

Contemporary collecting may indeed seem more like journalism than normal history writing, but material collected honestly and thoroughly will be valued in the future, even if the judgements made on it at the time become dated. In any case, such judgements will themselves be part of the future historian's source material that leads to understanding of the way people were thinking at the time. Similarly, an oral historian concerned with ordinary life today may seem to be straying into sociology, which has been using oral material in the form of surveys for decades, and which pioneered the concept of the life story. Social history can resemble a backward-looking sociology very closely, but there is a difference between the way a historian approaches a topic and the way a sociologist does, or a journalist. What sets oral history apart is the sense of history in the collector, a constant attempt to stand back and see things happening over time and as they will be seen in the future. A historian's perspective is concerned with the processes of change whereas the sociologist's is more concerned with the way things function at a given moment, and there is a value in having both at work. There is no need for too much heart-searching about whether a project is history or not; the important question is whether it is doing a worthwhile job.

NOTES AND REFERENCES

1. *Lifetimes: Something in Common,* 1975, Manchester Polytechnic Institute of Advanced Studies, p. 1.
2. *Ibid.,* pp. 45–59.
3. R. Samuel, B. Bloomfield and G. Boanas (eds), 1986, *The Enemy Within: Pit Villages and the Miners' Strike of 1984–5,* Routledge & Kegan Paul, pp. 177–9.
4. *Ibid.,* pp. 240–2.
5. *Ibid.,* pp. 72–7.
6. E. Dunphy, 1976, *Only a Game?,* Kestrel, pp. 13–14.
7. *Ibid.,* pp. 92–3.
8. *Ibid.,* p. 161.
9. J. Liddington, 1989, *The Long Road to Greenham: Feminism and Anti-Militarism in Britain Since 1820,* Virago, p. 228.
10. *Ibid.,* p. 229.
11. *Ibid.,* pp. 232–3.
12. *Ibid.,* p. 233.
13. *Ibid.,* p. 234.

CHAPTER SIX
Oral History and the Mainstream

If oral history is seen as having its own focus and its own subjects distinct from those of of 'real' history, then, as is the case with folklore, or folk life studies, or ethnology, or popular culture, or social anthropology, or any other name for what is essentially the same thing, 'interesting in its own way, but...' will continue to express the attitude of most historians towards it. In my university library, books on the past experiences of women and racial minorities will mostly be found not under history, but sociology, and this is a situation that needs to be changed. Oral testimony can make a unique contribution to our knowledge of the past because of its unique qualities, but it is important not to let this fence it off in a ghetto. There is nothing inevitable about the selection of areas with which historians mostly concern themselves today: modern historical studies have naturally been defined by the concerns of the higher strata of European societies since it was here that they were born. Male historians have developed the traditional idea that history is a chronicle of the affairs of nations and of the men who have led them.

Oral history can be seen as a modern response to this, but it already existed when academic history was developing among the educated strata of society. It was a community-based tradition, serving the rest of humanity according to their own interests. Most societies have always recognised the worth of preserving and passing on some kind of knowledge of the past, but this has rarely been seen as an active and creative task, rather one of protecting an accumulating heritage. Communities and royal houses in oral cultures acknowledged the skills of those whose job it was to learn, preserve, and pass on the stories of the past that told how the group had begun and how it had been shaped, and some people devoted their entire lives to these activities. An accessible portrait of a modern exponent of this tradition appears in Alex Haley's famous but controversial book *Roots*, in the shape of the griot who has preserved tribal traditions from the time when Alex Haley's ancestor was kidnapped into slavery in Africa in 1767. For those interested in pursuing this further, Jan Vansina's work on Africa, notably *Oral History: A Study in Traditional Methodology* (1973), brings out the great complexity of this type of role, for such people actually did shape history as well as record it, but they did – and do – so almost unconsciously, according to community rules.

The main aim of oral tradition was to explain the present and provide a moral justification for the way the community functioned. In this country, folk songs, stories, customs, and beliefs all bolstered the culture of the rural population and passed down over the generations a view of itself that satisfied its members. However, state education and the mass media have created a society that is culturally more closely integrated than ever before, both in class terms and in regional terms, and oral traditions have far less of a clear purpose to keep them autonomously alive. The old separation of cultures is impossible, but this leaves academic history stranded as much as the oral tradition, for as it has developed it cannot claim to speak for the broader-based nation we have become, except by denying all traditions but those of the elite it has primarily served. The continuing changes in emphasis in scholarly history over this century have made increasing numbers of historians aware, in any case, that our own studies are constrained by modern concerns to a much larger extent than many would like, and by a need to validate the society of today. Much of the current debate on the teaching of history in schools clearly revolves around this point, while many academic historians no longer claim to have a map of the past that will serve all purposes, and no longer see any possibility of constructing one.

Lawrence Stone's *The Past and the Present Revisited* (1987) provides an excellent introduction to the way methodologies have changed as part of general social change, and the way the questions we ask of the past are shaped by the issues of today. It also shows the growing awareness that social history is not just the wallpaper of the historical process, the backdrop against which the action occurs, but which has no influence. Communities may seem primarily social institutions, but their power and wide ramifications make them a crucial determinant in economic performance as well. It is not seeking refuge from the real issues of history to investigate the way people organised and made sense of their lives in the past. If we believe change is a broad-based phenomenon, as I certainly do, then the study of communities at a local, regional, and national level is crucial to understanding why a particular society or nation made the choices it did in the past. It will take a long time to overcome the preponderance conventional history has built up, if only because it has had a monopoly for so long and because of the scarcity of other types of sources, and it is hard to see how we can do so without oral testimony. We need, however, to consider ways of linking oral material with more conventional sources so that it generates real understanding rather than description alone.

Even though the extracts in this book are so fragmentary, I would expect most readers to have gained something from them beyond the descriptions of particular places and events, because of the sense of breaking new ground that they convey to those unused to this sort of material. All history must begin with the collection of facts, moreover, for until we have some idea what happened, when, and who was involved, we cannot move further. It would also be pointless to collect this information without making the results available in an accessible format, for then every researcher would have to waste time going over basic facts that had already been established. The *Oxford History of England* is an example of narrative history done well, and I am a great admirer of the series as an accessible and reliable reference work, even though most of the volumes are now thirty to forty years old. Many of the interpretations in them are now dated, but our knowledge of the sequence of events changes very little in this sort of well-trodden area. The minutiae that are subject to fresh discovery would not justify rewriting such a general narrative for many years, as has been the case here. What they do is stimulate us to ask whether we have an adequate understanding of why the things that we all agree happened, happened as they did.

We have to be concerned with cause and effect, with why and how things came about, rather than simply what and when. In contrast to purely descriptive history, the potential here seems almost limitless, and it should be no surprise that this is where most professional historians' effort goes. Good narrative history analyses as it lays out the facts, purely analytical history needs to take knowledge of the basic facts for granted, and pure analysis cannot therefore be an alternative to narrative in a new field. The farm servants of the East Riding lived on the edge of one of the most urbanised areas of Europe, and yet their existence was hardly acknowledged by the existing literature. Oral history is operating in a similar way to archaeology at the moment, asking analytical questions of data as it accumulates even though our knowledge is inevitably very imperfect, and a major discovery can still necessitate wholesale rewriting of large sections of the basic pattern. With our knowledge of most of human societies outside the European elites so patchy, giving a high priority to collection is neither an indulgence or an avoidance of working to high standards, but a necessity. Those elites represent only a fragment of humanity and the traditions that contain the past of all the rest are under grave threat of extinction in the foreseeable future.

Wherever possible, oral testimony should be linked to other sources, for we should not be content to be the modern equivalent of Alex Haley's griot, passing on an accepted view. Like it or not, the vast majority of us are outsiders to those we tape, even if only in terms of the gulf between generations. The long-term future of oral history as an active subject depends on asking questions and linking into all appropriate methodologies, within history and outside its traditional boundaries as well. Only a minority of collectors will want to go far down this road, just as few conventional local historians try to rival their professional colleagues in the universities, but some will, and professional historians using oral testimony must. We must therefore look at the nature of oral testimony as evidence, and the limits to memory that make it appropriate for many enquiries, but inappropriate for others. All investigations into the accuracy of memory in general support the view that, used as indicated in this book, there is no reason to fear wild inaccuracy. Paul Thompson gives a thorough survey of this subject and the literature on it in his classic book, *The Voice Of The Past* (1978, 2nd ed., 1988). For those who wish to see a deeper discussion of whether oral history is history, and of the way academic history evolved from the earlier oral forms in Europe, this and *Listening to History* (1987) by Trevor Lummis are so comprehensive that there is no need for me to add anything here.

The most ambitious attempt in this country to marry together oral testimony and academic history was Paul Thompson and Thea Vigne's enormous computerised survey of 'Family Life and Work Experience before 1918', the most accessible product of which has been *The Edwardians: the Remaking of British Society,* from which I have already quoted. Following a sociological approach, 500 people were interviewed to give a quota sample that would be as nearly perfect a geographical and social representation of Edwardian Britain as could be obtained. *The Edwardians* is a social history text book that integrates life stories with more conventional analytical chapters, also partly based on the oral material, in an attempt to interweave the personal and the general as life does. All social classes are represented, and the themes are those that best encapsulate what drove this distinctive period. It has proved highly successful and it gained an enormous amount of publicity and recognition for oral history. It turned Essex University, where Paul Thompson was based, into the natural centre for oral history, but it should not be forgotten that the oral material does not stand alone. He said in *The Voice of the Past* that it was originally 'conceived as an overall reassessment of the social history of the period rather than a field-work venture. But I fairly soon discovered that although there was a wealth of printed publications,... much of what I wished to know was either treated from a single, unsatisfactory perspective, or altogether ignored.'[1]

Alun Howkins' use of oral material is more integrated with conventional sources in his *Poor Labouring Men: Rural Radicalism in Norfolk 1870–1923*. This is described as 'the first detailed account of the relationship between the farmworkers, trades unionism, and political and social radicalism.... The main themes are the shifts from religion to politics, from Liberalism to Labour, and in more general terms from local to national consciousness.'[2] Of necessity, it begins before oral material can be of much help, but the recordings of East Anglian teammen or horsemen that come in to the later chapters make an interesting addition to those of George Ewart Evans. They concentrate not on contributors' skills but on their memories of the rebirth of agricultural trade unionism in the first decade of this century. One of George Ewart Evans' great strengths was that he located his folklore investigations against a social and economic backdrop, and this book reinforces the point that the farmworker's culture copes with the present as well as drawing on the past. The world of the frog's bone was also a world where agricultural workers were trying to claim a share in shaping their changing society. The social and economic material thus comes to the fore, the community setting and rural culture becomes the backdrop. Both are essential: neither should be neglected.

Trade unions kept written records, of course, but they frequently do not survive and they are far from comprehensive. They tell us little of the rank and file, like 'Billa' Dixon, of Trunch in Norfolk, who served in the First World War and

> returned from Flanders to an ill-paid job in a saw mill where he was sacked for leading a strike. From 1919 to the summer of 1923 he was a casual worker, spending the winters as 'second corn' in a threshing crew and the summers working where he could get it.
> 'Course they was having their own way, the farmers was then ... they were putting us just anywhere ... they wouldn't have cared

whether you lived or died. An course them days there was a lot of unemployment, them days. When you worked on a farm like, there was always one or two people what was unemployed looking over the gate where you worked.'[3]

Labour history easily becomes a tale of heroes (whichever side the historians themselves are on) and villains, but the story of Womack William Ringer who farmed in Titchwell, Norfolk, and a strike by his employees in 1921 shows well the complexities of real events that are probably only recoverable through oral history. Farming was in a poor state and tension was building between masters and men throughout East Anglia, and then Ringer proposed to tie his men's wages to the market price for wheat. He was

> a traditionalist and a paternalist – in short 'a good master'. His workers were well housed, regularly employed and received extra payments on the birth of children.... Nor was his workforce unionised, with a few exceptions.... Even when the strike was under way this powerful influence continued:
> 'If Mr Ringer wanted anything done he'd go to one of them tell them to go and get a load of straw or this and that then come back out on strike again. They always stood on the corner at Titchwell, the Chalk Pit Corner we called it, and when my father got there he [Ringer] said "Well come on together", and walked up the street, and they all went bar three others and my father.... Mr Ringer came back to these four and said "You got some rotten B——s in your union as well as I have in mine ..." and of course when the strike was over he didn't take them four back.'
> This points to the other, inevitable side of paternalism.... He owned all the cottages in his villages and single men were 'lodged' on the married ones with 'never a by your leave'. He forbad the keeping of animals by any of his workers depriving them of some little independence. He owned the lease of the pub and was a major figure on the school governors, and like all paternalists of the old school he linked religious and secular power by standing at the church door to make sure his men attended.[4]

Links between people had traditionally run vertically up and down society in this manner, rather than horizontally according to economic class. Groups had regarded themselves as 'interests' dependent on and looked after by some superior figure, reminiscent of the family on a grand scale. There were many paternalists like Ringer who tried to keep this going, but he was now seemingly trying to turn the clock back even beyond this state of affairs almost to feudalism, requiring 'his' men to share the hazards of his business. This was quite exceptional and went to such lengths that he even undertook 'to find them all the flour they wanted at 2s 6d a stone, and what meat they required at 1s 2d per lb. for the best joints, as he considered tradesmen were profiteering and charging more for meat than they should.'[5] In the past they might have acquiesced, or even been grateful for the protection that this implied, but in a modern society his ideas were just anachronistic. No-one accepted his terms and he gave up the attempt, but as general wage reductions loomed, the dispute merged with a wider strike about wages, which failed. This is in itself instructive, for with the exception of a few short periods when market conditions favoured them, if we judge farmworkers' history in terms of strikes and disputes, their struggle for better conditions can easily seem hopeless. Their main strength lay in the trouble that stubborn resistance could cause, making it plain that 'progress' could only be had at a price.

In a context like this it is particularly important to be aware of all these undercurrents that could persuade non-unionists to strike for nearly a year against Ringer, as they did, and to understand that conflicts are rarely the simple matters they may appear on the surface. Traditional histories of farming deal with the labourers only as a problem: passive participants in the progress at best, conservative hindrances to it at worst, and never partners with the farmers. On the other hand, I found things in print, in locally-published pamphlets and newspapers, for instance, that the oral evidence could not have supplied. Take the hiring fairs held every Martinmas, where farmers and farm servants met in the market towns to negotiate contracts for the next year as an example. They were in many ways the highlight of the servants' year even though the weather was often poor in November, for the throngs of people, the large funfairs that came, and the conviviality that resulted more than compensated for the weather. This was the only time when they had money in their pockets and no responsibilities, and the pubs did a roaring trade as the lads blew off steam after a year on isolated farms.

These hectic and colourful scenes usually went entirely unreported in the local newspapers, for farm servants did not buy newspapers and the middle class, who did, usually disapproved of these events. A bare listing of wage rates, with sometimes a short paragraph on the attendance and the state of the labour market, was of interest to farmers and appeared regularly, often in the commodity sales section. Just a few times descriptions of fairs did appear, but it was usually evident that they were an outsider's view. Later there might also be court reports concerning those who had celebrated too well. Though infrequent, these last were the only reportage consistently available, and as they inevitably centred around the excesses of the day, any researcher working from them alone could not help but get a twisted view. Local clergy castigated the fairs as a source of moral degeneration in the 1850s and 1860s and a number of pamphlets were published demanding their reform or abolition. The few books that notice the fairs, then or now, either on a local level or a national level, mostly take a similar line. Thomas Hardy's famous picture of a fair as a virtual slave market in *Far From The Madding Crowd* supports this view and Joseph Arch, the great trade unionist, fully agreed with it. Indications that not everyone saw things this way do exist in print, but they are few and small. The newspapers therefore provide wage rates and specific fair dates, and these were very useful, but otherwise the picture that exists in print is one of fairs as a public disgrace. The oral testimony is so different that it is hard to believe that they concern the same events, but can we believe old men reminiscing about their youth when conventional sources agree so well on a different story?

My reasons for doing so are simple. First of all, the oral evidence hangs together at least as well as the rest, so there is no intrinsic reason to rule it out. Then we must ask which version actually fits the real world best. The conventional sources show a system that was basically rotten, with no real purpose and yet causing great drunkenness, debauchery, and uproar. Why then did the authorities not take much firmer measures and why would lads go along with it, year after year? No one forced them to: newspaper advertisements provided an alternative way of finding jobs when the system was winding down in the late 1930s, and could have done so sooner. Girls were persuaded in the late nineteenth century to change to a system of registries like those widely used in towns for domestic servants. When the newly-formed York Labour Exchange set up temporary branches at all the fairs in 1910, however, it had to admit no interest was shown at all. The oral version gives clear and logical reasons why people liked the fairs. Since servants had little money and less leisure through the year, it is not surprising that some did get extremely drunk, but most did not and they used the pubs as part of an intense week's socialising when they renewed their friendships and met relatives. They walked round the town, got hired if they needed a job, chatted, bought the things they needed for next year as well as presents for their relatives and girl friends. The hirings were a key element in resisting the dislocation that leaving home at the age of thirteen, followed by frequent changes of job, could have brought to the county's working-class community.

Martinmas was also the time when grievances were settled, which kept feuds from disrupting life, and work, on the farms during the year. One of the chief complaints against the fairs was their rowdiness and it is true that pub yards and side alleys saw plenty of fights, but, accidents apart, they only involved those who wanted to fight. The police recognised this and my contributors agreed that they turned a blind eye to everything that did not get out of hand. Drunks and the randomly violent were held at the police station till things had quietened down and then were released. The newspaper court reports concern those few who were seen as a genuine danger to themselves or to others and so were charged. They often had long records of wild behaviour and had usually offended persistently on the day in question. They are in no way representative of the average lad's behaviour or experiences. Anyone who could see them as the norm is thus shown to be out of touch with ordinary people, which is not surprising in the case of the local Anglican clergy, who wrote many of the condemnatory pamphlets, given their own backgrounds and the fact that farmworkers were Methodists, either Primitive or Wesleyan.

In judging the fairs as labour exchanges, we have to see them in the context of a labour market which was, as we have seen, in balance in the county. Unlike Suffolk horsemen or Thomas Hardy's Dorset farmworkers, lads were not afraid to refuse jobs, and when they bargained for wages they were capable of forcing more out of a farmer than he wished to pay. The fairs helped them in this, for had they been meeting the farmers privately, lads might well have felt intimidated, and the inconvenience involved in seeking another offer would certainly have been a strong incentive to take this one. There was strength in numbers, and in the fact that they knew that the farmers could get no horsework done until they had hired new lads. They checked up on farmers they did not know by asking friends, and those who fed their lads badly always found it hard to hire. It is impossible to do justice to the fairs' complexity here, but it should be clear that the oral evidence shows a system that worked, and the survival of the system up to the Second World War proves this is closer to reality than the other version. The few fairs that survived in the south were demonstrably different. The huge surplus of farm labour there meant farmers could get all the labour they wanted on a casual basis, so for the most part they ceased to hire, except where it suited the farmer to have a boy available at all hours, or to have a skilled man like a shepherd tied to them. Written contracts were used to remove all the customary protection of the traditional oral contract, and to increase the obligations laid on servants. Negotiation was usually a matter of the farmer stating his terms. This explains the disapproval of men like Arch, who admitted he had no experience of northern fairs. If East Yorkshire farm wages were low by the standards of industry, and they were, they were still far higher than southern equivalents.

Understanding the way farm service worked is a matter of

assembling all available evidence and putting it in the correct context, not of taking too local a view or too dogmatic a view about good and bad sources. This is worth doing because it had been an essential part of English farming from the times of the earliest reliable records. Ann Kussmaul's *Servants in Husbandry in Early Modern England* (1981) was the first attempt to see servants as more than a different kind of labourer, and is inevitably based entirely on documentary sources. She concludes that the role of the servant evolved to carry youths through adolescence to adulthood. Though they were hard-worked, they were better fed and housed than any father working as a labourer could have managed for them, and it is worth noting that in 1864 the Medical Officer of the Privy Council declared the East Yorkshire servants the best fed working-class group in the country. Much internal family conflict was also avoided by their absence from overcrowded homes.

Farm service was far more than a way of hiring labour, for it was central to the shaping of rural society. Saving, for instance, was virtually compulsory, with only one pay day a year, and when a lad got married, his wife would almost certainly have been a servant herself, with her own savings. Together they might have the capital to take a farm or start a business, and as long as such things were realistic prospects, it was worth delaying marriage into the late twenties to save more money. The age of marriage remained high in East Yorkshire into this century, in fact, even though most workers could only aim at a foreman's job since farms were large and highly mechanised. Late marriage helped limit families, since a good part of a woman's most fertile period had gone by before she began having children. Recent work on the demographic background to the industrial revolution suggests that this mechanism played a crucial role in controlling population levels before that time, matching them to resources and preventing the classic Malthus catastrophe. The twentieth-century East Riding was vastly different from the same county of a hundred and fifty years before, yet with wages kept up by the nearness of the industrial West Riding, farmers also had an incentive to stay with the system. The hind or foreman had a respected quasi-managerial post and this gave lads something to aim for even after it had become clear that there was no future for them as farmers. Many left farming when they gave up being hired, but this usually meant leaving the county and so a few years as a servant still made sense until they were old enough to become a policeman, or get a job on the railways, or try their luck in Leeds, or whatever. This explains their ready acquiescence in a seemingly archaic system, and it also shows that it did not survive by being insulated from the modernising pressures of industrialisation.

The East Riding of Yorkshire, outside Hull and its suburbs, is described in several census reports as one of the most wholly rural counties of England, but its relative prosperity and its transformation in the eighteenth and nineteenth centuries into one of the most up-to-date farming counties in England, depended on the West Riding's demand for food and raw materials. It was an integral part of an industrialised regional economy, able to concentrate on growing food because it could buy in all the manufactured goods it needed. It preserved a decidedly pre-industrial work pattern, while those areas that gave up servants, notably East Anglia, were actually de-industrialising. Progress and modernisation are dangerous concepts if we assume that there is only one way forward. Ann Kussmaul showed what could be done to understand farm service through conventional sources used in an imaginative way, and enabled me to link my own work back to the early modern period. The distinctive contribution of the oral material was to give dimensions to the story that she could never have recovered, making it more comprehensible and helping to explain both its longevity in some areas and its sudden decline in others. The two books are complementary, just as modern written sources complemented my oral sources when carefully handled.

Industrialisation was not a simple process even in the West Riding, one of its classic locations, but even for a subject so far removed from the obvious concerns of oral history and so far back in time, oral testimony can make a contribution. Edward Thompson's famous book, *The Making of the English Working Class* (1963), set out to consider the way industrialisation affected the common people of England at the end of the eighteenth century and the start of the nineteenth. His thesis was that this period saw the birth of a sense among English workers of their status as workers and of an inherent conflict between their interests and those of their employers and rulers, in stark contrast to those vertical ties William Ringer was still trying to preserve in Norfolk a century later. A dearth of source material on movements like Luddism was almost inevitable for many Luddites were either illiterate or nearly so, and the death penalty hung over everyone who swore the oath of membership, so no documentary records were ever kept. However, a pioneering piece of oral collection in the last century, though seemingly just of local interest, offered an alternative to such things as reports by government informers, who had a clear interest in building up sinister conspiracies to bolster their usefulness and justify what was often highly unpopular work.

The Spen Valley, which lies between Leeds and Huddersfield in the heart of the textile districts of the West Riding of Yorkshire was at the centre of the Luddite disturbances in the West Riding in 1812, when there were more troops deployed in England against its own people than in Spain against Napoleon. Born in 1831, Frank Peel spent most of his life there and had a keen interest in local history, contributing regular articles to his local newspaper, the *Heckmondwike Herald,* which were often based on conversations with old people. He traced the long local history of nonconformity in religion, of which he was part, and he was also fascinated by the less obvious but equally pervasive radical tradition. Only those who had been there could put the Luddites' own case, and it is Frank Peel's achievement to have realised how important this was. With the passage of time, people were prepared to talk and a series of his articles recalled *The Risings of the Luddites* in 1878. Popular interest led to serialisation in about a dozen other newspapers and to a book in 1880. Though far from enthusiastic about the methods used, he gave a voice to those such as the man

> who had stood as a stripling in the Luddite ranks, and had often joined in their wild defiant songs as they plied the sounding shears, called himself an 'old rebel', and not without cause, for he had been mixed up with every movement against constituted authority that had sprung up in the West Riding during his life-time.... [He] repeated to me with wonderful fire and energy the impassioned speech made by that staunch old democrat [John Baines].[6]

John Baines was a well-known Halifax radical, and this reinforced Edward Thompson's conviction that such men were not isolated figures but were central to the disturbances that were occurring in many parts of the country at that time. Luddism has entered the English language as a word to describe mindless opposition to change. The machines that were broken, it is held, were the key to modernising British industry and giving it a world lead in cloth production, which would provide many jobs to replace every one destroyed, and bring great wealth to the country. In fact, machine breaking was a symbolic act as much as a practical one, and the troubles of 1812 centred round a clearly perceived threat to the very existence of tight-knit, semi-rural communities, as Frank Peel was told:

> There are many people still living who in their younger days knew intimately everybody in the village, and could say whether they were married or single... who they married, how many children they had and all their names and distinguishing peculiarities. The whole population in fact seemed at that time to consist of one large family.... No member of it could see any impropriety in discussing the private affairs of another in a way which would now be considered not only offensive but insulting. This familiarity had, without doubt, occasionally an eminently disagreeable side, but it had its redeeming

111

features also. Then all the members of the community stood pretty much on a level, and a far stronger bond of sympathy existed amongst them than obtains at the present time.[7]

The new cropping frames took over one of the few jobs in the West Yorkshire cloth manufacturing system that was done by men who depended on wages for their entire livelihood. They cropped or shaved smooth the rough woollen cloth produced by families in their own homes. Earlier machinery had, after a few hiccups of opposition, been welcomed because it could be fitted into the existing organisation of the trade: the spinning jenny, for instance, was devised as a household implement, not a powered one to be used in factories. Factory hands in the new textile towns of the mid-nineteenth century must have been hard-put to share the employers' enthusiasm for the new way of doing things, for they had lost all claim to a share in the profits and they could not be expected to take the long view. Their plight was exactly what the Luddites had set out to avoid, and Luddism is seen in Peel's work as a disciplined, community-based attempt both to control change and to force the sharing of some of the benefits of progress. Moreover, Yorkshire's success in wool textiles meant the end of East Anglia and the West Country as important manufacturing areas, so the theory that the machines created more work than they destroyed is not nearly so clear if the wider perspective is taken. It was this loss of industrial jobs in the south that contributed so much to the overstocking of the southern farm labour market in the nineteenth century, and to the atmosphere that forms the backdrop to the work of both George Ewart Evans and Alun Howkins. India suffered similarly at the hands of the Lancashire cotton industry, so the implications of localised changes can spread far and wide.

Opposition to mechanisation in this period stemmed from a fear of loss of control over one's life and livelihood. Property was not destroyed randomly and there was overwhelming support for the Luddites: despite all the troops, in West Yorkshire not one Luddite was ever caught in the act and no attack was ever betrayed. The eventual convictions and executions that ended the affair in the county were all based on the information of one man, and the accuracy of that is by no means certain. The same spirit of resistance revived at intervals, showing the tenacity of the idea that communities had a right to resist those who were perceived as enemies. This longer struggle was recalled in a much enlarged edition of Frank Peel's book, which now became *The Risings of the Luddites, Chartists and Plug-Drawers* (1888, new edition 1968). It was largely discounted by historians until Edward Thompson showed that where facts could be checked, it stood up. He found, for instance, that a story about a soldier who refused to fire on Luddites attacking Rawfolds Mill in Cleckheaton was confirmed by military records, though it had always been dismissed as romantic nonsense. His book is widely recognised as a turning point in historical study, even among those who disagree with it, and if work in the last two decades has led to many qualifications of its central theme, the fact that such work has been stimulated is adequate proof of its power. Though it did not, of course, depend on Frank Peel's work, the significance of its contribution can be seen from the fact that Edward Thompson wrote a long introduction to a modern edition of his book.

Oral testimony is much more clearly the basis of one of the most rounded attempts to study the actual process of change in one industry, *Living the Fishing* (1983), by Paul Thompson, with Tony Wailey and Trevor Lummis. There are few direct quotations, but several extensive oral history investigations were linked to all the forms of documentary source materials available, building up a picture of the fishing industry over the last century and a half. However picturesque and unchanging fishing harbours may look today, a key point of the book is that all of them have actually undergone vast and nearly continuous change in that time. Hull and Grimsby developed enormous distant water fleets from nothing in the second half of the nineteenth century, and have now once more virtually ceased to exist as fishing ports. Smaller centres like Whitby (in Yorkshire), Buckie (near Aberdeen), Shetland, the Isle of Lewis, and the various East Anglian ports have all been responding continuously to changes in the habits of the fish themselves, in markets and the transport facilities available to reach them, in boats and fishing methods, in the availability of workers, and in the methods of financing the purchase of a boat. Each port has its own highly distinctive mix of these factors, and even within one port, like Fleetwood in Lancashire, there may be two or more separate communities based on different types of fishing.

Success or failure is relative and either may suddenly be turned around by factors beyond human control, or by events such as the recent extension of foreign 200-mile limits over most of the fishing grounds on which the distant water fleet depended, sealing its fate in a way British fishermen could do nothing about. This type of fishing had been organised from its inception as a modern industry, for deep-sea trawlers had always been far too expensive for anyone but companies to finance. The workforce had little say in the enterprise and received wages rather than a share in the profits, as was common in the more traditional inshore fishing. The companies had no involvement in the communities where the boats were based and treated fishing as they would any industrial activity. For many decades it earned them high profits and inshore fishing looked doomed in the face of such a rival, but when *Living the Fishing* was written in 1983, this was the sector that was thriving, with its smaller, more flexible operators turning their hands to a multitude of activities and often getting a premium price for a quality product.

Despite the increase in the prices of the boats needed in virtually all branches of fishing, the most successful fleets were now those where the crew had a stake in the catch and boat ownership was widely spread among ordinary families rather than companies. Personal involvement encouraged adaptability, which was essential in such a changeable environment. With so many small units competing against each other for the catches at sea, but co-operating otherwise and unable to keep secret for a long time any innovation that significantly improved catches, a near-perfect environment for encouraging innovation had been created. Innovation is not an act of God nor the product of great individuals or firms. It often arises, particularly where there is no pre-existing research and development structure, precisely as this type of small-scale problem solving, which cumulatively can lead to great things. With so many different enterprises all seeking solutions, with all of them watching each other and learning from each other, and with clear rewards for success rather than threats as a driving force, progress occurs on a broad front.

The big companies' profits had depended on despatching standardised trawlers to places where the fish swarmed reliably in vast numbers. The boats were expensive and they tried to maximise profits by cutting time in port to a minimum, driving crews relentlessly, and setting individuals against each other for more effective control. From the start conditions were appalling and the Humber fleets relied extensively on getting orphans apprenticed onto trawlers as a captive labour force. They made up a third of Grimsby's sailing smack crews in the 1870s. All crews, moreover, were subject to a savage disciplinary code and men could be imprisoned for being absent when the boats were due to sail. It was in Aberdeen where this type of labour relations probably reached its nadir in the early twentieth century, and the disgust aroused in everyone linked to the trade played a large part in its demise after the Second World War. Serious domestic violence had become the rule in the trawler families, with the men brutalised by spending the overwhelming majority of their time in the cramped conditions of the boats and worked to exhaustion and beyond.

If we want to understand Britain's initial success in industrialisation, and her later and continuing inability to adjust her economy to cope

Plate 6.1 A group of boats at Whitby, North Yorkshire, one of the ports in which information was recorded that contributed to *Living the Fishing*. It still is an active fishing port, with a reputation for fresh, high-quality fish and is probably the leading centre for the hire of boats by amateur fishing parties. It has attracted increasing attention over the last two decades because it remains so much of what a fishing port ought to be in our popular consciousness, and yet a central point of *Living the Fishing* is that photographs such as this one, redolent of tradition though they genuinely are, may disguise the reality of constant change in the fishing industry.

In the foreground we have a clinker built coble (pronounced cobble) stacked with lobster pots, a type of boat that is peculiar to the north-east coast and has many echoes of Viking ship design. Equipped with engines they remain the most popular boats for this very local type of use, and with plastics used for both the netting and the ribs of the pots, an adaptable tradition is evident in the fishing technology as well as the boats. Behind it lies a bigger coble with a wheelhouse, ideal for fishing parties, and behind that lies one of the big modern trawlers that have recently taken over the more distant fishing that is based at the port, though there are no big companies here. The state of trade, the nature of the catch, and the organisation of the workforce are still changing all the time.

with competition from the USA, Europe, and Japan, there are strong parallels to be found in the reasons why some of the most successful big fishing firms seemed to succumb almost without a fight when conditions changed. Those involved in doing the work were alienated from those who controlled the industry and innovation was seen as a threat both to wages and employment. Those in charge often remained heavily involved in trading, the original source of their capital. In

115

Aberdeen such men found that, once the initial boom was over, they made more money from selling fish, supplying ice, or insuring vessels than they did from fishing, and then they bought fish in from outsiders or deliberately neglected their fleet to save money. As long as it went to sea, subsidiary companies made large profits even as the ostensible basis of it all, the fleet, decayed and made losses year on year. Investment in boats and equipment was given up in a return to operating a commercial network.

Nationally, it is hard to find any single economic or political cause for the failure of this country's industry to build on or even retain the enormous lead it built up in the mid-nineteenth century when it had a near-monopoly on modern industry. The same retreat from actual doing into commerce is clearly a contributory factor, and the same refusal to allow the workforce any creative role was remarked on by many American commentators at the turn of the century. Given the urgency that this now has as a contemporary issue, it is a subject worth pursuing, and orally based studies have the capacity to contribute important facets to this and other related subjects. The Elswick group, quoted earlier, who prepared the history of the leather works in Newcastle were explicit about their desire to draw conclusions from their own experience that had implications for the wider regional and national communities of which they formed a part, and in turn for the story of British industry in recent decades. No such study on its own is going to have much effect on our attitudes to big historical questions, but in a mass, they may transform them.

Attitudes to life both shape and are a product of the working environment. Communities, their value-systems, and the pressures they exert on their members are all a vital force in determining what course human history follows. Opportunities are seized by some societies, while others prefer to lose out rather than do something perceived as dishonourable, or impossible to carry through in the face of vested interests. This is not to deny obvious economic and political factors, but to assert that they cannot explain things on their own. In *Living the Fishing,* for instance, the importance of family relationships in explaining the dynamism of some systems and the collapse of others is forcibly argued. This links to the work on Lancashire women and their role in industrial society that we looked at before. The feminist perspective on women's position in society is that they have always been an exploited group with fewer rights than a man on the same level in society. The reminiscences from working-class women quoted so far, however, indicate that most had a positive view of their domestic role. Thus, one of Elizabeth Roberts' Lancashire contributors had gone out to work in the First World War but lost her job when the men returned:

> Well I knew I was engaged to be married and you see in those days as soon as you were going to be married you left a job, you knew you were going to be a sort of housekeeper and be at home all the time you see. That's the only thing we girls had to look forward to, if you understand, getting married and sort of being on our own, and getting our bottom drawer together and various things like that. Yes, that was the ambition of girls then.[8]

Apart from special places like the cotton weaving towns, Elizabeth Roberts' statement of the traditional attitude to the idea of working on after marriage must be accepted as typical:

> Women at home did not envy their neighbours in full time work. Rather they pitied them. In some cases the image of the full-time working mother was one of a downtrodden exploited being, forced to work by unfortunate circumstances such as widowhood. One old lady told how her own mother, whose husband was a chronic drunkard, was finally forced to work at the mill after the bailiffs had twice taken all her furniture to settle the family's debts. Her sisters used to bring the baby to the mill gates to be breast-fed.... A woman's perceived duty was to her family. It is interesting to note that in the two cases in Lancaster where the woman chose to continue to work full time after marriage (and was not forced to do so by adverse conditions), two related preconditions were fulfilled. Both women had one child only, and both had living nearby an able-bodied grandmother willing and able to cook, clean and act as a surrogate mother. There was a general consensus of opinion in both towns that unless these conditions were fulfilled, it was not possible for a woman to care adequately for her home and her family.[9]

Yet she felt that this was not subservience to their husbands,

> but rather that they were partners; and that this relationship of partnership can be partly explained through the economic role and status of the working-class wife within the family... [for she] was an economic necessity to her husband; she was indispensable. If she did not do the housework, he could not afford to pay anyone else to do it. Indeed if a wife died, it was a lucky man who escaped breaking up his home and seeing his children in the workhouse.
> 'I remember one young woman her mother died, I think it was T.B., and her father had to go out to work, he was on a farm, labouring. Do you know there was six children and the neighbours used to help. But I always remember the School Board coming and what they were going to do with the dad. They explained to it and they got somebody to come out of the workhouse, an old lady out of the workhouse, as it was then, to come and house for them, and I think she got about half a crown [12$\frac{1}{2}$p] a week and her food. If you lost your mother, well you broke your home up. My father did.'[10]

We have seen that housework was hard work, and that women controlled the family finances, even down to denying the men pocket money in some cases. They made the decisions about where to live and when to move. They were the arbiters of moral and ethical standards, often dictating to their husbands about matters like church attendance. It took all their time and energy, and they were constantly aware how important the tasks they undertook were. If they had little choice in the life they led, no more had their husbands. Their jobs were often heavy in the extreme and in the aftermath of industrialisation they brought little of the satisfaction of the old craft operations. Only by battling together against a hostile world, with others in the same situation, could they come through, and both their roles were vital. The suffragette message seems to have had no appeal to such women, and those who were politically active saw the priority as improvement in the conditions of the entire working class. Feelings of oppression were directed at the rich, far more than at their partners. One woman was asked if her father felt exploited:

> Oh, I'm sure he did. He would occasionally get drunk, not really drunk, but well oiled and he used to grind his teeth and you could hear them…. Sixty years he worked for those people with very little remuneration, very little. Of course it's through that John Willie Scott who is commonly known as the Duke of Buccleuch, it's through that, that my father's family…. the five of us, there was four boys and me of course, made Socialists of us, the Duke. He didn't know he was doing that but that's how it turned out. You see they were pirates these people, the fore-fathers of these, lord this and lord that, and duke that, they were pirates. There was no doubt about it that they helped themselves to all these enormous places that they live in.[11]

This raises an issue that has particular force for women but is relevant to the majority of oral testimony, and that is how far to accept the almost universal protestations that people were content with their lot. When even Tommy Morgan, bringing himself up in a travesty of a family in the East End of London could say this, it clearly does not mean what it seems to. If housework was so essential, it could have been shared out differently and it should have been given a higher status, and its identification with women was not inevitable, either in theory or in practice. Mr Harper, who was born in 1900 in the East Riding, did not become a horselad when he was first hired into farm service:

> I was two year in house as a kitchen boy, do you see, with two sisters and a brother. And I used to have to get up at five o'clock at morning, get fire going – and it was an old fashioned fireside in those days, you know…. We were at it from five o'clock of a morning till

seven at night i' those days....

Were there many places kept lads in service?

In my young day, round about that way [Scagglethorpe, near Malton]
there was more young lads in house than what there was maids.
'Cause they could trust you better. For doing things. But when the
war broke out it knocked it all on the head. (Tape 17/1)

His weekly schedule included helping with the Monday washday,
washing up after meals, making beds, scrubbing tables and floors,
cleaning dairies and poultry houses, washing bedroom floors, and,
when a party was being held, he spent the evening waiting at table. He
saw it as in no way a degrading job nor one that was likely to attract
mockery. Moreover, Jill Liddington's contributors from the
Lancashire weaving towns had turned the normal attitudes to
housework on their heads: they could not imagine how they would fill
the day if they were at home. We have to note, however, that the
reason given for working was that their earnings kept the family
respectable, so this is not the flouting of conventions that it may seem,
merely a reworking. It is surely significant that the struggle for the
suffrage did become a burning issue for working women here. Once
even partially outside the home they felt like individuals and wanted
individual rights, so it cannot be said that the Barrow and Lancaster
model of family life was better or more inherently satisfying. If women
had had a real choice about taking on the caring role, no-one could
doubt them if they said it was all they wanted out of life, but they were
prepared for this from birth and, if this process had not been so
successful, many would certainly have chosen differently, as they do
today.

Catherine Hall's investigation of 'Married Women at Home in
Birmingham in the 1920s and 1930s', also from *Oral History* (1977)
explicitly looked at this question a generation later in Birmingham. In
some senses the backdrop is the same, Mrs Wilkinson had enjoyed
working at Cadbury's while she was single, but she said, 'He (my
husband) didn't want me to go on working. I thought that was lovely. I
used to go and visit my friends... I thought it was a grand life.'[12] Mrs
Gardiner

had worked as a domestic servant before marriage and she was
delighted to be able to stay at home. She described how the most
important thing for her was that she should keep her husband happy –
she had no children but she made a very full life for herself looking
after family and neighbours. She had looked forward to having her
own home whilst in service and never had any ambitions for a
different kind of life –

Plate 6.2 Millicent Caunce photographed at the door of her brand new semi-detached council house in Newton-le-Willows, Lancashire, in 1952 by her husband Wilfred. She had grown up in a traditional terraced house less than a mile away, and Newton is not a large town, but even such a move meant a transformation of many aspects of her way of life. The houses were modern and had large gardens, but the estate had no shops, churches, or community facilities. This was not too important on a small estate like this, but in the cities the results were much more dramatic, as Catherine Hall records.

> 'I've always been happy in my home, of course, I wasn't ambitious, I was perfectly happy if I could be at home... I was always at home when my husband came home for a meal, I was always there, everything was always ready and I think that's what brought us the happiness... When he came home, there was always a meal, there was always a fire, he was always looked after.'
>
> Mrs Gardiner's objective subordination to her husband's work and politics, for he was very active in the Union and the Labour Party, are quite clear in the interview – she organised her life around him – but she does not appear to experience any resentment at all about this. The woman's sphere is the home, her main tasks loving and caring and those definitions are held to.'[13]

This is, however, a study of a crucial moment and place in working-class history. The big new suburban council estates of the interwar years offered families space and facilities they had never had before. The regional economy of the West Midlands was prosperous and as it was the better-off who moved onto them, it was unlikely that their lifestyles would remain unchanged. Families were shrinking, moreover, and housework was losing some of its drudgery for those who lived in modern houses with access to new appliances. There were few community facilities provided, and what there were tended to be inadequate. Husbands worked in scattered and distant places, so common employment could not forge a bond among residents. Relatives kept up their links, so this was not a place where everyone was isolated, but the clear roles of the women of Lancashire and their supportive community life were both being taken away at once. The obvious model to copy was that of middle and upper-class wives who had long been assigned a more ornamental role. As they lost their centrality in the life of the household, the work that remained became ever more openly that of an unpaid domestic, and the inherent subservience of those who lived within the family rather than in the wider world became apparent. This left women in a cleft stick, for objectively they were better off, but they lacked the tradition of independence that sustained the working wives of Blackburn, as well as the sense of a hard job well done that was observable in most other places. As yet, few were prepared to query the value of the new ways, but this helps to explain the transformation in women's views of themselves that has occurred since and is still continuing.

Both Jill Liddington and Elizabeth Roberts combined their oral material with every other source that could be used, looking at employment patterns, wage rates, illegitimacy rates, child mortality, and anything else that helped produce rounded studies. In both cases their *Oral History* articles form the basis of later books, *One Hand Tied Behind Us: The Rise of the Women's Suffrage Movement* (1978) and *A Woman's Place: An Oral History of Working Class Women 1890–1940* (1984) respectively. Their challenge to stereotypes from all parts of the spectrum shows how oral history can illuminate areas that would otherwise be dominated by conclusions drawn from totally inadequate evidence, from inference, and from extension of the historian's own beliefs. They show that even on an issue as basic as women's relationships to men, class has a bearing, but they also show that any attempt to say that it is the sole determining factor is nonsense, for women from the same class in the same county came to lead quite different lives. Elizabeth Roberts's contributors' lifestyles depended on the re-emergence of stable, self-regulating communities out of the maelstrom of industrialisation, which had undeniably been revolutionary in Lancashire. It also depended on mens' wages keeping a family, which was not true in the weaving towns, and this concept of the family wage became one of the worst barriers to the re-entry of women into paid full-time work in recent times. In its time it clearly had practical benefits for both sexes, however, for the weaving towns were one of the few areas where men and women competed for the same jobs, and this must have contributed to low male wages.

Traditional communities largely restricted individual choice to minor things, laying down rules for life that were inculcated into people of all sorts so successfully that they were hardly aware that things could be done otherwise. The collapse of farm service in the East Riding in the 1930s was due to several factors, but one undoubtedly was the opening up to the world that was the result first of mass service in the First World War and then of the arrival of the cinema and the radio. It became clear to most lads that hardly anyone else was living like them, and they wanted to join the consumer society rather than wait a year for their wages. I can find no evidence that they suffered lower wages or a worse standard of life through being farm servants, so there is no case for condemning the system, but the general acceptance of it that was such a feature of the county, say in 1900, was as much due to lack of knowledge of any alternatives as to positive choice. People may disagree as to whether the choices apparently open to all today are real or illusory, but understanding a system that worked without them requires of us a great effort not to judge it by modern standards, but not to condone brutality and oppression either.

Oral material, then, cannot be taken at face value any more than any other source, but it is as useful as any for history at any level as long as the subject is appropriate. It is not just about reminiscence and description, but is capable of deepening and widening our analytical understanding of the world of the past. Moreover, the failure of the statistical historians to sweep the field as they may have expected to do two decades ago is part of a realisation that since history is about people, it is complex and many-faceted. Statistics are invaluable where things can be counted and measured, and I have used them myself wherever they seemed appropriate. History is much the better for the more rigorous approach to quantitative data that has developed in recent times, but no one approach holds the key to everything. People's own stories can and should be in there too, and it is interesting to see Lawrence Stone in *The Past and the Present Revisited* arguing for social historians in general to move away from purely analytical approaches back towards the narrative format to promote accessibility.

NOTES AND REFERENCES

1. P. Thompson, 1988, *The Voice of the Past: Oral History* (2nd edn), Oxford University Press, p. 86.
2. A. Howkins, 1985. *Poor Labouring Men: Rural Radicalism in Norfolk 1870–1923*, Routledge & Kegan Paul, back cover.
3. *Ibid.*, pp. 136–7.
4. *Ibid.*, pp. 140–1.
5. *Ibid.*, p. 141.
6. F. Peel, 1968, *The Risings of the Luddites, Chartists and Plug Drawers* (reprint of 1895 3rd edn), Frank Cass, p. xi.
7. *Ibid.*, p. x.
8. E. Roberts, 'Working Women in the North West', *Oral History,* Vol 5, no 2, 1977, pp. 9–10.
9. *Ibid.*, pp. 16–17.
10. *Ibid.*, p. 13.
11. *Ibid.*, p. 9.
12. C. Hall, 'Married Women at Home in Birmingham in the 1920s and 1930s', *Oral History,* Vol. 5, no 2, 1977, p. 74.
13. *Ibid.*, p. 74.

CHAPTER SEVEN
Starting Out

Everyone has access to memories that would contribute to at least some of the topics covered so far, and it is time to look at the practicalities of oral collecting for those who want to do more than read, to examine the planning and running of projects of all types and consider how to use the material that they produce. Few people have experience in this, even if they have been undertaking conventional research, but the basic skills required are actually only adaptations of some that most people possess anyway. For instance, running an effective session depends mostly on the ability to get someone talking freely, so it is positively harmful to imagine that no-one can start without special training and expertise. There are certainly ways of working that are better than others, and there is no point in not taking advantage of others' previous experience wherever you can, but making a start is in itself a vital part of training yourself. All the early oral historians began this way and worked their rules out for themselves.

A beginner with no clear aim would do well to join an existing project, or to work in such a way as to make the tapes compatible with one. A valuable first contact could be the Oral History Society's voluntary regional network 'of accredited individuals who are all members of the Society, experienced in oral history and willing to assist anyone new to oral history or wanting to discuss their work in detail with someone who is sympathetic and knowledgeable.... All represent the Society in their local area and will lend an ear.' The list is still being added to and will change over time, so consult the current issue of *Oral History* for names. Otherwise, a reference library or a museum are obvious places to contact. Even if they are not involved in anything themselves, they should be able to pass you on to someone who can help with advice at least. Funding for individuals or groups is never going to be instantly available and has to be sought in the usual way, through applications for grants and direct money-raising activities. Borrowing equipment may be possible, though it should not be relied upon, and there are institutions which regularly train and use volunteer staff. One of the contacts listed for West Yorkshire, for instance, Kirklees Libraries and Arts Service, has a sound archivist based at Red House Museum, Gomersal, near Leeds, and they are always interested to hear from local people who wish to have a try at oral history. Remember, however, that this does mean making a commitment and any volunteer programme will expect you to accept training and take it seriously. No-one will allow strangers to act in their name, or trust them with expensive equipment, until they are sure that they will act responsibly.

Many people will wish to pursue their own course, either because they have a clear idea of what it is they wish to do, or because they are shy of getting involved at too deep a level until they have proved to themselves that they can cope. This should not be an excuse for working to low standards, however, even if your aims are very modest. Even the smallest and most intimate project runs better for being taken seriously and, in my experience, those who see working rules as preventing a friendly informality actually create the ideal environment for turning minor misunderstandings into serious disagreements, either between co-workers or between collector and contributor. At first there are few things that can go wrong but trouble later is both certain and all the harder to put right, so it is best to be systematic from the start. For example, where several people are involved, it is important to keep track of equipment and make sure collectors can rely on getting a recorder when they need one. If you are working alone, have a routine for checking that the recorder works and that you have tapes and batteries before you set out. Tapes of sessions must be stored properly, with a record of who is on the tape and when it was made, so avoid the temptation to record as much as possible at first and sort them out later. Backlogs are rarely cleared, in fact, and once they have built up, their very existence makes getting organised seem a hopeless task.

Testimony can be collected without making arrangements or keeping records, but the results will be of little use to anyone, even you, if the only documentation is in your head. To be effective for more than a short time a group needs formal co-ordination, but if the tasks involved in co-ordinating the activities are rotated round the members, everyone experiences personally the difficulties involved in doing the job, and, hopefully, is more understanding as a result. Similarly, rules should be open for discussion, which produces the mutual confidence essential for a genuinely relaxed atmosphere to develop. Build up your systems as you go according to your needs and keep them as simple and straightforward as possible, for there is no point in tying yourself in organisational knots trying to anticipate every circumstance that may arise.

Selecting a subject for your project needs a sense of realism, and full account must be taken of limitations such as the need to restrict yourself to one town or village because of lack of time or transport. It is much easier to scale up something that is going unexpectedly well than to scale down a grandiose effort that is not working. There is no harm in modest beginnings, especially as it is almost inevitable that an oral history investigation will grow as it progresses. Breaking new ground, one of oral history's greatest attractions, is incompatible with precise descriptions of what the conclusions will be before the first question has been asked. The sensible way to start is to establish a clear general framework within which detail is deliberately left vague. Do not become so committed to something in advance that it is difficult to disengage if it is patently not achieving its aims. It is always tempting then to follow the line of least resistance in the hope that things will work out, but mostly they will not, and the project will either break down or turn into a random set of tapes. Shape and adapt things as you go, but start from a position worked out as clearly as possible. This is the essential foundation that stops such a process reducing the project to shapelessness.

Defining areas for investigation and intended methods as far as possible brings out inconsistencies and weak points that will not show up if everything is left at a woolly, unchallenged stage. Statements like 'I want to know more about Edwardian childhood' need turning into manageable work programmes. Your ability to pass on a coherent picture of your aims when you begin contacting contributors is a good test of how successful you have been, as well as showing them that you are not going to waste their time. A starting point can be fairly generalised, such as recording all the old residents of a particular street or village, as long as there is a rationale behind it. In this case it would be to build an archive of a locality seen in its own terms, which may be quite different from the agenda that an outsider would impose, and the recordings are tied together by a sense of place and shared experiences and attitudes. The project can then be developed by filling any perceived gaps, and subjects raised but not covered in detail can be revisited. A completely random set of contributions from a wide area, done to no plan and with nothing in common, is different altogether. It does preserve memories, but randomly, so there will be no clear use for it and even as an archive it will be neglected since no historian will see it as likely to yield much of interest.

George Ewart Evans wrote in the preface to his first book, *Ask The Fellows Who Cut The Hay:*

> I have to confess that the book, as originally conceived, had no purpose at all. Shortly after coming to live in this village seven years ago I became aware of the material that was waiting to be collected and went out in a desultory way to do so. Later the colour and the wealth of the material overcame my natural laziness and hesitation about starting a new project, and eventually worried a pen into my hand.[1]

This should not be taken too literally as he was already then an experienced radio broadcaster and writer with an instinct for producing results, and once started, the project naturally shaped itself into a rounded view of a rural community. Farm horses and horsemen already figured and he decided to research this subject more intensively, leading to his more specialised books. Louise Brooks' comment on inspiration, quoted in the first chapter, is relevant here: the seeming spontaneity of early film directors hid the fact that years of experience had given them immense resources on which to draw, and younger men who tried to manage on spontaneity alone got into difficulties. Do not be afraid to draw inspiration from others and to ask for help. It may even be worth modelling a local investigation on one done elsewhere, or trying to get intensive coverage of one area on a subject already covered more loosely on a national scale. Thus, I was involved for a short time in an adult education class in Leeds which aimed to run a parallel local study to Paul Thompson's national project on the Edwardian era, using the same interview schedule.

Motivation may come from a generalised interest in your locality or a more specific one in a particular family, firm, or trade. It may come from working with elderly people and becoming interested in their stories of the past, while many teachers are aware of the educational possibilities of oral history for all age groups in schools. It has a place in the national curriculum and specialist materials are now on sale to help those interested. A local history group could turn naturally to oral collection as part of a project in progress. If you have a strong interest in fairly recent events and contributors ready to hand, resist the feeling that this is less important than searching for some crucial but unknown witness to an equally unknown event who must be found and recorded before they die. When any old person dies something is always lost,

Plate 7.1 A group of school children collecting testimony during a workshop run by Bradford Heritage Recording Unit in 1987, using equipment loaned by the unit, and helped by a unit member (the woman on the right facing the recorder). The enthusiasm with which children normally respond to oral history is clear from the postures. Many teachers find such schemes motivate children to a high degree, and run under their own steam. Naturally they need adult help in framing questions, and a questionnaire is a good idea in most cases here, but they are not shy of asking questions once they get started and very impressive results can be obtained.

and it is true that there are chasms in our historical knowledge because no-one took a tape recorder to particular individuals or groups. This, however, is a natural process that has been going on since time immemorial and the efforts of one collector will never halt it even at a local level. The *New Statesman* enthusiastically reviewed George Ewart Evans' *The Horse in the Furrow* as 'probably the last book to be written with the personal aid of the men who served the horse when it was still the prime mover of all field-work'[2], in 1960. In fact it helped stimulate a torrent of interest in heavy horses, including my own, and there has been a steady stream of books of this type ever since.

Farm horses did not vanish overnight and men are still around thirty years later who knew what it was like to work in an industry based completely on horsepower. Others who worked with horses but knew that they would soon be replaced by tractors will be around for many years to come. Each generation appears to have lost something compared with the one just gone, but usually it is a progressive, incremental loss, not a catastrophic one, just as we saw with harvesting technology. Each generation right down to the present has its own history and its own special skills or knowledge. With a group of very elderly people who like to talk about the past, it makes sense to capitalise on that by going as far back in time as possible with them. However, Iona and Peter Opie's work with children showed that, though they were too young to have accumulated much personal history, they were the unwitting preservers of centuries of customary behaviour, and the young here could go further back indirectly than the elderly could have done directly. Elderly people probably make the best contributors in that they have often reached a contemplative stage of life when they themselves are trying to make sense of their past, and the recording process becomes a natural part of this. Remember, though, that their view of the world of their childhood is a child's eye view, modified by later experience, but still lacking elements that only an adult would know about.

There is much about East Riding farming which my tapes do not cover. My own interests and awareness have changed as I have grown older, and there are questions I now see as important which I do not have the information to answer. I would like to compare the lives of female farm servants to those of the lads, for instance, for I know that there were many differences, but I have only fragmentary information on this group on my original tapes. Building it up will now be very hard, though not impossible. Even worse will be to cover the labourers, the married men of the village. They were mostly in their late twenties at the very least, and while there will still be a few who knew the system while it was still intact in the 1920s, their experience will be tinged by the general awareness that times were inexorably changing. Ideally it is the cohort that began work before 1914 that should be recorded, but very few will still be around now. While there are exceptions in communities with a strong surviving oral tradition, such as parts of the Scottish Highlands and Islands, the difficulty in this country of going back beyond personal experience is one of oral history's most obvious weaknesses.

My choice of farm horsemen as a group to study is also worth examining, for it resulted from the combination of several strands of interest and opportunity: it was not a driving ambition of long standing. In 1972, when I finished my BA in history at London University, I felt my studies had had little connection with my own experiences of life in an ordinary family from a small manufacturing town in the north of England. I did not doubt the importance of what I had been learning, but the lives of the vast majority of the population had been virtually ignored. Folklore seemed to offer a possible path to an alternative history, one passed on by word of mouth by the ordinary people. I also felt that history often seemed too free-standing, too neglectful of the insights that other disciplines could bring to it. There was no originality in these thoughts, for it was a time when all sorts of avenues were being explored in search of better historical understanding, and much local history was undertaken from similar motivations. Even collecting oral testimony was only partly my choice as a method of working, for at the Leeds University Institute of Dialectology and Folklife Studies (a long name for a small institution), where I went to undertake my research, this was the standard approach.

Picking horses as the subject for my research was again part chance. Direct contact with horses in my home town was rare – even riding ponies were not common then. The only evidence I can give of any predisposition to study them is that I am told I had an obsession as a very small child with a horse-drawn milk float which toppled over with spectacular results at the bottom of our street. I have already described how the older men with whom I worked on my summer jobs while at university often harked back in conversations to the use of horses, and this definitely contributed to an awareness that there was something here that warranted studying. There was a clear dividing line between these men, who could probably still have harnessed and driven a horse, and the younger workers, whatever our origins, who would have had no idea. It seemed symbolic of a deep change in working methods and ways of life. While I was searching for a subject at Leeds, I read George Ewart Evans' books and Yorkshire Television discovered Geoffrey Morton and his farm at Holme on Spalding Moor in the East Riding, where he still used nothing but horses. Today he is a tourist attraction and holds open days, even though his primary aim is still to run his farm in the way that he wants, but until then he had only been known about within a small area. I now had an interest, a model to follow, and a potential central contributor. I advertised in the local newspapers for older contributors, to add the authentic memories of the past, and got several responses. The way seemed clear, after Mr Morton agreed to talk with me, to emulate George Ewart Evans' work in the north of England, and also to study the economics of horse farming at a time when ecological concerns were suggesting that it might be of more than nostalgic interest in the future.

It did not work out like that. Mr Morton was from County Durham, not the East Riding, and was also, understandably, actively seeking ways to change traditional working methods to keep his costs down and to cope with the fact that farm machinery suitable for use by horses is no longer easy to come by. I would have to look elsewhere to find out about the traditional methods of the East Riding, though I gained valuable insights from Mr Morton into the practicalities of horse farming. Letters from older men, however, offered a chance to put things back on course and I arranged a programme of visits. I started the sessions believing I was talking to men who had been the skilled elite of the arable farms of the county, like the Suffolk horseman who 'was in a special class among the farm-workers: he did not lose work through bad weather, and he had a number of privileges that gave him a steadier and more comfortable living.... The horseman's skill was recognised in his wages,'[3] as George Ewart Evans said. Only after years as labourers could they become a horseman, and only illness or incapacity would make them give up the work. The answers to my first questions obviously did not make sense in these terms. The notion that there would be a traditional framework intended to preserve the superior status of the horsemen was obviously a non-starter, for horselads and labourers had separate places on the farm and neither was superior to the other. In terms of the project as I had envisaged it, I could hardly have done worse, but I had also been presented with an enormous opportunity, for here was a system of farming that had never been written up before, and one that fascinated me right from the start. The number of points to follow up that arose in my first session with an ex-horselad, Mr Pridmore, is still almost unbelievable:

> 'We used to get hired in November.... You left your last farm on November 23rd – that was what they called the leaving day. You had a week off and you used to go to the markets, to what they called the statuses, you know. They were held anywhere in the farming districts where farmers used to congregate and take their produce. You used to go there if you wanted hiring and the farmer would come to you and ask you if you wanted hiring and what could you do? 'Can you plough, can you stack, can you thatch, can you do this, can you do the other?' You answered yes to all the lot you see. So this is how you used to get hired. If you accepted, of course, they used to give you what was called a fastening penny, that was when they hired you they'd maybe give you two bob or half a crown and that was what they called a fastening penny. You were hired to that man for that year then once you'd got that fastening penny. That went on, oh, every year when you got hired, you see.... It was only the just the men hired in the farm house [that used the hirings], young single men that were were hired in the farms – they used to leave. Sometimes they'd ask you to stay on for another year, but I didn't believe in staying two years at one place. I liked a change.... It was never much money, of course – you had to make do with what you'd got. I remember once I wanted a sub off a farmer and he didn't want to let

me have it – middle of the year, 'cause I'd run out of money, dost
see, 'Oh,' he said, 'you're not supposed to have it while year end.'
(Tape 3/2)

If I had spent months preparing a Suffolk-type survey in great detail,
and if I had become committed to my original concept, then I would
have had good grounds for despair, but these possibilities rapidly
crowded out any thought of examining horse farming along those lines,
or in a technical way. As I had already arranged my first sequence of
visits, I had no time for elaborate pre-visit research and as it turned
out, this was lucky, because there was so little in print about these lads,
and much of what there was was actively misleading, as I have shown. I
had to rely at first, therefore, simply on getting the conversation going
and then picking up on issues that emerged as they talked. This is a
perfect illustration of why it is always sensible to run a trial project to
see how things work before tackling a large-scale enterprise, even
where there seems to be the clearest possible path to follow. It must be
conducted as a project in its own right with its own aim, which is to
discover what will be the most productive lines to follow later. It is
sensible to limit the numbers of contributors at this stage, until it
becomes clear that there are certain areas that seem to be historically
significant, and about which the contributors are willing and able to
talk, and then the investigative phase can be ended and the main
project defined.

Ignorance is no barrier to success in oral history, and it can be an
asset if used wisely. A contributor who thinks you already know a great
deal about your subject and are only in search of assistance on specific
points of detail is unlikely to offer the sort of general accounts that
make good archival material. I knew absolutely nothing and had to
encourage the fullest possible accounts. This is a vital point, separating
out real oral history from the mere use of a tape recorder to round out
more conventional research. The recordings are meant to have a value
in their own right and the contributor must therefore be encouraged to
do more than answer questions. There was no real risk of sessions
missing the point entirely, moreover, because horsework had been a
specific phase in their lives and they knew in advance that it was what I
was interested in. As often as possible, I went back for a second
session, and in some cases more followed, though this was where I
learned how limiting a reliance on public transport was when covering
a country subject. Unless two contributors lived in the same village,
each interview meant committing at least a morning or afternoon, and
often a whole day.

I have gone into some detail because the preliminaries of research are rarely described. A newly-finished building has no trace remaining of the scaffolding that surrounded it while it was being built, yet during construction the whole site was a mess, with little sign for the public of what was going to emerge, and without that scaffolding there would have been no building. Historians do their construction in private and rarely have a blueprint to follow, just a list of sources to search and their own skills in unearthing relevant material and linking it together. When they have finished it is easy to assume that they moved inevitably and irresistibly to the polished conclusions that they now present to the world, but they went through the messy stage too, when nothing seemed clear, so do not be discouraged by the need to rethink your approach from time to time. Where detailed results are perfectly predicted from the outset, there must be a strong suspicion that research was deliberately shaped to provide support for an existing theory, rather than to look honestly at all the facts. Work out what questions to ask, not what answers you expect to get. Working with people is what can make oral history so personally rewarding, so do not allow fear of the unknown to deprive you of its possibilities – be prepared to adapt to circumstances.

People are, indeed, the essence of oral collecting, and finding the appropriate ones is therefore essential. An established network of contributors, such as relatives or neighbours, will obviously make starting out easy in some cases, but it is by no means essential. Moreover, even among those people you know personally, some may not want to take part, some may need persuading to open up enough to make a worthwhile contribution, and you may need to seek others to get the right balance. A pre-existing relationship between collector and contributors can help, but it can act as a barrier as well as a bridge. At its simplest, reminiscences may be cut short because the contributor remembers telling the same story before. Harder to deal with is the fact that we all project an image of ourselves, and complete honesty on many subjects may endanger that. Those who grew up in great poverty may wish to deny that it ever happened, lest it detract from their standing in their community. Those ostensibly proud of having done well after a bad start may baulk at giving details that seem demeaning, relishing the image of a poor childhood, but not wishing anyone to know what it really entailed. Adult/child relationships are hard to break out of, and if questioning becomes personal, a relative may feel threatened. Outsiders who simply collect facts and who promise anonymity might get more openness in all these situations. It is worth noting, however, that sessions can become emotionally charged in any circumstances and this can be difficult to cope with.

Image preservation is also something to be aware of with groups as well as individuals. They may be proud of their street, town, or trade, or else defensive about it because it has generally been maligned or laughed at. People from districts like Elswick, or from towns like Wigan which have been the butt of jokes for years, are often sick of this public image their home has been given and may be very reluctant to perpetuate it, or may consciously try to put a contrary case. They will not then willingly come forward with the seamier side of things, unless they are convinced by the collectors that it is both necessary and desirable. One of my contributors let slip, while talking about the spartan conditions that prevailed in farmhouses, that many horselads used toe rags rather than socks, and his wife took him to task – he had been under instruction to avoid such subjects. No-one told me that servants were expected to relieve themselves on the midden rather than use the family toilet, and I discovered this from written reminiscences, though another collector knew of it.

Local networks can achieve great intensity of coverage over a small patch, with each contributor unknowingly verifying or casting doubt on the testimony of the others, and the knowledge that romancing is likely to be detected will keep it to a minimum anyway. Enthusiasm for a project can create a group dynamic that encourages more and better recall and stimulates new contributors to approach of their own volition. There is a natural audience for the results, and the boost that a group can get from publishing them is one of the best ways of ensuring that it does not lose heart and fizzle out. The very intensity, however, leaves a danger of parochialism, concentrating on one of the trees to the extent that there is no concept that it is part of a wood, much less that its place in it needs defining. Customs commonly found over whole counties, regions, or even nations are often fondly assumed to be local oddities because no-one involved has checked, and the course of national history is seen as irrelevant.

Any closely defined group is bound to generate internal tensions and where the contributors deal with each other directly rather than through the collector, these may interfere with the project. They themselves, and the way they operate, say a good deal about the nature of the community involved, but one group of contributors may end up withdrawing. A recorder of historic buildings told me recently about a pair of farmhouses separated by a field, both of which were of interest to him, but whose inhabitants had been feuding with each other for decades. Keeping in with both involved a lot of very judicious nodding of the head and smiling at stories of the latest outrages the others had committed, without becoming identified with either, and he had managed to keep his neutrality intact for several years. It is difficult, however, and the personal contact inherent in oral history collection makes keeping this kind of distance even more of a problem.

It is natural to expand the original group by asking for introductions to others, but this is not always as easy as it sounds, for sharing a mutual friend or acquaintance may not be a good enough recommendation for a new contact to open up to a collector. A personal introduction breaks the ice as well as vouching for your honesty, whereas simply arriving on someone's doorstep on the off-chance, expecting confidences, is very optimistic, especially in this time when the elderly are continually warned to beware of strangers seeking to gain access to their houses. People are remarkably willing to co-operate, but this should not be presumed upon. When going beyond friends, take steps to reassure potential contributors: any project with official backing, whether it is a school, an adult education department, a local authority, a church, a university, or whatever, should give its collectors the best identity credentials that it can. A formal identity card is the best solution, but is often out of the question. Anyone should be able to provide a letter of authorisation bearing the name of the collector, however, with an address and a phone number to contact for verification or more information. Also, a group has a duty to keep an eye on the activities of its members. If anyone fails to respect the standards contributors expect, this could damage the name of a whole project, even if they feel that they have done nothing outrageous, and remember that someone may join a project precisely to gain access to houses.

Building a network without prior personal contacts needs more effort, of course. Elderly residents of a particular locality can be most easily contacted through day centres, specialist organisations, sheltered housing schemes, and residential homes, which again help to prove that the project is a genuine one. Projects with access to libraries, museums, community centres, or other appropriate premises can also get potential contributors to come to them by setting up exhibitions on the subjects to be covered, and by holding events, such as day schools. These can be very effective as long as there is a system for people to leave their names and addresses easily. There may be a high rate of second thoughts, but it should still be worthwhile. Some museums with oral history programmes have instructed attendants to keep an eye open for people who seem particularly interested in relevant exhibitions. These are then approached to see if they are interested in becoming contributors, and this is an effective way of keeping a long-term project going.

Research into a particular trade can begin by using the Yellow Pages and other local directories to find individuals and firms still active in it. They may offer direct help, but more likely is the provision of a list of people who have retired and who might be interested. I find it best to write rather than phone, as there is a good chance of the switchboard operator genuinely not knowing to whom this type of query should be passed, whereas a letter can be thought about and passed round, and if no answer comes after a while, it makes a good excuse for a follow-up phone call. Even if you write to the wrong people, they may well tell you whom you ought to be contacting. Trade unions and trade associations are well worth approaching, where relevant, though they often have small staffs and may be slow in replying. Officials who are too young or busy to help personally can usually pass you on to someone with local knowledge who can be approached directly.

Be enterprising when compiling a list of possible contacts: many firms or associations call themselves after their main activity and will then be listed under it in the alphabetical section of the phone book. Associations often take the name of the town or county in which they work, so check that, and, if it seems appropriate, look under 'British' or 'National', as a trade that is highly localised may have a national trade association based nearby. Thus, the Leeds phone book tells us that the city is home to such bodies as the British Equestrian Trade Association, the National Federation of Fish Friers (because a high proportion of their equipment is made in that area) and a host of local branches of national bodies. Libraries often know of local societies, such as a local history society, that may supply names or make enquiries on your behalf. Do not be disappointed with a poor response to such queries, though, for many societies exist mainly to organise lecture programmes and all rely on volunteer administrators who often can give little time to this work. In such a case, it may be worth approaching them again later when you could offer to give a talk on the progress of the project as a way of making direct contact with the membership, for most societies are permanently on the lookout for speakers.

Newspapers and magazines are the most effective way of contacting potential contributors directly, of course, and you should write to as many as possible because it is difficult to be sure which will get the best results. I used the *Yellow Pages* to prepare a list of all the newspapers serving the East Riding and also wrote to the *Yorkshire Post* as the regional daily paper covering the county as well as several magazines that ex-horsemen might read, such as the *Dalesman*, a monthly devoted to rural Yorkshire life with a large and dedicated readership.

Studying old photographs at Linthwaite Library Local History And Heritage After-noon were Kirklees Local History Librarian Lesley Kipling and visitor Pauline Pog-son

Photo: Simon Morley

Reliving the past at village library

A DIALECT quiz was one of the novel items at Linthwaite Library Local History And Heritage Afternoon.

Over 30 Linthwaite villagers filled the library to capacity to swop memories and examine old photographs and memorabilia of the area.

In the dialect quiz 10 sentences and a poem were read out and people had to translate the old words such as "ackled" and "addled." "For some of the older people it was easy, second nature," said lib-

rary assistant, Valerie Stead.

Visitors were invited to take a mental walk down Hoyle House with an 1890 map, next to a modern map for comparison. There was a display of coloured postcards of the village, and collections of old household items, such as charcoal irons, and toys including wooden hoops, apple barrels, metal bullys and whip and tops.

Lesley Kipling, Kirklees local studies librarian, gave a talk on the Luddite Connection with the village.

A number of visitors re-

membered that the garage opposite the library used to be stables aound the 1920s and 30s, said Valerie. "We would be very interested in any photographs of what it was like then," she said.

"I think everyone enjoyed reliving the past. A number of people remembered one particular Linthwaite shopkeeper who always had migraines. They said they never saw him without a vinegar cloth wrapped round his head."

Valerie stressed that visitors to the library are welcome. "They do not have to be members."

Plate 7.2   This newspaper cutting records a reminiscence session in the Colne Valley above Huddersfield, West Yorkshire. This sort of local community event can be a very effective way of contacting contributors who would not respond to a more formal appeal, and of mobilising a sense of general involvement in a project. Local newspapers are usually very supportive.

Trade journals, like the *Fish Friers Review,* which is based in Leeds, are good for specific projects, and trade unions usually have their own newspaper or newssheet. I did not use local radio, but other projects have. I expected to contact most horsemen through the local papers published in the market towns, yet it was the *Yorkshire Post* that produced the most replies and the best, perhaps because it covers farming topics extensively. On the other hand, other projects with which I have been involved have shown that, in the long run, the close contacts that are possible with small papers can be very productive.

There is no reason to pay for an advertisement, as most papers will print a letter appealing for help, though none can be relied upon to do so instantly and some may wait a considerable length of time before using it. They might well be interested in running a piece on the project, if supplied with the right material, and this attracts far more attention. Offering an appropriate old photograph which has no copyright restrictions on it – in other words, if it is borrowed or purchased, make sure that you are not expected to pay a reproduction fee or to keep it private – is usually very effective. They get a good reader response and also fill a lot of space, which is a consideration on many short-staffed operations, especially the free ones. As well as a caption, write a brief and clear appeal for assistance, making sure you do not bury it deep in a complex explanation of who you are or of what you are trying to do. Everything that matters should appear in a short, clear first paragraph, for a lot of people only skim through a paper, and they will miss the fact that you want help unless it stands out. Make sure an address for replies is prominent in any letter or article, especially if it is not the same as your own letterhead. A short account of your project is a good idea, but keep it to the minimum, and the whole thing should always be less than one side of A4 paper unless you are specifically instructed to write more. Try and make it interesting rather than scholarly, for neither the newspaper nor its readers will take much notice otherwise. Type it if at all possible, double-spaced, and give a phone number to let them get in touch quickly for more information.

A friendly newspaper contact can help to keep stories appearing through the life of a project, and all newspapers value any reliable source of printable items. Repeated coverage does help, for most readers tend merely to note the first and second mentions of something new without really taking it in, but to absorb it as real and lasting as it continues to appear. When there is a response, follow it up immediately. A letter again seems best to me, for anyone who is prepared to correspond probably has more than a passing interest in the project, and something written down is less likely to be misunderstood. It also gives you the chance to mention things like assurances of confidentiality, where appropriate, and to explain what will happen to the recordings. If you are operating from an office, or have a private phone which will have someone near it most of the day, then it may be worthwhile including a phone number in appeals, but phone contacts are more open to misunderstandings and more casual than a letter. Many calls may come from people who just wish to have a brief talk there and then, whereas real contributors have to be willing to give time and effort to helping you. Be especially wary of anyone offering another's name and address on the phone as they may be doing so without authorisation. It is inevitable that a percentage of even the best-sounding contacts will actually lead nowhere, but be friendly and sympathetic at all times. If there are too many replies for you to visit all your contacts soon, or if a project is delayed, be sure to write and explain what is happening.

Newspapers should produce much more of a random sample than a network that co-opts new members with similar interests. Neither is automatically better, but to ensure that what is being recorded is not just a partial story, different perspectives are essential. Between the farmworkers' trade union, newspapers, and some personal recommendations from interested people not themselves able to help, I contacted ex-horsemen who had worked in all parts of the East Riding, virtually none of whom knew each other. In some instances I met two or three linked people as a result of one initial contact, but in no case did two people from the same village or circle of friends write to me directly. I finished up with twenty-six contributors who had directly relevant experience, and this was all I could handle. I could, however, have used them as the starting point for building separate local networks if I had had co-workers, or had been able to follow up my initial work more intensively later. My sample was more effective than mere numbers would suggest because of the farm lads' general belief in changing jobs regularly – in many cases once a year. Since they rarely stayed close to home once their first year or two were over, I covered well over a hundred farms (and the number may have been double that) scattered all over the county and its fringes. Moreover, they themselves were well aware that not every place functioned in the same way, which made their reminiscences more wide-ranging.

Such a sample, though, is still self-selected and therefore not random in a statistical sense, nor could any attempt be made to balance it to cover different classes, age groups, or any of the other factors that a sociologist would take into account in a contemporary survey. Those with really negative views are less likely to come forward than those with good memories which they wish to share, unless they feel a need to set the record straight. This is not to say that all reminiscences will be drenched with rosy nostalgia, or that the bad side of past experiences will be edited out, but that, on balance, they have emerged from their trade, their street, their way of life, or whatever, with positive feelings. Investigating the experience of ethnic groups arriving in this country and the extent of racial discrimination they suffered, however, may well suffer the same effect in reverse, with those with negative experiences being the highly motivated ones. Few projects can afford to pick and choose contributors, however, especially those working with the elderly, even though in an ideal world we would begin with a sound sample.

The clearest attempt to achieve such a sample on a major oral history project was in the Essex University survey of Edwardian life. Here it was decided that there should be 444 people, selected according to occupation and place of residence, so as to stand for the entire British population as it appeared in the census of 1911. In actual fact, it took 500 interviews to fill the necessary categories satisfactorily, and the effort that went into finding and interviewing so many people clearly shows that only the most major projects could undertake anything so precise over such an area. It may be possible to do it with less effort over a county or a locality, but the smaller the catchment area, the greater the chance that some categories will simply not be filled because no suitable volunteers come forward. Balance is more often achieved by making allowances in the use of testimony, but there is a limit to this and where contributors only come forward in tiny numbers, there may be something fundamental wrong with the design of the project. A rethink is more in order then than a renewed search.

One method of finding and motivating contributors that should be firmly resisted is to pay for information. Apart from occasions when legitimate expenses must be reimbursed (and this is rare as most collectors visit contributors rather than vice versa) money should not change hands. There are strong ethical arguments against the purchase of information, but the practical ones are so strong there is no need to consider any others. Once it becomes clear that offering interesting stories is a way of earning money, the incentive is there both to keep providing them and to keep them interesting, and since there is no way of checking on the authenticity of most of them, a good number may be invented or embellished. Contributors may also try to keep the collector interested by shaping genuine recollections along the lines in which the collector seems most interested. This would normally stand out if a normal network had only one such person in it, but if several are feeding dubious or erroneous information into the general pool, the distortion will become severe. The fact that contributors get no material benefit out of their activities is the greatest guarantee of good faith.

Many elderly people are lonely and get back something from oral history without being paid – indeed, a visit may have a significance you do not suspect, so do not miss one lightly. Make appointments unless you are absolutely sure that simply dropping in is acceptable. Just because someone is retired, do not assume that they have no objection to spending half or all of a day waiting for a collector to turn up. Near neighbours and personal friends obviously do not need formal letters, but even then, the collector should keep a comprehensive diary of commitments made and not rely on memory, because mistakes occur often enough even when precautions are taken. For instance, an estate steward once offered to arrange appointments for me with two men who had retired after many years among horses on the estate. When I arrived at the first house, I was invited in and tea and cakes were produced, but I gradually realised that they had no idea who I was and what I was there for! The other family were prepared when I went on to their house later, so this was obviously just an accident, and as they were all clearly happy to have company, and to talk about the old days, no harm was done. To have been the one at fault in the misunderstanding, however, could have meant that I had wasted the best part of a day for nothing, for getting to their village meant an hour's train journey, then a wait for one of the few local buses, which took me four miles to a crossroads, and then a walk of two miles or so with a heavy tape recorder on my shoulder.

Avoid overbooking because a properly conducted session can be very stressful. The collector should be constantly aware of where the session is going and making mental notes of things that may need clarification. This always requires concentration and empathy from the collector, and where the contributor is not in good health or has difficulty in maintaining their own concentration, it can be a strain. It can be exciting when it goes well, and things get easier when you have built up a relationship with a contributor, but I have never known an initial session to be the relaxing experience that might be imagined. Feeling drained at the start of the second or third session of the day is no way to build up good relationships, and the contributors may feel you are not putting much into it, though when recording miles from your home base, as I usually was, you may have no choice. A heavily booked day leaves only a short fixed time for each session, moreover, and there is no chance of capitalising on the one that goes unexpectedly well. Find out how much you can do by careful experiment, but do not feel you are proving anything by cramming in extra sessions. A people-centred approach to history has to take account of the people involved in the present, as well as trying to capture the experiences of years ago.

It is important to end sessions properly for this reason. Most contributors will want to chat more casually than they have been able to do with the tape running, and this is where a collector can open up and join in rather than trying to keep themselves out of it as much as possible, as must be done when the tape is running. Cups of tea are usually offered and it is polite to accept, quite apart from the fact that you will probably need it. Try and disengage yourself in a friendly way: usually this is easy, but on one occasion an old man with whom I had spent the morning offered me a meal, and then clearly wanted to talk for a while. I had someone else to see, and had to leave hurriedly, and his disappointment was only too clear. This period at the end of the session can also show if contributors have things they want to say that the tape recorder inhibited, so it should not be cut short. Arrange another meeting if one seems necessary, and once a sequence of sessions is complete, you should send a letter of thanks. This also gives the opportunity to clear up any missing details, or spellings of names and places that were missed or were unclear on the tape.

NOTES AND REFERENCES

1. G.E. Evans, 1956, *Ask the Fellows Who Cut the Hay*, Faber, pp. 16–17.
2. *Ibid.*, back cover.
3. *Ibid.*, pp. 73–4.

CHAPTER EIGHT
Gathering Material

Moving from reading about oral history to the active role of collecting will almost certainly seem daunting. While it is not a good idea to launch straight into serious collection, there is a lot to be said for trying it out right at the start simply as an icebreaker. Oral collection has a public element built into it that worries a lot of people and delay often makes this worse, whereas sessions usually go well enough in practice. Talk initially to a sympathetic elderly relative, with or without a tape recorder, about a topic like childhood games which most people find interesting to talk about, and keep the session short to avoid running out of steam. If problems do arise, be positive about them, for now they have been identified they can be overcome before any harm has been done. At this stage, your main aim should be to gain confidence in yourself.

There is no single ideal relationship with contributors and what works in one situation will not work in another. Every collector is different and their relationships with different contributors are moulded by the combination of their personalities, but productive relationships generally depend on politeness and respect. Everyone has the knowledge of their own past within themselves, but very few can spontaneously edit and organise their experiences so that they illuminate the wider experience of their community or nation. The collector helps in this process, shaping the material that is recorded, but it is essential not to treat the contributor as a mere source of information. They have offered to help for no reward other than company and the satisfaction of seeing their knowledge valued: anything received from them is a gift. The collector focuses the session, prompts, and offers encouragement – but never drives or interrogates. I use the words *collector, contributor,* and *session* because I have never liked the connotations of being an *interviewer,* running *interviews* with a *respondent* or an *informant,* which are common alternatives. Other people use them happily, and I respect this, but I prefer words that seem more neutral to me. *Informant* seems particularly unfortunate with its connotations of spying and police work, but the others suggest a passivity that is inaccurate.

In starting an investigation, factors like age, sex, class, and ethnic differences must be all be allowed for. If the investigation hinges on ethnic issues, for instance, collectors should ideally come from the same community as the contributors and if sessions can be conducted in the contributor's mother tongue, they are likely to be fuller, richer, and more natural. This can be difficult, however, both in terms of finding collectors with the necessary language skills and in using the transcripts later. Where there are genuine cultural clashes between one community and another it is important to try to understand them and to set them in context, so avoid the stereotyping that results from collecting nothing but accounts of disagreeable incidents, and seek out positive material on the way a community sees itself. Otherwise, the group in question is seen purely as a problem. There will be no easy answers, but this is a subject where the more information that can be gathered and analysed, the better.

The average elderly woman will find it hard to discuss intimate matters with a young man, although it is not impossible if handled correctly. Steve Humphries' *A Secret World of Sex* examines sex before marriage in Britain in the first half of the twentieth century, and draws out confidences from people who had often never talked to anyone else about this subject. Even so, he noted that his first attempt to tackle the subject attracted a good deal of hostile publicity which forced him to give it up, and even when he returned to it

> I knew my own inhibitions would make me shrink from asking a 92-year-old lady... about her orgasms. What intrigued me much more was the way in which sexual experience or inexperience influenced young people's lives.... My first interview proved to me that it was possible to break down the taboos which normally block conversations about sex with people of this generation.... The interviews themselves were the most moving I have ever done. They often started awkwardly: there would be an atmosphere of tension and embarrassment spiked with difficult silences. But after fifteen or twenty minutes the talk would generally flow much more freely. Long ago hurts would come back, lost loves were remembered, the joys and injustices of the past were relived, often with laughter, less often with tears.... Perhaps surprising was the fact that my being a man didn't seem to make any difference.[1]

A refined accent may provoke deference or resentment from a working-class contributor, and either will colour the answers that are given. Some people will take moving straight onto first-name terms as a sign that you see them as an equal, but others will see it as overfamiliarity, and there are times when the formality of the respectful 'Mr' or 'Mrs' will create the right atmosphere for the handing down of information. In the divided society of Alabama, for instance, Nate Shaw was acutely aware of the significance of titles. For instance, when two policemen came to investigate information that he had been selling whiskey, and his wife denied it, they said,

> 'Auntie, we believe you, we believe you.' They called her 'Auntie' because that was their rulin then. If it was a man, they'd call you 'Uncle', 'Uncle so-and-so'. A young fellow, they'd call him by his name if they knowed it. I didn't worry bout what they called me because I knowed they weren't goin to call me nothin but what they wanted to anyhow. We took that – there's colored people all through this country now, white folks still callin em uncle, auntie. A good crowd of em comes here and calls me 'Mister'. They can call me 'Mister' as much as they please; I know that they don't want to do it.[2]

Closer to home, an anonymous ex-worker from the leather works in Elswick remembered the Quaker brothers who owned and actively ran the factory before the 1950s:

> The Richardsons were upright and real gentlemen. You held them in respect and answered 'yes sir' and 'no sir', not like today where they treat gaffers as equals and call them all names.... You looked up to them and just accepted it. I wouldn't say they were very class conscious. It was just that they kept you in your place.... A lot of the older men would doff their hats, and all the directors used their Christian names, and it was Mr Lawrence, Mr Gilbert, Mr Frank or Mr Alaric. They never called them Mr Richardson.[3]

You may make lasting friendships out of a project, but, while the tape recorder is running, personal feelings of affection or dislike – and they are bound to arise – should not affect your attitudes. Avoid coldness, for showing an obvious appreciation of what is being offered is the best way of stimulating more, but stand back to avoid projecting yourself onto the tape. Personal remarks are best saved until the tape is off, when it is natural to have a more relaxed chat. Opinions on the causes of some particular event, or of a political nature, that you might challenge or agree with in ordinary conversation should simply be accepted. Florence Atherton, for instance, ended a section on her trade union activities in a Lancashire cotton mill with 'Employers did use the workers for their own ends those days. They got as much out of you for as little as possible. Now today it's gone the other length, hasn't it?'[4] This can be more than just a matter of keeping to your subject, for while you may disagree about the value of extreme corporal punishment in improving the character, say, a contributor's opinion governs their thoughts and actions, and understanding is only possible on the basis of accurate information. Disapproval may arouse animosity or lead them to conceal their opinions, or even to end the session. Where it seems relevant, return to such things later to find out if they are based on knowledge, hearsay, or supposition, if they are part of a wider set of beliefs, and if they are open to challenge. A good way to tackle a difficult topic, and to try to get a broader explanation of anything at all without directly challenging statements made by the contributor, is to say, 'I've heard it said that …, what do you think?'

If a group is recording itself, interplay between members is inevitable and desirable and it is best to make each session a genuine group event. If it is difficult for the person who is responsible for the tape recorder to join in fully, they can stay silent and everyone can take a turn at this job. In general, group working produces very different results from sessions done on a one-to-one basis, and we saw an example in Chapter 5, with Frank talking about his experiences as an incomer in this country. This has its own merits, but I believe that the average project is best conducted by single working. Contributors are then cast as teachers offering their knowledge and are encouraged to explain their past rather than just recount it. They are free to talk without fear of contradiction or of any unconventionality being pounced on, for a group has standards and customs, and individuals may well be reluctant to voice some thoughts in front of friends and neighbours. Similarly, unless there are specific reasons for recording in a social setting, like a pub, I would not do it. For research into community entertainment or folk song, there probably is no better environment for observing the subject of study in action, but even here it is best to have some quiet sessions trying to analyse and dig down into exactly what has been observed. Friends provoke each other and jog each other's memories, but one story is commonly met with another and often companions try to top each other's efforts, so truth is not at a premium. Try out different locations if it seems appropriate, but, in judging the results, do not look just for liveliness. Listen to the content and judge it critically.

Purely exploratory sessions can be both the easiest and the hardest to run, since the only way to find out which subjects will produce the best reminiscences is to cover a lot of ground. This very formlessness makes it easy to go nowhere at all, especially as most ordinary people will try to recall the things that made the headlines in their younger days unless they are prompted to do otherwise. It obviously helps to have done preparatory reading, for prior knowledge may save a lot of time and effort, as long as it does not predetermine the results. Although I was unable to apply George Ewart Evans' work directly to the East Riding, I gained enormously from it. On the other hand, the point of an oral history project is to do oral history and if the reading threatens to take over, re-examine either the decision to use oral methods or the project itself. Oral history will be the junior partner in some investigations, but then the non-oral research must be conducted in its own right, not as a preliminary. The only real exception to this is interviewing at the top end of the social scale, especially if it is about specific events or activities. Someone who perceives her- or himself as important and busy will frequently object to a slow, exploratory technique and may feel slighted that you do not seem to have taken much trouble to prepare for the session. They are also the ones most likely to shape their responses, consciously or out of habit, and you need to be ready to challenge statements that seem to run against the known facts. In some cases it may be necessary to be abrasive, if they are people who themselves operate in this way, but this is a difficult technique, for, taken too far, it becomes intolerable rudeness and ends the session.

Questionnaires may seem like an answer to most problems, but they are something over which there is deep and, in my opinion, usually sterile disagreement. Good work has been done both with and without them, and there are, in fact, a wide variety of types. As far as I can see, someone with a loose and flexible questionnaire is really doing nothing very different from someone else who keeps a mental checklist of points of interest and covers them all eventually, though in a seemingly random manner. Writing things down or not is then more a reflection of ways of thinking than anything else, just as some people cannot shop without a list while others hate them. It is when we contrast the use of a detailed set of questions that dictate the course and content of all sessions with a genuine case of playing everything by ear, that we see a real difference. Resolving it is hard because those putting either case tend to caricature the opposition's real position, making it more extreme than it really is.

Many differences in approach are the products of temperament, confidence, and the nature of the project. Since my research was a voyage in the dark, for the early sessions at least, it made sense for me to trawl fairly widely for as much relevant information as I could get, feeding back to the contributors comments they made and asking for more information, leaving the organisation of what I found until afterwards. It suited me and it worked. Paul Thompson's survey of Edwardian life started with a strong set of guidelines from contemporary sociological practice that allowed him to define closely the areas about which he wanted information. Sociological interview techniques provided an obvious model, and the statistical analysis the interviews would later undergo made it essential that they should all be directly comparable. As a result, a computer can now compare the experiences of different regions or social groups for those things covered in the interviews, giving complex breakdowns of the answers. The resulting massive archive at Essex University is an impressive testament to this way of working and since the collectors were scattered the length and breadth of the country, there was good reason for tight control of the way sessions were conducted. Lengthy notes gave advice on how to handle the points where difficulties might have led to individual interviewers amending the interview schedule, which is reproduced at the end of *The Voice of the Past* in an appendix significantly titled *Model Questions*. This begins with the comment that 'these questions are *not* a questionnaire but an outline interviewer's guide.... Where there is a question mark, the form of the question is as suggested; elsewhere, points for questioning are in a summarized form and need expanded wording in use.'[5]

Any questionnaire must be used with sensitivity or it will stultify a session: there is no point asking the son of a labourer elaborate questions to find out about the living-in servants his family kept. Be prepared to vary the order of the questions where a contributor naturally moves on to something you will be asking about later. As long as you cover everything eventually, the order in which you do it usually does not matter, and it helps to move away from an atmosphere of interrogation. Similarly, if contributors clearly want to expand on an answer, let them, and only step in to drag the talk back on course once you are satisfied that they have gone completely off course. A constant need to cut short contributors as they digress in particular directions indicates problems, as does a persistent lack of response to particular questions, or responses that indicate that the questions, are framed in a way inappropriate to the contributors' experience. For instance, we have seen that the Blackburn women with whom Jill Liddington talked would have found questions baffling that assumed that married women gave up full-time, paid jobs for work at home, or for relatively informal jobs that fitted in with their family commitments. Yet, over most of the country such questions would work well.

New questionnaires, and even informal approaches to sessions, should be reviewed after a few pilot sessions to be sure that they are working correctly. Changes may mean that the first few tapes become incompatible with the ones done later, but this is a small price to pay for improving the results. The questions themselves may be a problem, creating an atmosphere where the contributor censors testimony to suit the collector. Thus, 'How did you get on with your parents?' is fairly neutral and encourages some explanation in the answer, but rephrase it as, 'Did you like your parents?' and neither is true any longer. Some people will tell a stranger straight out that they did not, but many would not, for in many communities respect for parents is a general requirement. 'Did you dislike your parents?', with no preliminaries, definitely puts the contributor on the spot, especially if it is said in a disapproving voice. It takes a certain amount of trust to confide in an outsider, as Maggie Fuller did for *Dutiful Daughters,* that,

> I don't love [my mother]...and even to this day I am no the girl who'll go up and kiss my mother. I won't kiss my mother if you give me a pension.... My mother was a whacker – oh my God, you didn't ask – you got punished, it didn't matter. Do you know what I really think it was? I hate my mother – I respect her but I don't love her – but I think it was because she had too many kids and she was so work-worn, the poor beggar.... I respect her and help to keep her, I've always said that, and I'd take her for a month's holiday. But, you know, now when I am grown-up and I see the life she had! I remember she once nearly killed me.[6]

This complex mix of respect and resentment is clearly a vital factor in Maggie's life and it needs time and sympathy to bring it out. The internal tension that can arise from coping with such feelings can explain a lot in a person's life. A quick, conventional answer would not be a deliberate lie, and should be looked at alongside any qualifications that come later, for they are both important factors in the lives of people. Thus, Catherine Hall found that

> on tape Mrs Cooling did not want to record statements about her husband that were critical. She presented a very positive picture of her married life – she did not appear to mind at all that her husband had a very full life outside the home and was away and out a great deal. Over tea, however, when she no longer felt that she was being interviewed, she started to tell me what a difficult man he was to live with in many ways, how he expected her to understand what he wanted without ever saying it and how her daughter still expects to be serviced in the same way.[7]

Great care must similarly be taken over digressions, as it is always hard to be sure what is really too far from your interests to spend time and tape on. Many revelations will be missed by rigidly refusing to allow the contributor to do more than answer set questions. For instance, Mr Harper's eviction story, quoted in Chapter 1, grew out of comments on the meetings of his trade union branch in the 1970s and the lack of realism, as he saw it, of younger militants who thought farmworkers should strike. Again, three contributors spontaneously mentioned that farmers for whom they had worked had also maintained some woodland and sold timber and plate 8.1 was shown to me as part of a group of farming photos. Because I did not cut these apparent digressions off short, and refuse the photograph, together they form a valuable record of this activity and would make a good start to a deeper enquiry. Mr Jarvis, for instance, recalled:

> They lived apart from t'farm, d'you see, wood waggon horses .... The biggest part of horses I had was broken down entires [stallions] what wouldn't pass .... They were as handy as could be .... [Some horsemen] said they were awkward, but I said it's the *man* what's awkward. I never had no bother with 'em. No, course I used to just shout at 'em, ... 'Stand there now', and they would stand, and then I used to say, 'Now for it!' and they would all pull together and it would go out [of the wood], that tree, as if it was on roller skates .... I said, 'I've horses that can nearly talk.' ...
> But anyway, we used to go to ... Malton station, deliver our trees. ... And at that time o' day they had a crane ... at t'station, and we used to drop off at side o't'crane, then the railway [men] used to take on then, one at each side, winding 'em up onto timber waggon ... Then when we were coming back, we used to stop at a pub called the Griffin.... I had a four-stone weight, I used thread halter through four-stone weight, and put it just on t' edge of t'footpath, you know, [the horse] thought he was fast then, so we used to go to t'pub, and then take it off. I said, 'Go on. Cheerio,' then we used head off home then. (Tape 12/1)

Too dictatorial an approach is unlikely to endear a collector to anyone, so sessions will probably be short and unproductive. Coping is a matter of sensitivity and of being able to spot ways of steering conversation back to the original topic without seeming rude. Most recorders have a pause button that arrests the tape temporarily and this is a useful way of avoiding the wastage of tape while waiting for a chance to intervene. If the button is on a microphone held in the hand, it can be used unobtrusively, but in using it there is always a risk of missing something important as the digression suddenly turns out to have a point, or as the contributor suddenly switches back to relevant material. Above all, do not forget that you have set the machine on pause or you will lose the rest of the session.

The problem is worst where the aim is to collect information on a specific event or period, but even here, be alert to what is offered as

Plate 8.1 Timber waggons making a delivery at Selby station on the border between the East and West Ridings of Yorkshire, c.1914. Although the area was largely under the plough, large estate owners maintained some woodland and sold timber. This was not directly related to farming or to farm servants, but even so three contributors had been involved.

well as what you want. When Theodore Rosengarten began his first session with Nate Shaw, his intention was to get background information about the Alabama Sharecroppers' Union. The old man

took off his hat and sat down with us by the fireplace. We asked him right off why he joined the union. He didn't respond directly; rather, he 'interpreted' the question and began, 'I was haulin a load of hay out of Apafalaya one day –' and continued uninterrupted for eight hours. He recounted dealings with landlords, bankers, fertilizer agents, mule traders, gin operators, sheriffs, and judges – stories of the social relations of the cotton system. By evening, the fire had risen and died and risen again and our question had been answered....

In March 1971 I went back to Alabama with a proposal to record Shaw's life.... I returned in June with a hundred pages of questions to ask Shaw. It became clear during our first session that I'd never get to a fraction of them. It would have taken years; moreover, my prepared questions distracted Shaw from his course. Since it was my aim to preserve his stories, I learned how to listen and not to resist his method of withholding facts for the sake of suspense. Everything came out in time, everything.

We would sit under the eaves of his tool shed and talk for two to six hours per session. Shaw would whittle or make baskets as he

spoke.... When it rained we would move our chairs inside the shed. There in the near dark, cramped among baskets, broken-bottomed chairs, sacks of feed and fertilizer, worn harnesses and tools, Shaw enacted his most fiery stories. I am thankful for all the rain we had, for it moved us to a natural theater and pounded the tinroof like a delirious crowd inciting an actor to a peak of his energy.... After sixty hours spread over sixteen sessions we completed the first round.[8]

This is like a dream come true for any collector. Nate Shaw was illiterate and a fine story teller in a true oral tradition, as well as being well aware that his recollections had a far greater significance than the facts they contained. I have never experienced anything to compare with this, and I would not expect to, but it does illustrate in an extreme form the limitations of questionnaires, even though they can undoubtedly give confidence to those with no previous experience. For this reason, a school project is almost certainly going to need one of some description, as children find it hard to be systematic in their approach. They can be very good interviewers, and usually get a good response from the elderly, but they do need directing at first. Operating without a questionnaire or interview schedule is not an easy option, for contributors asking what you want to know will not be impressed by a response like 'anything you want to tell me'. Giving contributors some idea beforehand of what you want to talk about is generally a good idea as it allows them to make some preparation, and even in a group self-recording project, it is sound practice to agree what to cover as a first step. The collector almost always has a responsibility to provide a framework for the sessions, questionnaire or no, as a way of getting them started.

Turning evidence into history always pivots around organisation and analysis. A questionnaire organises the material as it is collected, so that analysis should be possible with a minimum of effort, while a free-form session must be organised afterwards. I prefer the free-form approach because I feel that I find out more, but I believe that in terms of its capacity to yield systematic information the material I produce is nothing like so far as might be imagined from that of the questionnaire users once it has been organised. The two methods can even be combined to a degree by preparing a detailed list of questions and then using them only as a guide to yourself. Working your ideas out is a necessary preliminary to any action, and writing questions is an effective way of doing it. Thereafter, an open session can be structured around the concepts that have emerged. Some of the written questions may never be asked, and the order will be quite different, but the end result will be a series of tapes with a common basis that can be

restructured later for analytical purposes around the original questions. Equally, a free-form start to a project may indicate a need for a more structured approach, and it would be foolish not to use a questionnaire where comparability was vital. A structured beginning may reveal that its premises are wrong, as mine were, and that only an open enquiry can provide the information needed to set matters straight, when a return to a questionnaire may be possible.

The most worrying thing about an open session for anyone new to recording is getting it going, or restarting one that has lost its way. What specific questions work best? First of all, for every contributor there must be a bare minimum of biographical information to put the sessions in context: their full name, age, and date of birth, together with the names of all the members of the nuclear family and their ages relative to the contributor. If asked for in a sensitive way, such family details will usually get a conversation going, though bald questions resembling a social security interview are unlikely to establish a harmonious relationship, especially with those who have been through the real thing. Most people like to talk about their families and give a lot of information that can be used later as the basis for extra questions, even though it may seem like a distraction for projects that are not oriented around personal or family subjects.

The place of birth and any later addresses should also be collected, and the occupations of parents and siblings. People rarely think of their family in a statistical way and will tell things in the way that makes it easiest for them to recall the details, so it is best not to be insistent about getting everything at once, especially if their family was a large one and if several members have died over the years. Lengthy comments on one family member or another can be a valuable source of facts that might not otherwise come out and which may provide a lot of insight into attitudes and psychology. It may take several starts to get all the facts, and you may have to finish with a deliberate attempt to fill in gaps. The result may be a tangled forest of information, for members of stable communities often define themselves and everyone else in them in terms of their genealogy and relationships, as Frank Peel has said was true in the Spen Valley in the early nineteenth century. At this period, and for some decades afterwards, the inhabitants of the nearby Colne Valley, running towards Lancashire from Huddersfield and so in the heart of the world's first modern, industrialised society, hardly ever used their official surnames, but knew each other as, for instance, Ben o'Bill's, or Sal o'Jane's. The older folk could extend this into a lengthy genealogy for all their family members. Nate Shaw named over four hundred people in his account

of his life, usually placing them firmly in a genealogical context when they came into the narrative. At times this produces almost biblical passages, and since multiple marriages and illegitimate children were common, they can be very complex:

> After my mother died, my daddy married [my half-brother] TJ's mother. She was a Reed, Maggie Reed.... Old man Jubal Reed's daughter and old lady Adeline – used to be Adeline Milliken and after old man Jubal Reed married her, him and her had one child and she went in the name of Maggie Reed. And this old lady Adeline Reed, who was Adeline Milliken before Jubal Reed married her, she had had other men before him. I knowed em: old man Coot Ramsey come in contact with her enough to have four children and they all went under the Ramsey name – Roland Ramsey, Reuben Ramsey, Waldo Ramsey, Hector Ramsey.... She weren't married to old man Coot Ramsey – he just gettin children by this woman – and she went in the name of Milliken, Adeline Milliken. And my daddy married in that family to the only child that that old lady Adeline Milliken and old man Jubal Reed had.... And she was a half-sister to old man Waldo Ramsey; Adeline Milliken was the mother to both of em. And I married Waldo Ramsey's daughter, in 1906.... That made Maggie Reed, you might say, my wife's half auntie.... Well, that drawed me in to be my stepmother's brother's son-in-law.[9]

Make a mental note if the talk strays off or something seems to have been omitted, but remember that the opening of the session sets the tone for the rest. To signal that it is to be just a question and answer session can stifle spontaneity and that is to be avoided at all costs. Contributors should feel free to go into detail and also to seem to contradict themselves, and completeness is probably a more relevant goal than accuracy for most sessions. Thus, a run-through of all the contributor's jobs breaks the ice at the same time as gathering facts for later questions, but 'When did you start work?' is an almost meaningless question for a working-class person born several decades ago. Does this mean work around the house (especially significant for girls); helping parents or relatives at their work; part-time paid work while at school; or the first full-time paid job? John Hallows of Manchester, for instance, was the son of a coal merchant, and seemingly a substantial one at that. We probably would not expect such a child to contribute to the family income, and yet he perfectly illustrates the variety of jobs many children had long before leaving school:

> At one time we had sixteen horses. Father died when I was very young and my mother was left with six children, of whom I was the eldest. She carried on the business for a couple of years but it became too much for her and my Uncle William took it over....

My first job when I was still at St. Thomas's School was taking papers round at six o'clock in the morning and half past five at night, then I went on to sell programmes at Hyde Theatre. When father died I worked part-time for the coal business, mucking in, collecting money, and everything else you can imagine – what I didn't do wasn't worth doing! I used to take the chain horses to Manchester and meet the wagons on certain hills; there weren't many motors about in those days.... We also did general removal jobs. A regular one was taking the scenery from the theatre on a Sunday; we might go to Rochdale, Sheffield or Huddersfield. I was only about eleven years old but I can remember sleeping all night in the furniture van on one trip to Yorkshire. Sometimes we would be away for two or three days. At twelve I had a half-time job in a weaving shed and when I left school at thirteen I was taken on at Ashton Brothers, working on the automatic looms; I worked there for 42 years altogether.[10]

There was clearly no sharp division between childhood and work. Moreover, despite growing up in Manchester, John Hallows shared many experiences with East Riding children, especially with Mr Johnson, whose father also carried coal among many other activities, and this is a warning not to compartmentalise the past. Indeed, when farm lads married, many looked for work with firms like the Hallows', capitalising on their skills with horses, rather than settling for the low wages of farm labourers. The half-time education system was another common bond between them. This began as a legal requirement that children employed in mills should be educated for half of every day, but in this century it had become a device allowing school-age children to work for half of each day in the districts where it survived. In the East Riding all the half days could be lumped together, as this suited farmers better, while in mill districts the employers preferred it in its original form, and many children there began work as half-timers into the 1920s.

Farm lads were given no formal training for work. 'It was,' Mr Carter said, 'straight off the mark. You maybe got a clatter o't'earhole, sometimes, i' them days. Yes. If you didn't do right. Or if you got a bit cheeky or anything.' (Tape 12/2) In his first job Mr Tate was immediately given three horses 'to feed, clean, look after, gear [harness].' (Tape 19/1) It was not their education that enabled them to live up to these expectations, but childhoods spent like Mr Masterman's:

At Camerton Hall, before I left school when I was eleven, twelve – eleven year old or so, I used to go wi' my father at six o'clock, I used go into the stable where they used to keep the trap horse, carriage horses and hunters. And I used to help the groom to do, look after the horses, clean the stable out – you know, do whatever there was to do..., work till about quarter to nine and then go to school. Come back at four o'clock when I left school and work till maybe eight or nine o'clock.

What did you get paid?

A bob a day. But I couldn't go home till the chickens had gone in cause I had them to shut up. But on a Saturday in summer I had to cut the grass with a Shetland pony. It was a great big lawn, cause they used to have tennis tournaments on it in summer.... They used to give me my dinner on a Saturday. (Tape 11/1)

Despite all this, people still regarded their first job after leaving school as their real entry into the world of work, and may omit the others unless asked. The John Hallows extract also shows how this simple start to a session can open up all the opportunities needed to continue it once the initial flow dries up. The business, and how well the family lived off it, is an obvious line of questioning. It would also be worth checking who ran the financial side of things while his father was alive – this was traditionally the woman's role where no outsiders were involved. Many other questions also arise, such as whether his mother faced any special difficulties in running the business as a woman after her husband's death. With sixteen horses they may well have employed men, but family labour might have sufficed, and plenty of interesting detail is likely to surface in establishing this sort of thing. How far did they go with deliveries? How did John get his job as a paper boy and was it his idea? Did he keep any of his wages? How did he feel about having to work like this? Did all his friends do likewise? We could ask him to go into detail about working with the horses and about his trips over the Pennines. Did all this interfere with his schooling and, if so, did he feel cheated? Did he always expect to work in a mill or was this a result of giving up the business to his relative? What work did he do there? We could ask about the theatre and his involvement. There really are immense possibilities from this one paragraph, and while not everyone will give so many openings, there is always something to pick up on. In fact none of these were relevant to the purpose of the actual session from which I have taken this quotation: it was concerned with his later service in the Manchester Regiment in the First World War *(The Recollections of Three Manchesters in the First World War* (1985)).

Try to keep to the point, keep the questions asked as open-ended as possible, make them intelligible for the contributor, and try to pursue areas where they show enthusiasm. 'Tell me about your childhood' may spark off some people, but on the whole such a subject is too vast. 'Were you expected to help out around the house when you were young?' is a more productive approach, and feeding back elements of earlier testimony in search of fuller explanations and descriptions is most likely to cause any session to take off. This works even where a brief initial answer seems to have written off a topic. It is often useful to try to pin memories down to one specific event or day, so, 'Can you describe one day at work that sticks in your mind?' will usually get a better answer than 'What was life like at work?' 'Was there anything about work you particularly liked or disliked?' is another way of seeking detail you don't have the knowledge to ask for directly. My most productive single opening was a request to Mr Johnson to take me through the farming year as a horselad saw it: the reply took over an hour. There will be times, however, when there is no more to be got from probing, either because the contributor is not interested or is unwilling to say more.

Mere quantity is no indication of a worthwhile session but a sound rule of thumb is that the relative amounts of time taken up by the collector and contributor give a good indication of its real value. One that is ninety-five per cent contributor is likely to be interesting as long as it is not pure digression, whereas one that is eighty per cent collector is almost certainly a waste of time. It is best to show encouragement and appreciation with nods and smiles rather than words as far as possible, as long as it can be done naturally, though it is a good idea to interject a phrase when a contributor points to something rather than naming it, or shows the size of something with their hands. Adding 'about four feet?' and getting confirmation then makes the section comprehensible later. Describing a process and asking if that was how it was done, however, is not the same thing and cannot be counted as real evidence, especially at the level of detail, because there is no way of knowing whether a 'yes' is meant to show total agreement, partial agreement, or politeness. 'Did your father ever hit you?' for instance, cannot be meaningfully answered briefly because it is regularity, reasons, circumstances, the force used, and whether the practice was general and approved of that give the answer a real meaning. Someone who was smacked once could answer affirmatively just as honestly as someone whose childhood was one long series of beatings, and it is the nuances that make up the real picture. Given the modern stereotype of extensive and severe physical abuse of children, the Essex University survey actually found a surprisingly low level of real beatings in Edwardian times right across the UK. In the Shetlands, indeed, corporal punishment was almost unknown.

A suitable photograph can be of great assistance in starting off a flow of reminiscences, either through explaining a technical process that is shown, naming people and giving their history, identifying locations

Plate 8.2   Another of Wilfred Caunce's photographs, which I came across while sorting out his possessions after he died in 1991. He was a keen amateur photographer, but concentrated entirely on the snapshots that fill the bulk of most people's albums and drawers. It would have been easy to throw them all away as of no more than personal relevance, and thousands of such images must be destroyed every year. I held on to them for sentimental reasons in the main, but I found many were of wider interest when a more careful examination was possible.

This one shows a scene in Earlestown market place in the 1950s as children are marshalled into lines before the start of the annual Walking Day at Whitsun. These were enormous processions by church and Sunday school members, with banners and bands, walking several miles round the town. They brought traffic to a halt for several hours throughout south Lancashire towns on the appointed days. This was the time of year when most children received new clothes and the procession was a good chance to show them off. For boys in particular, on the other hand, it was often preferable to avoid taking part and spend the time poking fun at their friends who were parading round in unaccustomed and often unappreciated finery, as I well recall. The walks were an important statement of communal solidarity, and of divisions as well, as shown by the separate Catholic Walking Days. These walks still occur, but on a much smaller scale and they no longer concern many local people since church attendance has fallen dramatically. Oral recording has been done on this subject, but they would justify more, and also the collection of more photographs.

and talking about them, or explaining the background to an event. The Thixendale farm photographs I collected from Mr Walker proved very useful in this way, besides prompting other contributors to get out their own. Most people have old snapshots around the house, but would not

Plate 8.3 Wilfred Caunce himself, seen here at work at the Vulcan Foundry, Newton-le-Willows. He was a highly skilled engineer and the Vulcan was world famous for its railway locomotives, both steam and diesel powered. It was one of the first locomotive works to be established anywhere, but sadly locomotive building is now but a memory, much of the site employing very few people as an industrial estate, and just a small portion still continuing to make diesel engines for use in ships. Again, not a dramatic photograph, but a rare one for very few photos are taken of work, and this records the closing years of a proud engineering tradition. He was certainly proud of his own skills and, like all the Vulcan workers, he found it hard to understand the logic that has led to their devaluation and to the closure of such works through progressive amalgamations with bigger concerns whose main interests lie well away from their acquisitions.

bring them out unless prompted, and they are a fascinating adjunct to oral history with a real value of their own. Eventually my collection numbered more than a hundred, and I saw more that were not of a good enough quality to copy. Such photographs will almost certainly be destroyed sooner or later if they are not copied. Even the Thixendale collection would never have been found among the negatives of an old photographer's business, which is the main source for the recovery of such collections if the surmise that the farmer took them himself is true.

The big old glass plate negatives from which the pictures were printed can survive astonishingly bad treatment – like being used for years as cloches in a vegetable garden – and there is now a widespread realisation of their value. More recent photographs are not yet accorded the same respect at all, and as their negatives are much more vulnerable to decay, there is a real danger that many photographic archives will achieve impressive coverage of the period up to the 1930s or so, and then virtually cease, perhaps restarting in the recent past with modern record photographs. Images of the 1950s already look a world away, as Jack Hulme's photographs of Fryston show, but few people make their collection a priority, even though copying photographs of any type is a technique with which any keen amateur can cope. Borrowing should be done systematically, for there will be justified bad feeling where originals are mislaid or kept for long periods. Each individual loan should be kept in an envelope, clearly marked with the name and address of the owner, the date of borrowing, and the items borrowed. Get all the details you can on the scenes and people shown, as well. Take the pictures out only for actual copying or other essential operations, put them back immediately, and return them to their owners as soon as possible, for it is the easiest thing in the world to mix up piles of photographs or documents that are left lying around. If originals are donated, the same information needs collecting and preserving.

Old newspapers can be found in most main libraries, together with facilities for copying them, and they are full of advertisements and evocative stories that can jog memories. An old flat iron could unlock a long session of washday reminiscences for an elderly woman, though the possibilities with such museum-type objects are much more limited as they are far more unwieldy than photographs, and if they are fragile there is always a risk of breakage. They also may be meaningless or uninteresting in themselves to the majority, where a photograph is more generally interesting. A compromise is to photograph objects or to photocopy a page of illustrations from an old trade or mail order catalogue such as that shown here. Museums often have such catalogues and they will probably allow photography of objects. Some have loan collections for educational purposes and others keep some items specifically for oral history use, but very few will be willing to make loans from their main collections for an outsider's use. A school-based project or a group working from a community centre could collect its own, which can be a productive exercise in its own right. Primary-age children are particularly likely to respond to the challenge to the imagination of actual contact with the things about which they are being told.

Old objects and photographs are much used in reminiscence therapy with elderly people who are becoming confused. They act as direct

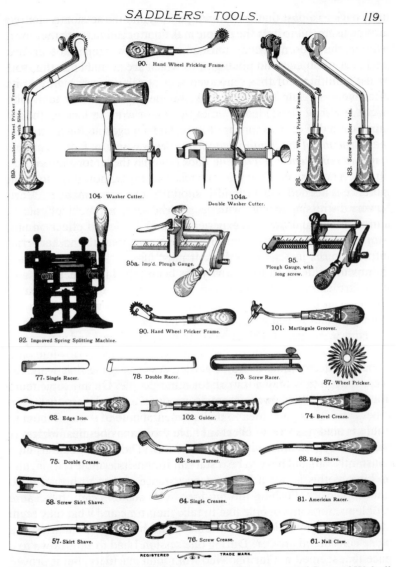

90. Hand Wheel Pricking Frame

89. Shoulder Wheel Pricker Frame, with Slide.

88. Shoulder Wheel Pricker Frame.

83. Screw Shoulder Vein.

104. Washer Cutter.

104a. Double Washer Cutter.

95a. Imp'd. Plough Gauge.

95. Plough Gauge, with long screw.

92. Improved Spring Splitting Machine.

90. Hand Wheel Pricker Frame.

101. Martingale Groover.

77. Single Racer.

78. Double Racer.

79. Screw Racer.

87. Wheel Pricker.

63. Edge Iron.

102. Guider.

74. Bevel Crease.

75. Double Crease.

62. Seam Turner.

68. Edge Shave.

58. Screw Skirt Shave.

64. Single Creases.

81. American Racer.

57. Skirt Shave.

76. Screw Crease.

61. Nail Claw.

REGISTERED   TRADE MARK.

Plate 8.4   A page from the Equine Album of Hampson and Scott of Walsall showing saddlers' tools. With the right contributor this can set off many reminiscences as the use of them all is explained, but it does not take a lot of organising and there is no risk of spoiling the original since a photocopy is all that is required. It can be left behind as a gift if the contributor is interested.

links back to a past that is becoming unreal and the session is centred around using this to help the people make better contact with their own lives in the present. Many museums have now prepared standard packages of objects and photographs which are available for this sort of use, and most of those involved seem to think very highly of its effectiveness. Help the Aged took the idea up, and their tape/slide package *Recall* (1981) led to an explosion of work in local authority homes and day centres for the elderly, and a magazine *Reminiscence: the Magazine of the Reminiscence Network* was set up. Faith Gibson's *Using Reminiscence: A Training Pack* (1989) is the latest stage in their efforts. The very confused do not respond easily, however, so great patience is needed and a friendly, supportive personal manner. It can be very distressing to work with people who are at a low ebb physically and mentally and my first experience had a profound effect on me. Moreover, the session is run to help the contributor, and historical information is just a by-product. It must also be said that the truly therapeutic side of all this activity has been called into question, and there are some people who respond very badly to this approach. However, it is at the very least a useful method for working with the elderly, and as it is also good for staff morale, there is no question of rejecting it, simply of scaling down extravagant claims and working to see if it really is a therapy or just an activity, albeit a worthwhile one.

Each collector finds ways of getting sessions going that work for them though they may not work for other people. On any topic there are questions that always seem to produce a better response than others and it is a good idea to make a mental note of some of them to hold as standbys. Every collector I have spoken to does this, whatever their attitude to formality in the session. There are sessions that constantly halt and have to be restarted, for no discernible reason, and as long as this is not a frequent occurrence, it has to be accepted philosophically. Pushing too hard for swift answers can often cause problems, for some people like to take their time and what may seem like a brief reply followed by silence could be the preliminaries to a more considered answer. During one session I had to slow down to a pace that seemed not far removed from total inactivity, but it proved worthwhile. If everything fails, do not lose your patience. Even the worst session usually produces something, and one of my least productive ones in oral history terms was suddenly transformed at the end when Mr Walker produced the collection of photographs from Thixendale.

The one thing to avoid in all circumstances is the exploitative approach, as typified by the tabloid journalists who would do anything

Plate 8.5 A page from the Harrods mail order catalogue of 1917 showing many different types of domestic irons. Since it was aimed at the well-off, many of these would be found only in a minority of homes, but since many young people, and especially young girls, worked in domestic service in the early decades of this century, this can serve a double function of starting off explanations of ordinary housework routines and of accounts of life in service.

to get a story, including making it up. History is about making sense of the past, and that can only happen when the data that is used is honestly based. Never allow probing questions to become tricks of the 'have you stopped beating your wife' variety. Even if your project involves contributors who are perceived as hostile to some degree, such as the working miner who contributed his views on the miners' strike to *The Enemy Within,* there is no point in setting them up to make themselves look foolish. This simply diminishes your work and its value to future historians. It is possible to get results from straight questioning in the unlikeliest situations. Thus in *Challenging De Gaulle: the O.A.S and the Counterrevolution in Algeria, 1954–1962,* Alexander Harrison obtained full details on the murders and torture French terrorists committed in the very dirty struggle over independence for Algeria, and the foreword notes that

> had it been published two and a half decades earlier, the author – having spilled too many beans – might well have met a speedy end through an O.A.S. car bomb or a lightning fusillade.... He deals ... with those ordinary footsoldiers who actually carried out the *ponctuelles,* the killings of the O.A.S.... He does not idealize the O.A.S. fighters, but explains what they did, why they did it, and what sort of people they were.[11]

Successful sessions are not the result of any mechanical application of fixed methods but of some sort of rapport between those taking part. Everything in this chapter is based on experience, mine or others', but that does not mean it is either comprehensive or a set of instructions to be mastered in detail. It is well worth paying attention to the radio and television, where a multitude of different interviewers are constantly at work, to see how they get people talking, though many of the lessons will be of things to avoid, for there is no real place for the abrasive style designed to get short, quotable answers. Take what seems useful from anywhere you find it and experiment to find the most productive way of working: the one that gets people talking most freely and recovers most usable historical evidence. The one essential element for success is some sort of underlying confidence in your ability to do this. Many experienced collectors get nervous before sessions, including me, and some never cease to find the experience a trial, but as long as you believe that you can do it well enough to override these fears, you can accept them and live with them. This is easiest when working in a manner that makes sense to you, regardless of how you arrived at it and working to methods you do not believe in is never likely to lead to good results. Diversity of approach is likely to give our best spread of results in the wide variety of research projects to which oral history can contribute.

NOTES AND REFERENCES

1. S. Humphries, 1988, *A Secret World of Sex,* Sidgwick & Jackson, pp. 9–13.
2. T. Rosengarten, 1974, *All God's Dangers,* Avon, p. 212.
3. Elswick Local History Group, 1985, *Richardson's Leather Workers: The Worker's Story,* Elswick Local History Group, Newcastle, p. 21.
4. T. Thompson, 1981, *Edwardian Childhoods,* Routledge & Kegan Paul, p. 120.
5. P. Thompson, 1988, *The Voice of the Past: Oral History* (2nd edn), Oxford University Press, p. 296.
6. J. McCrindle and S. Rowbotham, 1977, *Dutiful Daughters,* Allen Lane, p. 116.
7. C. Hall, 'Married Women at Home in Birmingham in the 1920s and 1930s', *Oral History,* Vol 5, no 2, 1977, p. 72.
8. Rosengarten, *op.cit.,* pp. xiv–xx.
9. *Ibid.,* pp. 12–13.
10. S. Richardson, 1985, *The Recollections of Three Manchesters in the First World War,* Neil Richardson, Manchester, p. 58.
11. A. Harrison, 1989, *Challenging de Gaulle: The OAS and the Counterrevolution in Algeria, 1954–1962,* Praeger, p. xiii.

CHAPTER NINE
Transcriptions

While tape recording is an excellent way of preserving voices, making available the information the tapes contain requires further work. It is much harder to skim through a tape than a book, especially as an oral history tape is the record of a conversation and so is much less structured. Original tapes are both unique and delicate, so they need careful storage, while providing the equipment to allow consultation of working copies can be expensive, and the very need to play them back on a tape recorder may deter some researchers. If tapes are simply put on archive shelves after recording, the information on them may all too easily be sterilised, even though it may never be lost. On the other hand, the same is true of most documentary archives when they are first collected, and would be true of notes made for a book if they were left in that state. Archivists and authors both spend considerable effort on organising and indexing, and so must oral historians, and this has to be seen not as a distraction from the real business but as a necessary investment, setting aside the personal satisfaction of rushing onto the next session and working instead on behalf of all the potential future users. Investment is always at risk when there is pressure for immediate action, but for an oral historian to record ever more tapes without following them up is just the same as archivists defining their jobs as cramming rooms with ever more paper, or authors refusing to write up their research because there is more to be done.

We have to face two separate but closely linked issues about what to do when we have made a recording. First is the need to make tapes accessible, so that every researcher does not have to replay them, listening to every word, to know what they contain, or even to find something they remember from a previous run through. Second, one person who makes an accurate transcript of the words on it saves everyone else from having to do more than copy sections from that. Word processors make this a doubly attractive proposition because material on a disc can be directly copied in seconds, and edited on the screen so that all the relevant sections of several tapes can be collated with ease. The tape, of course, remains the actual historical record and the transcript could not be relied on as authentic unless the tape was available to check it against whenever there was a doubt. It is merely that for most purposes, written words are easier to work with, to reorganise, to edit and re-edit, and to do all the other things a researcher needs to do in shaping raw material into finished history.

A clearly typed transcript is guaranteed to be comprehensible, whereas a poorly recorded session may only make sense to the people who were present at it, and not always to them. It is ironic that oral methods open up history by turning from the written word to the spoken, and yet largely close off what has been discovered unless it is then written out, even though there is a quality to listening to the original words which can never be captured on paper. When there is a chance to incorporate original extracts in talks or broadcasts, or even to publish tape cassettes of extracts, it is not to be missed, but the plain fact is that these are few and far between, compared to the uses that can be made of a written version. The extracts in this book are reaching a far wider audience as a book than they could ever hope to as taped material unless they were broadcast on radio or television, and then they would probably be heard only once. In an ideal world, every tape would therefore be readily available as a copy of the original recording and as a full, typed transcript. Sadly, like so many ideals, this one is rarely realised for two main reasons: lack of resources and boredom.

Transcribing is not easy work, even for someone trained in taking down dictation, for the recordings may be of variable quality, accents may obscure relatively normal words, and technical or dialect words make life hard. Every false start to a train of thought, every 'you know', and every significant pause needs to be indicated on the transcript if there is to be total reliability, and this takes great patience. Some go further and include slight pauses, coughs, ums, ers, and so on to give an exact sound picture of what was recorded. In my experience a good tape will take at least six times as long to write out in longhand as it does to play; a bad one, like that of Mr Harper from which I quoted in the first chapter, will take much, much longer. A knowledge of shorthand would speed up any manual transcription substantially, but this seems to be a skill rarely possessed by collectors. The primary goal must be accuracy, not speed, in any case, for a misunderstood word could alter the sense of a whole section. I have been told of one

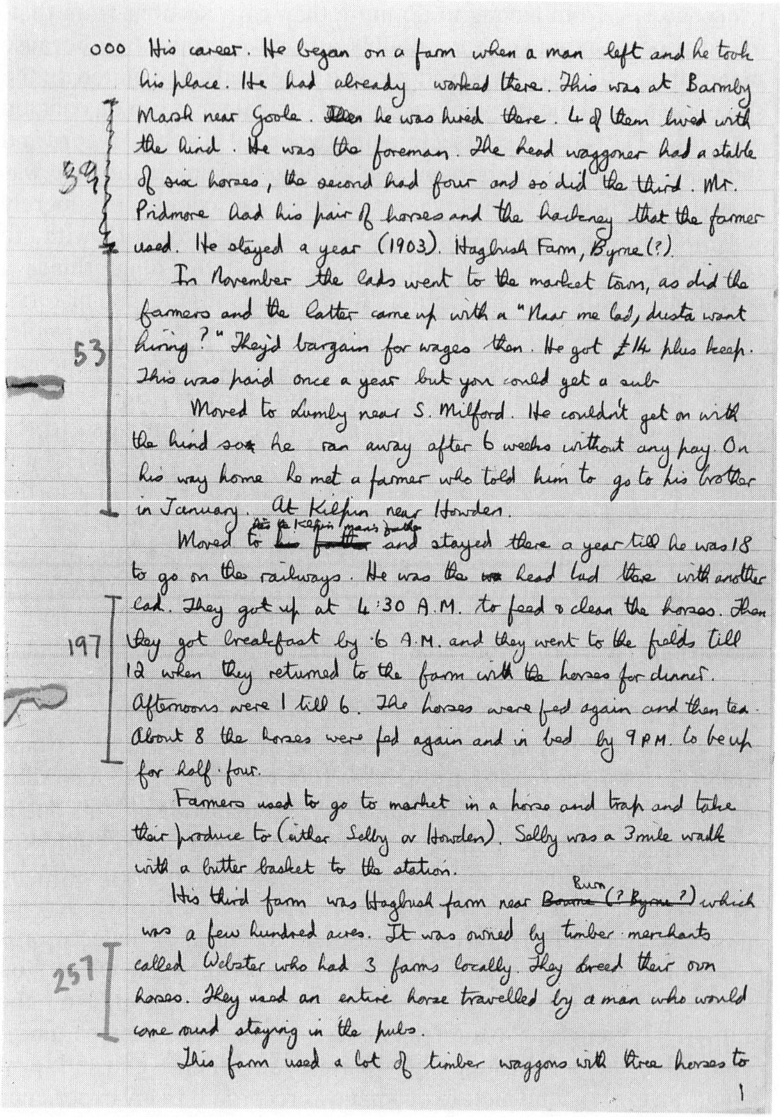

000 His career. He began on a farm when a man left and he took his place. He had already worked there. This was at Barmby Marsh near Goole. Then he was hired there. 4 of them lived with the hind. He was the foreman. The head waggoner had a stable of six horses, the second had four and so did the third. Mr. Pridmore had his pair of horses and the hackney that the farmer used. He stayed a year (1903). Haglrush Farm, Byrne (?).

39

In November the lads went to the market town, as did the farmers and the latter came up with a "Near me lad, dusta want hiring?" They'd bargain for wages then. He got £14 plus keep. This was paid once a year but you could get a sub

53

Moved to Lumby near S. Milford. He couldn't get on with the hind so he ran away after 6 weeks without any pay. On his way home he met a farmer who told him to go to his brother in January. At Kelfin near Howden.

Moved to Kelfin man's brother and stayed there a year till he was 18 to go on the railways. He was the head lad there with another lad. They got up at 4:30 A.M. to feed & clean the horses. Then they got breakfast by 6 A.M. and they went to the fields till 12 when they returned to the farm with the horses for dinner. Afternoons were 1 till 6. The horses were fed again and then tea. About 8 the horses were fed again and in bed by 9 P.M. to be up for half-four.

197

Farmers used to go to market in a horse and trap and take their produce to (either Selby or Howden). Selby was a 3 mile walk with a butter basket to the station.

His third farm was Haglrush farm near Burn (? Byrne?) which was a few hundred acres. It was owned by timber merchants called Webster who had 3 farms locally. They breed their own horses. They used an entire horse travelled by a man who would come round staying in the pubs.

257

This farm used a lot of timber waggons with three horses to

1

Plate 9.1 An example of a transcript summary from a session with Mr Pridmore. The various marks and numbers are explained in the text, but note the sixth line from the bottom where a place name had to be checked and changed. I have deliberately not selected a perfect looking example, or cleaned it up, for on a small project it is better to have a system that works than one which looks beautiful but tells you nothing.

young typist who transcribed 'pawn shop' as 'porn shop', for instance. Place names and personal names may be difficult to get clearly, but every effort should be made, with all dubious ones listed for checking with the contributor. The occasional lapse is inevitable, and some things may be beyond resolution but doubtful sections should be marked as such. On occasions, it is necessary to clarify the spoken record where gestures amplified or filled in the words of the speaker: pointing to a particular object in the room, perhaps. Only the collector can provide this clarification and though few people enjoy transcribing, it is not a straightforward clerical task that can be handed to any typist and forgotten.

A group may find that one member is better at transcribing than others, while an institutional project will probably employ skilled clerical labour, or it may even be able to afford the high fees charged by specialist transcribers. Full-time transcribers within a group can easily come to feel they have been given the part of the work the collectors least wanted to do, and as a major part of anyone's workload it can soon become burdensome. Some people do enjoy it, however, and making sure that things run smoothly is very much a matter of working to the abilities and needs of individual staff members. At the very least, the collector must check the initial transcript against the tape before it is accepted as an accurate record, but in a small amateur team the preparation of a transcript has to be treated as part of the recording process. As such it is the responsibility of the collector, and apart from anything else, the knowledge that any backlog of transcription work is a personal backlog helps to impose a discipline that prevents the reckless accumulation of tapes. A schedule should be established that requires transcription to take place within a specified period of time, and this should be both realistic and enforced. If it is chronically ignored in practice, recast it and rethink what you are doing or a two-tier operation will develop with a fictitious schedule that looks impressive, but where people actually do what they can according to the pressure of immediate needs.

It is worth stressing that even though full transcription is rarely achieved in practice outside fully professional and very well-funded operations, and often not even in them, it remains the best option. Accessibility can be achieved with less, however, and this is the overriding issue, for even a transcript will not tell anyone unfamiliar with the session what subjects are covered in it and whereabouts to look for them. A summary that is comprehensive and clarifies any obscurities, without pretending to reproduce the words of the speakers otherwise, can be made without extensive replaying to get everything just right, and sections of the tape which are worth transcribing for use can then be located with little difficulty. For anyone whose aim is to go beyond the creation of an archive, this method is especially attractive and it is the one I used myself. It encourages the rapid construction of an index of the tapes because of its subject-orientation, and this index is the most valuable tool any researcher can have. It must be complete, however, with digressions noted as well as the main material, and nothing should be excluded simply because it is not germane to your particular enquiries. Asking researchers to donate a copy of any exact transcriptions made using the index may lead to quite full transcription in the end.

To give some idea of the real quantities of work involved in this type of operation: I produced something like 37 hours of relevant recorded material on 29 tapes from the East Riding, which produced over 150 A4 sides of summary in longhand, at approximately 650 words per side. These I then indexed using file cards, and from the cards, transcribing only the best extracts on any subject, I produced an organised verbatim transcript 400 sides long, though at a lower average wordage. This latter probably covered a third of the spoken words and filled a lever-arch file. It took so many hours that I doubt very much if I should ever have finished complete transcripts at all, and I found working on related extracts both an effective way of clearing up obscure points and of avoiding transcribing material not good enough to use. If something later turned out to be worth adding, there was no difficulty in doing so, and by cross-referencing any extract touching on two or more topics, I produced a very effective data base that is capable of being used for many purposes besides my original research aims. Word processors were unheard of then and the labour involved in recopying the extracts I finally selected for use, and often the further recopying through different drafts, was a major task that can be completely avoided today by using one. This also means that without excessive work or the destruction of the original transcript, an archive that transcribes onto disc can keep complete transcripts and reorganise them into subject-oriented compilations.

It may, in fact, seem logical to cut out the summaries and simply note down the subjects that are of interest on a run-through of the tape, ignoring the rest and producing an index directly. It is, however, impossible to predict how an open-ended investigation will develop, and which lines of enquiry will prove most productive. Every time something that originally seemed of little importance turns out to be worth attention, all the tapes must then be searched again for relevant material. The temptation will be strong to put off any searching at all

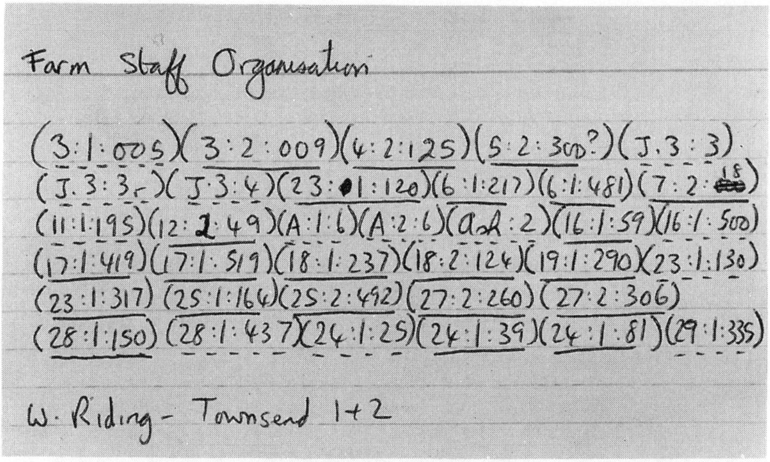
Farm Staff Organisation
(3:1:005)(3:2:009)(4:2:125)(5:2:300?)(J.3:3)
(J.3:3.)(J.3:4)(23:1:120)(6:1:217)(6:1:481)(7:2:18)
(11:1:195)(12:2:49)(A:1:6)(A:2:6)(a&h:2)(16:1:59)(16:1:500)
(17:1:419)(17:1:519)(18:1:237)(18:2:124)(19:1:290)(23:1:130)
(23:1:317)(25:1:164)(25:2:492)(27:2:260)(27:2:306)
(28:1:150)(28:1:437)(24:1:25)(24:1:39)(24:1:81)(29:1:335)
W. Riding - Townsend 1+2

Plate 9.2 An index card compiled from the transcript summaries, in this case covering the way the farm labour force was organised. The brackets keep the entries separate and those that have a full underline will have been transcribed under the heading 'farm staff organisation', or else a cross-reference there will say where the full transcript is located.

until it is clear that no new interesting material is going to alter the overall picture, but this is one of those goals that retreats in front of the pursuer. The likely end product is a large mountain of unindexed tapes that has become too daunting to tackle. It is common sense that if the tapes have to be gone through in their entirety over and over again, the time spent on collating information from them will multiply, rather than add up, as it does in producing and then working from a single index. The first run through should produce enough detail to allow any consultation of the tapes thereafter to be done from knowledge rather than as a trawling operation.

Lists of the major subject changes on each tape, almost like the table of contents from a book, are no substitute for summaries as they are too brief to be comprehensive. They can give general guidance for searching transcripts quickly, just as a table of contents does in a book, but that does not not remove the need for a proper index and no more does this. Even where a collector has worked through a rigid questionnaire meticulously, no two sessions will proceed at the same pace and answers may include all sorts of sidelines, so it is impossible to be sure where on the tape any particular subject is dealt with. This is exacerbated by the fact that while recorders usually have a digital tape counter like a car mileometer, to show how far the tape has run, there is no standardisation and the numbers derived rarely correspond to leisure time

Mr. Pridmore (8:1:000)

"These farm lads used to sit on t'wall and they used to talk about what they'd done during t'day - you know - all been ploughing and drilling or whatever they'd done. And we did so and so in such an such a field and so and so - they used to talk about one another you know. And they were all a jolly sort of lot o' lads. They was all entertained one another in the village - you understand what I mean? All congregated together and, of course, they hadn't money to go into t'pubs with, in them days, although beer was only 2d and 3d a pint. You see they hadn't the money to do it with in those days so they had to sit on these walls, and 8 o'clock they'd got to go back again in winter time to feed their horses and be off to bed just turned nine, you see. Because they had to get up at half past 4, so that they needed to get off to bed, you see."

[margin: Summer evenings in village]

Mr. Johnson (6:1:40)

[Was there a lot of drinking went on?]

"Oh, I don't know there was any more than there is today. No, I don't know. Some did and some didn't. No I don't know. No, I wouldn't say there were, well - only on really - if they did get drunk it was generally Saturday night or Sunday. I mean there weren't time other times to start playing games, weren't time to play games, you know. We used to play football sometimes but I could never play - I could kick a ball about, but we had to do it summertime - you Saturday afternoon, you know, you were working Saturday afternoon. No I don't know that there was a lot of boozing. They couldn't afford a lot. Then, it'd be 3d a pint in a pub. See we used to - a lot of the farmers a terrible lot used to have a barrel o' beer in - never out all year round - a barrel o' beer. And, see, t'foreman - when he lived on a place with himself, most foremen, he had beer in t'cellar and he used to be in charge o't beer you know. But, you know, some of 'em used to think - one place I was at, we hadn't in all year round, we had to get so many barrels of beer in for harvest - that was it - see there was no more - so many barrels - and I used to tap it and give 'em their beer, so much like, and all these fellows thought - you know - that I was on a winner when I had these barrels o' beer to go at, but if they'd but known it they had a lot more beer than I had - those days, I never touched it. Course they used to buy that - I think they used to buy it - course they got so many barrels they got it a bit cheaper, but it'd cost about 1½d a pint. It weren't quite so good as tap beer, you know, but it wasn't bad stuff."

Mr. Fisher (6:1:30)

"You more or less made your own entertainment. You know, you'd get wintertime on, you know, when you got your horses - it used to be about eight o'clock and you hadn't much time. You were beginning to feel ready for bed because you'd been up since quarter to five. And then they got a charge,"

Plate 9.3 A transcript sheet compiled from the index. The line down the side is merely an indication that I used the quotation in *Amongst Farm Horses*.

those of another model. Counter numbers have to be used in indexing, but always note down which machine they come from. Where two or more different machines are frequently used, it is a good idea to construct a conversion table by playing the same tape on both and comparing the numbers.

Interview no.1 with Mr A.M. Pridmore, ex-farm servant

Tuesday July 9th, 1973

<u>Tape 3, side 1</u>, commencing counter no. 292

```
292    his career
317    hiring fairs
357    daily schedule
390    traps and trap horses
407    Hagbush Farm
422    stallions
435    forestry and timber waggons
445    breeding horses
452    breaking in
488    day labourers
530    end of side 1
```

<u>Tape 3, side 2</u>

```
000    personal details
009    day labourers
022    working on the railways
052    leaving farming
066    marriage
069    personal details
082    education
085    father's job
105    friendship with boatman
158    part-time jobs
178    feeding the horses
187    caring for horses
201    learning the job
209    stacking
246    thrashing days
268    harvest money
275    meals
310    labourers' pay
370    railway pay as comparison
379    Martinmas holiday and hiring fairs
416    Trade unions, lack of, and comparison to situation on
       railways
523    harvest suppers
533    end of tape
```

Plate 9.4 A guide to the contents of the session with Mr Pridmore from which the tape summary in Plate 9.1 was taken. It is useful for fast searches for substantial quotations, but a comparison with the summary sheet will show how blunt an instrument this is for any other purpose.

Selective transcription requires attention to detail to be effective. First, it is essential to show, in the index and on the summary sheet, which sections have been transcribed, both to show that transcripts exist and to indicate where they can be found. On the summary I put a line in the margin down the full length of the section transcribed, and next to it wrote the page number where it would be found in the transcription file. Where an extract was relevant to several sections, I put it under the most appropriate heading in the transcription file, and entered cross references in the others. In the index I put a solid line under a section's tape counter number, and where I had listened to the section and rejected it, I used a dotted underline. Each fully-transcribed section had its contributor, tape number, tape side, and counter number recorded above it. This means that the system can be entered at any point, from the index, the summaries, or the filed transcripts, according to which is the most appropriate on any particular search, and at each of these places all the information needed for writing a reference or extending the search was recorded. The system was flexible, effective, and minimised the work needed to provide the access I needed to my tapes, so they illustrate the general principles to be followed. Most successful systems that I have seen are similar, though they vary in their details. With full transcription, of course, things are simpler because it is only necessary to index the transcripts as you would any document, but the index must still be exact.

The essential details of what the tape is and when it was made must be accurately recorded on both the tape and its box. The tapes need numbering for any system to work properly, however few there are, and this number should be used to tie together all the different pieces of documentation. A comprehensive index must be maintained, recording contributors' details and relating them to the tapes that they have made, but to protect confidentiality, it should never be available for public inspection. Apart from this, accessibility is the overriding priority so avoid over-complex, over-specialised, and idiosyncratic systems. Any tape really worth making will be of use to others in a wide variety of ways when you have finished, and any archival system must allow the average person to follow it without difficulty. Use obvious and consistent headings when organising transcript sections by subject, and avoid building in shortcuts that depend on your own personal knowledge, because others are then excluded. Ask yourself whether the system would carry on working if you literally vanished without warning: any sound system should pass this test.

The actual presentation of the transcripts also needs some consideration. Writing down what is on the tape is not as simple as it sounds. I have already noted that some transcripts are fuller than others, including every sound rather than just the speech. If this is seen as over-complex, as it usually is, how do we define what should be recorded? Silences can contribute a lot to the rhythm of speech, and there are all the ums and ers that everyone incorporates into spoken sentences. Are they just padding, or part of the total picture? If they can be sacrificed for clarity's sake, what about 'you know'? It can occur every few words, dominating the flow and obscuring real meaning, yet these are real words, not inarticulate noises. If we edit them out, should we go further and clean up the transcript generally? A tape recording preserves all the false starts and cul-de-sacs down which we all run from time to time both in speaking and writing: are they worth preserving? Moreover, the normal rules that govern the use of English, or of whatever language is used, are often inadequate, since unrehearsed speech usually includes slang and dialect, and punctuation is often difficult to reconcile with speech rhythms. Are these difficulties faults that need setting right?

Few would disagree that the primary transcription has to be of a sufficient standard to be treated as the equivalent of the tape and since any editing moves the transcript away from the tape, it should be avoided at this stage. Putting things in the primary transcript does not force their later inclusion in an extract in a publication, as we shall see later, so any word spoken should go in, including swear words of all types, and any inarticulate noise that has become incorporated into speech. Background noises do not seem to me to fall within this unless they impinge on the flow of talk, and pauses should likewise be shown when they matter, not otherwise. A pause for thought is not the same as a pause for effect. On rendering punctuation, grammar, and spelling, my solution to these problems was essentially pragmatic and seems to be in keeping with the majority of oral historians. English spelling is not phonetic in any but a loose sense, as with words like cough, bough, and bought, and special spellings that seek to bring out the pronunciation often just leave the word looking bizarre. In many cases, many local pronunciations are no further from the Standard English spelling than the Received Pronunciation is and some may be closer.

I, for instance, was puzzled for years by a common literary practice illustrated by a passage from *The Cruel Sea* by Nicholas Monsarrat, representing a scrap of dialogue from the bridge of a wartime convoy escort: ' "Any sign of submarines, sir?" asked Gracey after a pause. He was a Lancashire man: he pronounced the hated word as 'soobmarines', giving it a humorous air which robbed it of its sting. Said like that, it was hardly a submarine at all, just something out of a music-hall, no more lethal than a mother-in-law or a dish of tripe.'[1] As a Lancashire man myself with an identifiable but not strong accent, when I say submarine I hear it with a 'u' not an 'oo'. I would transcribe the officer's version as 'sabmarine', and it would seem equally comical to me. It is far more sensible to agree to differ, since we both understand the word both in written and spoken form, than to claim that one form is more accurate than the other. This way we avoid the patronising connotations of the comments which end the quotation. English belongs to all those who speak the language, not just to one group, and to imply that its written form represents only the speech of certain groups is to belittle and marginalise the rest. Putting in our own versions of pronunciation does not work because only someone who shares our particular vowel sounds will be able to reproduce the sound that we are describing. This is the basic reason why no proposal to produce a phonetic spelling scheme can work, though the subject is regularly raised, for whose pronunciation is to form the basis of it? Moreover, I recently heard a Welshman speaking Standard English with no discernible accent, yet the rhythms made it unmistakeably Welsh. How could that be shown on paper?

Theodore Rosengarten felt strongly on this issue, and said of Nate Shaw's Alabama dialect, 'I have not reproduced a southern or black dialect because I did not hear it. I did hear the English language as I know it, spoken with regional inflection and grammar.'[2] There is, on the other hand, still an active tradition of dialect writing in this country, where strenuous efforts are made to reproduce exactly every nuance of speech, and this extends to the growing amount of Black British dialect that is being written. The effort involved in reading it back means that it could never rival Standard English as a normal medium of communication, even for those who naturally speak the dialect without thought. It is an exercise that writers and readers enjoy rather than a serious rival to conventional spellings, which is fine as long as it is mutually acceptable, but is it acceptable for more general consumption? David Adams recorded many ex-farm servants from the area between Aberdeen and Dundee and produced a fascinating account of a very unusual way of life, told clearly and in a lively manner. They had many things in common with servants in the East Riding, but they lived in outhouses known as bothies and cooked and cleaned for themselves. It provides one of the clearest comparisons with and contrasts to the East Riding version of what is clearly the same system at root, and the two together allow us to understand the basis of the farm servants' place in farming much better than we ever could from the study of one alone. He decided to write his quotations

> entirely in local dialect as it was told to me. This may have made it more difficult to read, not only for outsiders but also for local dialect speakers who are only used to reading and writing in standard English. However, I felt that the first-hand accounts from ex-bothy dwellers ... would have much more truth and immediacy if retold using only their actual vocabulary, incorporating many turns of phrase, expressions and anecdotes, illustrating their dry bothy humour. To be continually using parentheses to insert Scots would be wholly artificial, and make it more difficult to read.'[3]

I agree entirely with the underlying sentiment, but not with the conclusions, for if men cannot read back their own reminiscences, how is their immediacy being enhanced? Using ordinary spellings where appropriate has nothing to do with altering genuinely different dialect words, phrases, or forms of speech: it merely enhances comprehensibility. The danger is shown by this description of part of the farming year:

> Eftir the auld neep dreels were ploo'ed and harra'ed, barley wis sawn in late spring, jist afore the Mey term.... Tatties like neeps needed tae be weel dunged and main crop varieties were planted in spring. Hey was cut aboot the end o June, eftir the *bloom* was aff as the pollen irritated the horse. If the mower needed sharpened at the smiddy this was duin on a rainy day, the blades ye cud shairpen wi carborundum yersel, but the fingers had tae be taen tae the smiddy tae get buffed flush.[4]

Though Lowland Scots is not a different language, as we saw earlier, it looks like it here, and the initial assumption must be that there is a great deal of dialect. The more I read it, however, the less need for special spellings I can see. 'Cud' is exactly how I hear myself say 'could', so I cannot see this as a particularly local variation from ordinary English usage, and likewise 'Mey' for 'May'. Within sixteen words we have 'sharpened' and 'shairpen', and whether this is intentional or not, it reads strangely. There are words that certainly need spelling as they were said, for instance 'neeps' and 'tatties', for to render them as 'turnips' and 'potatoes' would clearly do violence to the authenticity of the record, but how many people anywhere do say 'potatoes' all the time, rather than 'taters', 'taties', 'spuds' or some other nickname? The humour of the contributors has little to do with spellings, standard or otherwise. There are no prescriptive rules by which any transcribing practice can be judged, so I am not saying this system is wrong: simply that to me, too much emphasis on the contributors' speech can make it very hard to view their lifestyle as a rational one. Even when it is done admiringly, hidden inside is the message that these people are not part of the mainstream of life but are an endangered species, confined to a special arena. Farm servants, however, flourished as part of a market-oriented agriculture in Scotland and Yorkshire, and while their identification with horses may seem nostalgic now, it was not then.

My transcripts, and those of others used in the book, including Theodore Rosengarten, do contain non-standard spellings, for a variety of reasons. Since consonants are much more phonetically consistent than vowels, they can be shown as said. 'Tiv' is East Riding for 'to' and clearly is not represented by the normal spelling. Dickens' famous inversion of *vs* and *ws* in Cockney speech is similar. Accurate rendition of what was said can be complex, as in the use of the definite article in northern speech, especially on a tape where the contributor is likely to be speaking 'properly' part of the time. At various times it will be used in full, omitted altogether, or reduced either to 'th' before a vowel, or the glottal stop in the throat that is usually meant by 't'. Each should be rendered as it is said. It seems legitimate to me, in addition, to retain the flavour of local speech by hinting at it with unobtrusive spellings like 'feller' for 'fellow', or 'tha' for 'thou' and this practice can be observed in a wide range of oral history material. The more pronounced the dialect, of course, the greater the unavoidable variation from standard spellings, and Scots in all its forms will clearly show this more than most English dialects.

Readers will barely notice a moderate number of variant spellings precisely because they do fit in, and they will have no idea of the trouble it may have taken the transcriber to produce this result. The complexity is apparent only to those who go into it, but it does give a constant reminder that this is not Standard English. If the accent is suggested on the transcript, a reader who knows how to will be able to read the written version in the way it was spoken, a stranger will get some sense of the sounds, and communication between any and all of us will not be hindered. The only way to show a phonetically accurate version is to use the International Phonetic Alphabet symbols, which can be found in most good dictionaries as a guide to pronunciation, but very few people can read long passages thus handled. A compromise method for those who feel that the reader should be given more than hints of the local speech, but who agree that the bulk of quotes should avoid this format, is to add an appendix where several paragraphs are given in full-blooded transliteration as an example, or to give the first few paragraphs in the main body in this way. In the final analysis, every transcriber makes up their own mind, but the excerpts in this book give a good sample of a variety of practices.

Any project which is concerned with a trade or with traditional ways of doing things, including housework before the introduction of labour-saving devices, will inevitably contain dialect terms which do not appear in standard dictionaries. Before creating your own spellings check other sources to see if someone else has done it already. Joseph Wright's *English Dialect Dictionary* (1898–1905) is the best starting point as it is a massive repository of words and is generally acceptable, though inevitably not complete. Any library with a local history section should be able to help you find out quickly if your area is covered by one of the many glossaries, word lists, or dictionaries compiled at some time in the past. The definitions may provide information about the word and its usage that you would not have suspected from a single use on a tape. Check if there is a history of the subject under study, or in the case of a craft, if there are descriptive guides to it. My book contains a glossary of horse words, as does Keegan's *The Heavy Horse* (1973). We have already seen Dave Douglass's mining glossary, and though this is short it refers to other sources. R. A. Salaman's *Dictionary of Woodworking* (1975) is the kind of modern work it would be wonderful to have for every craft: it has masses of information and definitions of terms, often with illustrations, and in such a case it would be perverse to go against what will definitely be the standard book in its field for the foreseeable future. Publications such as *The Transactions of the Yorkshire Dialect Society* contain many articles that cover this sort of thing. Be wary of locally published material unless it is relatively modern, however, as it may be of poor quality, and also of books with only fragmentary references.

If spellings seem over-complex and artificial, or if there is nothing to be found – and there is no point in searching forever – then create your own, using the simplest spelling that conveys the sound. Above all, resist the temptation to construct weird and wonderful trains of vowels to convey tiny nuances of sound. Slang should be treated in the same way even though it often has only a very short life. It is particularly common among children and while my daughter was passing through primary school, for instance, the accepted child's word for 'large' progressed from 'mega' through 'macca' to 'jocker' before settling down to the use of 'mega' as a standard. In a few years terms can become incomprehensible, but *A Dictionary of Slang and Unconventional English* (8th ed 1984), conceived and edited originally by Eric Partridge but kept up to date since, is a reliable source for definitions and spellings. Consistency is vital, so keep a list to avoid spelling the same word in two or more ways. The end product is a glossary of your own, which may be worth publishing in its own right with an explanatory text.

Grammar should also be rendered as close to the original as possible, even where you are sure a mistake has been made. You may be wrong, or the correction you make may not be accurate. If it seems likely that a reader will not understand, an explanatory note should be inserted in the text, as a footnote, or as part of a glossary if it is a feature that crops up repeatedly. Punctuation is undoubtedly a part of written rather than spoken English, so there is no reason for variation from standard practice in search of a scheme suited to a particular locality.

However, its origin in written English often makes it difficult to apply normal usages to speech of any kind. On tapes there are long pauses, sentences that continue interminably, digressions that change the direction of a sentence, and many more things that are not provided for. I found the dash a very useful addition to the normal symbols, both for long pauses and for abrupt changes of direction for which a comma was inadequate but, as with spelling, there is no point in inventing new symbols or systems to do the job accurately because, however well intentioned and well thought-out they may be, most readers have no chance of being comfortable with them. Aim to help the reader recreate what was said in the manner in which it was said, but don't use punctuation to bring order to what seems an untidy piece of prose when it is written down.

The result of transcribing should be a mass of material that is accessible as an archive and, if possible, ready for use in publications without more than superficial editing. Transcription is an unglamorous task, but without it hardly anything can be achieved in oral history. It is not an end in itself, but a vital link in a chain of communication of ideas, and an effective system will ensure that working from the original tape is kept to a minimum, not endlessly and laboriously protracted because of minor oversights. One of the main worries over the lasting impact of oral history must be that a large percentage of the tapes made over the last two decades have never been properly transcribed or even summarised, so that in time they may have to be discarded as more or less unusable for serious historical work because of the lack of information attached to them.

NOTES AND REFERENCES

1. N. Monsarrat, 1956, *The Cruel Sea,* Penguin, p. 224.
2. T. Rosengarten, 1974, *All God's Dangers,* Avon, p. xxiv.
3. D.G. Adams, 1991, *Bothy Nichts and Days,* John Donald, p. vii.
4. *Ibid.,* p. 55.

CHAPTER TEN
Using Recorded Material

Probably the bulk of all material collected has never been published in any form, so it would be quite wrong to imply that collecting and publication are inseparable, but recording can never be an end in itself. Reminiscence therapy apart, if the fate of oral history recordings is to be left in a bedroom somewhere, and then finally taped over, thrown away, or accidentally ruined, they may as well never have been made. Even fully documented and transcribed tapes serve no purpose if no-one knows they exist or has access to them, and so while simply preserving memories that seem likely to be lost is a worthy aim for an oral historian, it is only fulfilled if the tapes are properly looked after in the long term and open to use. For many collectors, archival deposit was not the reason they undertook a recording project, but making arrangements to put tapes somewhere safe where others can use them after their primary usefulness to the collector has ended is vital. If a project does decide to keep its own master tapes, it should at least make clear written provision for what is to happen if it is wound up at some future date. It may seem pessimistic to do so, but there is always a chance that this will happen and it is good practice to be prepared for it. It can avoid the tapes being thrown away, or ownership being disputed in a time of crisis.

A local library or museum which sets up or sponsors a project will usually expect to hold the tapes and all related material, of course, but an individual or a relatively informal group, such as a local history group or adult education class with no premises of their own, must make their own decision on where their tapes will ultimately be kept. Material is best placed where it is most likely to be used, but there can be no hard and fast rules about how this is best achieved because many factors have to be taken into account. The sensible course is to find an existing institution that will hold them on mutually acceptable terms. Some accept any tapes that are of good enough quality, but many have restrictive collecting policies to cut down the duplication and fragmentation that uncoordinated collecting produces. Some institutions, especially those funded by local authorities, concern themselves primarily with a particular place, area, or county, while others are subject oriented, like the Imperial War Museum. Some would be happy to allow a group to operate their own collection as a separate entity under their general umbrella, while others would simply integrate all tapes received into the main collection. Some have a very high profile and easy access while others are little known and have very limited periods when their holdings can be consulted.

Even public access must not override the need to safeguard the tapes and fulfil any promises made about confidentiality. Material collected for a special purpose may not be appropriate for general consultation, and it may be that it should be withheld for a stated length of time. The census imposes a hundred-year secrecy rule on enumerator's booklets for instance, as they contain personal information on us all and a local archive may well choose to restrict access to the raw materials they have collected to bona fide scholars, making available only selected extracts to those who merely wish to browse. Confidential sections of tapes that are otherwise unrestricted should be removed from access copies. There can be a temptation to say that the contributor will never know what use is made of material, and that serious researchers can be trusted to use it sensitively, but neither statement is automatically true and both are a breach of trust. Awareness of such considerations and a willingness to enforce them should not be taken for granted, especially if few tapes are held. A library or other institution that has no tapes at all and no facilities for dealing with them, should only be considered if it will make a commitment to using the deposit as the start of developing a real oral history section, and only then if the local element is the most important strand of the recordings.

The Directory of Recorded Sound Resources in the United Kingdom (1989), edited by Lali Weerasinghe and published by the British Library National Sound Archive, lists most oral history collections of any size. As the title suggests, collections are not limited to tapes, but include records, phonograph cylinders, piano rolls, and so on. 489 collections are listed, and the entries make it clear which include oral history. Many are very small: Bedford Central Library has six hours of tape, for instance, and of that only an interview with a retired alderman counts as oral history. Folkestone Central Library has eight discs and nine hours of tape, including local history topics but also things such as the Parliamentary debate on the Channel Tunnel. Kent University Library, not far away in Canterbury, has 16,000 tapes, including videos, but again not all are oral history. The North West Sound Archive in Clitheroe Castle, Lancashire, has 50 discs and 20,000 tapes and the National Sound Archive itself holds c.750,000 discs and c.50,000 tapes, including videos. These are all public institutions, and, between them, a few of the larger ones actually hold the overwhelming majority of tapes. Nevertheless a substantial proportion of collections are private ones held at home. Access is bound to be restricted in such a case, but appointments must be made even at some of the biggest institutions, including the BBC Sound Archives, with their 130,000 tapes, which also charges outsider users. *The Directory of Recorded Sound Resources in the United Kingdom* is a pioneer work as yet, and so is far from complete, but the major institutions are all included and it is the best guide available when considering what to do with your own tapes.

Museum experience has taught me that maintaining collections of local interest material always creates a tension about where to locate them. There is a natural desire to keep things as near as possible to the place of origin to make local access swift and easy. However, a study of an industry might actually be better located with a museum devoted entirely to that industry, even though it is very distant. Truly local access logically requires a local studies centre for every district, each of which would contain only a handful of things, would be impossible to staff and run properly, and would rarely be used by outsiders. At the other extreme, having only one national centre would ensure that those interested in any subject could be sure that any information in existence would be there and facilities would be as good as they could be, but only professional historians and those lucky enough to live nearby would ever use it. More realistically, large regional centres like the North West Sound Archive can group together sufficient similar material to make travelling to consult it worthwhile, and the evidence is that such collections are well used. Local availability can actually be enhanced for they can organise schemes such as that run by the NWSA which allows its collections to be consulted through many local libraries in Lancashire.

General economies of scale mean that good facilities can be offered and kept open for longer, especially where they are shared with or provided by another institution, as happens in Bradford where the Central Library houses the tapes of the Bradford Heritage Recording Unit. Centerprise Trust, of Hackney, has been one of the most active local oral history groups, with a string of publications and a determinedly community-based ethos, yet it finds it best to use the London History Workshop Centre as the place where listening copies of tapes are made available to the public. (Working copies should of course be retained, which has the additional advantage of insuring against loss, deterioration, or the accidental wiping of any particular copy.) Bradford have listening facilities for original tapes, with an index to the tapes available for listening and summaries that give some detail of each one. They will copy individual tapes to order and they always have on sale a very successful set of six pre-recorded tapes of examples selected from a wide variety of originals. Most people probably first hear oral material in this sort of format, not by listening to original or directly copied tapes. The Leicester Oral History Archive probably has made available the widest range of such tapes. In practice, a truly local project is likely to serve its audience best by making such specially worked-up tapes.

Even where there was no original intention to publish, making such tapes, or simply performing routine transcribing and summarising, can generate a desire to make the material more widely available and the simpler forms of oral history publishing are so straightforward that there is no need for anyone to shy away from having a try. The most direct way of using extracts is to capitalise on their unique quality, the fact that they are sound recordings, by playing them directly to an audience, usually in talks and lectures, but this also covers broadcasting on the radio or television and using them to support museum displays. Use only good quality recordings, for imperfections always seem to be amplified more than the voices. In a talk it is essential to get all the extracts in the correct sequence on a special tape rather than trying to find sections on a copy of a real session, for this cannot be done without trying the patience of any audience.

It is possible to weave together reminiscences so that they need no support, but anyone capable of this is certainly in need of no advice from me. Besides complexity, it also rules out offering the audience your own insights and so it is only suited to special circumstances. It may be appropriate simply to run one extract after another, say, to give the residents of a small area a chance to hear selections from the reminiscences you have gathered, but otherwise they should be integrated into a normal talk. The copying and editing must be done carefully so as not to leave the impression that the original has been butchered, and I like to use short chunks that make a point rather than long atmospheric extracts. Leave very short gaps between extracts as a few seconds of blank tape can sound like an eternity with an expectant audience sitting in silence. I always try to make available transcript sheets for the audience: people often deny using or needing them, but when I have tried to do without the difference is clear. Unfamiliar accents and words are all clarified by seeing the written version. Where the recordings or the copies are unclear, or where the acoustics or sound system is poor, I prefer to read the extracts myself, even if it is a poor second best to the real thing. Listening to an incomprehensible noise is even worse.

Well-chosen reminiscences are inherently interesting to many readers and can be put out as a leaflet with just a title and an introductory sentence or two to set them in context, so anyone unsure of their own writing abilities need not worry about this. As a rule editing and reorganisation of the taped material is a necessary first stage in even the simplest publication but with something like a leaflet on a place or trade, it can be very simple and direct, using large sections from one or two tapes to illustrate a common theme. Extracts about a particular place lend themselves well to this because the locality gives it unity. Alternatively, small extracts, perhaps just single sentences, can be gathered together according to a common subject. They achieve their effect by a cumulative weight and can be very effective, and since the readership is mostly local there is no need for much background: they are really triggers, setting off people's own memories. A local project will not find this constricting and it allows quick, popular results to be achieved, which themselves can feed back new contributors and enthusiasm among the team.

At its simplest, a single sheet of A4 paper, folded twice like the omnipresent publicity leaflet, will hold a surprising amount of text. Four hundred words fit easily in a large typeface in each of the six panels of such a format, though illustrations, the title, and subheadings will all reduce this. Desk-top publishing on a micro computer is the best way to produce such a leaflet as it allows anyone to get high-quality results that would have been quite impossible two decades ago. This sounds frightening to those who have never tried it out, but, with training, it is both easy and fascinating and after only a few hours, anyone can produce something. It is not necessary to buy equipment, for local councils or educational centres often make systems available and it is worth asking around to see if such a service exists in your area. They may be targeted at the unemployed as skills training, they may be part of arts provision, or they may be accessible through an educational programme. Few people can know all these possibilities so ask widely before accepting that they do not exist. An alternative way to get a good-looking result is to involve a school or college art department, who will often welcome the chance to work on a real project, or to contact a local graphics company and see if they will undertake the work as a community project in return for a mention on the leaflet. It is a very small piece of work for a professional, so it is not asking much of them.

Text can alternatively be prepared easily on modern electric typewriters which usually have clear, sharp typefaces, or on a word processor with a clear printer (not the faded grey dot matrix type), though the letter size is very large by printers' standards and this reduces the number of words. Many photocopiers allow an original to be reduced in size, and if they are thus cut down by 10 to 20 per cent, which still leaves a comfortable size for reading, the result can be hard to distinguish from conventionally printed text. Turning this into a leaflet requires you to create a replica of what you want by cutting and pasting the typescript, which you then use to print from. It is not hard, but it requires attention to detail and neatness. The text must be typed in columns, allowing for the reduction in width that will occur after typing, and this is best gauged by experimenting. Do not make columns too wide, as a gap of at least a centimetre between them on the leaflet is essential to keep them readable. A final width of 8.0 cm or 8.5 cm per column is a sensible size. Cut out the text, preferably with a craft knife rather than scissors, and keep a duplicate of everything, as you may want to try again. Stick it down with one of the solid glue sticks available from any newsagent onto stiff, straight white card, or even heavy white paper, using faint pencil marks to show where the pieces should go. Avoid making dirty marks and make sure the glue goes right to the edge of the original. The edges of the different pieces will not show up when copied, as long as the cutting and sticking are neatly done, and if things are not quite right, this glue gives you a few seconds to move the pieces around or peel them off and try again before it sets. A title can be prepared with the dry transfer lettering that all stationers sell in a huge variety of styles and sizes of typefaces. Illustrations can be either line drawings or photographs, which can also be reduced to the correct size by photocopying. Line drawings usually come out very well, but photographs also usually photocopy clearly as long as the original is not murky itself. Make a single photocopy of the result to test out that it really does work, and that when it is folded the panels run in the order you want.

For short print runs, certainly anything below a 100, the cheapest way to print is by photocopying and folding the leaflets yourself, but the copyshops to be found in all towns offer more economical printing as numbers go up to the thousands. They probably will also undertake the creation of the design if you cannot manage it in any other way, but this costs money, of course, and they will rarely give much time to it. This apart, the real cost in this type of operation is making a printing plate, and since this only needs to be done once however many copies you print, costs per unit decline rapidly with quantity. Extra leaflets may hardly raise the price at all as you are paying for little more than the paper involved. Again, a local firm may be willing to do the job at cost price, or even free, if given a credit on the finished product, or else local sponsorship can be sought. A series of such leaflets prepared in a common format can cumulatively provide a level of coverage of an area that would have frightened everyone off if it had been tackled at one go, and it can do so very quickly and have great local impact.

Larger pamphlets can be prepared on the same basis, but they are harder to do properly, unless a member of a project group has some skills in this area. However, local councils will probably have an arts officer of one type or another who will know of organisations that can help. A page from the booklet *Windybank: It's What You Make It*, published by the Windybank Book Group about their council estate near Cleckheaton in the Spen Valley is reproduced in Plate 10.1. The group summed up general attitudes to their estate in two quotes, 'Windybank! You don't live there do you?' and 'Windybank! What do you want to go there for?' and the booklet 'is part of our work to change that image.'[1] The result is 46 pages of text, maps, drawings, and photographs of a really professional standard. The group had never undertaken anything remotely like this before, but Kirklees Council, the local authority, gave financial assistance and an organisation called Artivan provided professional expertise without taking over. It is not all oral history, though this makes a substantial contribution and as part of the general historical background, links are made back to Luddite times, for this is Frank Peel's territory. The estate is only a mile or so from Rawfolds Mill where the soldier refused orders to shoot at machine breakers. Heavy unemployment brought by modern mechanisation has contributed a great deal to the estate's problems, so the connection has some force.

The Yorkshire Art Circus is another West Yorkshire organisation which has helped people produce many oral history publications in a variety of formats. Some of them are deliberately modest in appearance, with typed sheets stapled together behind a printed cover sheet, but chapters of short extracts relating to specific aspects of life in one village add up to substantial booklets. To a large extent, they are prepared by the communities involved with help from an editorial team. *Nothing Interesting Ever Happens To Me,* which we have met before, is a good example of what can be achieved in this way. Other

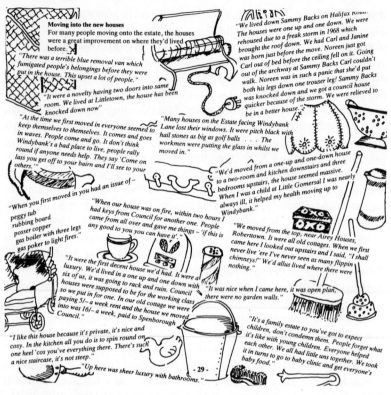

Moving into the new houses
For many people moving onto the estate, the houses were a great improvement on where they'd lived before.▶

"There was a terrible blue removal van which fumigated people's belongings before they were put in the house. This upset a lot of people."

"It were a novelty having two doors into same room. We lived at Littletown, the house has been knocked down now"

"At the time we first moved in everyone seemed to keep themselves to themselves. It comes and goes in waves. People come and go. It don't think Windybank's a bad place to live, people rally round if anyone needs help. They say 'Come on lass you get off to your bairn and I'll see to your others.'"

"When you first moved in you had an issue of –
peggy tub
rubbing board
posser copper
gas boiler with three legs
gas poker to light fires."

"When our house was on fire, within two hours I had keys from Council for another one. People came from all over and gave me things – 'if this is any good to you you can have it'."

"It were the first decent house we'd had. It were a luxury. We'd lived in a one up and one down with six of us, it was going to rack and ruin. Council houses were supposed to be for the working class so we put in for one. In our old cottage we were paying 5/– a week rent and the house we moved into was 16/– a week, paid to Spenborough Council."

"I like this house because it's private, it's nice and cosy. In the kitchen all you do is to spin round on one heel 'cos you've everything there. There's such a nice staircase, it's not steep."

"Up here was sheer luxury with bathrooms."

"We lived down Sammy Backs on Halifax Road. The houses were one up and one down. We were rehoused due to a freak storm in 1968 which brought the roof down. We had Carl and Janine was born just before the move. Noreen just got Carl out of bed before the ceiling fell on it. Going out of the archway at Sammy Backs Carl couldn't walk. Noreen was in such a panic that she'd put both his legs down one trouser leg! Sammy Backs was knocked down and we got a council house quicker because of the storm. We were relieved to be in a better house."

"Many houses on the Estate facing Windybank Lane lost their windows. It were pitch black with hail stones as big as golf balls . . . The workmen were putting the glass in whilst we moved in."

"We'd moved from a one-up and one-down house to a two-room and kitchen downstairs and three bedrooms upstairs, the house seemed massive. When I was a child at Little Gomersal I was nearly always ill, it helped my health moving up to Windybank."

"We moved from the top, near Airey Houses, Roberttown. It were all old cottages. When we first came here I looked out upstairs and I said, "I shall never live 'ere I've never seen as many flippin chimneys!" We'd allus lived where there were nothing."

"It was nice when I came here, it was open plan, there were no garden walls."

"It's a family estate so you've got to expect children, don't condemn them. People forget what it's like with young children. Everyone helped each other. We all had little uns together. We took it in turns to go to baby clinic and get everyone's baby food."

- 29 -

Plate 10.1 A page from *Windybank: It's What You Make It*. A lively visual effect like this can be achieved with simple drawings, typed transcript extracts, scissors, and paper glue sticks, and its preparation requires no special equipment. The drawings are traced from a children's picture book, and tracing is also a way of turning colour photographs into a format that can be reproduced easily. The oral material is used directly with no editorial comment, achieving its effect because the sections all have related themes that fit with the drawings. Despite its simplicity, great care went into this layout, and this is the key to a good appearance.

similar organisations exist all around the country and the plethora of leaflets and pamphlets that oral history has produced is a testament to the determination of groups of all types to get their material into print. Oral history has also been used as the basis for drama by groups specialising in community or educational theatre. It is essential to have a play that works dramatically, so it is hard to be true to exact words here, and of course it is almost impossible to have one character stick to the words of one contributor. However, given that drama is not expected to apply the same standards as historical writing, even when it is obviously trying to evoke the past, this is not a criticism and some very powerful evocations of the past have been the result.

Creating a more integrated piece of oral history that does meet the standards professional historians expect, obviously demands greater efforts from the editor than the simple selection dealt with so far. For instance, even though a biography may well consist entirely of the contributor's own words, it is inconceivable that it will have been spoken into the recorder in a form that requires no alteration. Nate Shaw was a brilliant natural storyteller, but Theodore Rosengarten could not use even his reminiscences without working on them. Creating a clear chronological order is usually the first task, especially where more than one session is involved. Thereafter, overlapping sections must be integrated and duplications removed, or else the readability of the complete text will be severely reduced. To save space, it may be necessary to omit sentences and phrases that seem irrelevant to the main purpose, even though respect for the spontaneity of the original recollection says it should all stand. It is vital to show the reader that what is on the page is not the full version wherever this is the case, and there have been plenty of examples of this throughout this book. Sections removed within a sentence are normally indicated by means of three full stops, and four show that the editing has run over into another sentence. Words inserted to help intelligibility should be surrounded by square brackets.

The only words spoken by a contributor that I have ever removed without indication are 'you know', and then only where there are so many that they are disruptive. To mark them as missing would be just as disruptive, and misleading in suggesting real editing. This is a purely pragmatic decision, and we all have to do this sort of thing occasionally, though it is always best to err on the side of caution. The aim should be to remain true to the spirit of the original. I also remove, with the appropriate indications, false starts that are clearly given up and verbally crossed out, but this is because any author has a right to amend their original efforts. While I have altered most sections of this book since I first began writing it – some of them repeatedly – the finished product appears before the reader as if I had never paused between start and finish. The tapes clearly show the contributors doing much the same thing, reconsidering and restarting certain trains of thought, and it seems right to me to implement these decisions. Repetitions and digressions cannot be treated this way, however, for they remain part of the narrative, and it has been stressed already that there should be no 'improvements'. This is a particular difficulty in those projects where the contributors do all the editing themselves, or

Plate 10.2   Oral history as drama: 'drawn from the memories of women and men in their seventies and eighties, *Echoes from the Valley* is the story of a Yorkshire valley and its people – from the beginning of the century to the Second World War. Using the music of the time, *Echoes* covers every aspect of life, from mill work to picnics, from childbirth to courtship'. Written by Garry Lyons and performed by the Major Road Theatre Company, this highly successful play has been performed in the USA as well as on its home territory, and was nominated for a Sony Radio Award.

are extensively involved by the collector, usually through asking for their comments on a transcript. The Elswick group produced their booklet on Richardson's leather works in this way and for biography especially it is a rewarding, if time-consuming, way of working towards a genuinely joint effort. If we accept that spoken English does not have the same rhythms and flow as written English, but is still impressive in its own right, then where the contributor is a good talker and unused to handling the written word, I am concerned that there is a danger of more being lost than gained unless the editing is confined to selecting from the transcript rather than adapting it.

Editing assumes a much clearer and more substantial role as we move into longer and more analytical work, and this is where a historian's skills come into their own. The type of work examined in Chapter 6 is the opposite end of a spectrum of editing strategies from those we have looked at so far. It is not a matter of stark alternatives, however. Any particular piece of work can be located at any point along this spectrum, as long as it is appropriate for your skills and the subject under consideration. For analytical work, themes must be selected out of the mass of reminiscences, and they must be made comprehensible to outsiders and set in a wider context. Working from transcript sections gathered together by subject helps here by making it obvious what had most significance for contributors, for it is essential to be guided by the recordings and not impose an artificial set of priorities. Isolated statements should never be selected just because they support the author's line, or used to prove anything above the level of the trivial.

The amount of space given to something by contributors is not an absolute guide, however, and may need to be queried as long as this is done within the context of the reminiscences. Thus, winter is as important as summer in real life, but it is less likely to be remembered with affection and so is more likely to be edited out of the memory. In the same way, sensationalism must always be rejected in favour of a search for real understanding. For instance, several ex-waggoners described to me times when they felt they had no choice but to resort to violence to keep order among the lads of whom they were in charge, and, by selective quotation, it would have been easy to create the impression of a Wild West atmosphere on farms. Discipline could certainly be robust and often involved physical chastisement of the youngest boys in a way that would be unacceptable today, but this needed serious investigation, not caricature. East Riding farmers had to keep a group of teenagers and young men working to high standards when they were usually out of their sight, and they had to do it without any of the usual sanctions open to an employer, such as the right to sack them or vary their wages, which yearly contracts ruled out. Work could also be disrupted by personal disagreements, given the conditions in which servants lived, yet all the evidence is that they worked long and hard and that fights were very rare on the average farm. Institutions like the hirings bled off tension, but what kept things going on a daily basis was really self-discipline, and a desire for a good reputation, which also governed the way farmers treated their lads. Farming dominated the East Riding so much that a good worker could expect to be recognised by the community at large, not just their workmates, and a mean farmer would become widely talked about. Physical violence was a last resort unknown on most farms and not the norm.

The average farm had only a few lads, most of them drawn from the surrounding area, and they knew what was expected of them. They all had a place in a rigid hierarchy that determined the order in which they did everything, from washing themselves to ploughing, and the fact that the lower you were in the farm pecking order, the younger you were likely to be made it easier for the waggoner to get his instructions obeyed. In addition, the special duties he undertook as head horselad, such as carrying bags of corn weighing anything up to 20 stones (127 kilograms), made the waggoner a heroic figure the lads were unlikely to defy. On big farms, however, farmers were less choosy in whom they hired and generally employed far more older lads, so the hierarchies were less age-based. This was the root of the real breakdowns in discipline that certainly occurred in such places. Studying them gives insights into the strengths and weaknesses of the normal system that can be derived in no other way, for when it was operating normally, it was so efficient that there often seemed to be no system at all. The temptation to eulogise this has to be avoided just as much as the urge to sensationalise, and we should not gloss over such things as the liberal use of 'boot-toe' as a remedy for slowness or cheekiness, or the much more serious mistreatment that a bully could hand out with impunity to a small boy unless someone took the victim's part.

Avoid the temptation always to use the most articulate extract, for this would exclude some contributors almost entirely. Some people are well organised, but others may tell a story in a more evocative way, and showing different personal styles is itself important. Humour has a valuable place, and it would be a rare recording session without any, but extracts should never poke fun at contributors. Someone satirising themselves or their friends is quite a different matter from an editor taking extracts out of context or selecting them solely to draw attention to accents, phraseology, or attitudes that seem quaint, thereby belittling those who have tried to help them. This treatment also builds barriers between us and the past by implying that people then were less capable of behaving rationally than we are. In fact, if used appropriately, quotations should be far more than illustrations bolted on to a text that would read intelligibly without them. They can develop analytical points as well as to bring them to life, and they may make up the largest part of some narratives. I have often found myself duplicating what is said clearly by contributors, restating it in an unconscious belief that my words have greater power and penetration.

If farm lads could describe life on the farms better and more graphically than I ever could, I can explain better how the farm servant system was developed and how it fits with more general history. For instance, physical abuse in this and other settings for instance, is often described with the rider that it was both normal and accepted;

however, it is clear from the descriptions that its acceptance is a product partly of the passage of time and partly of later having exercised the right to do to others as had been done to them. Lads never have enjoyed being kicked hard, and there is no reason to sheer away from discussing this. There is no need to make the average person appear brutal for doing nothing that would attract censure from their contemporaries, but there is every reason to examine critically this legitimisation and perpetuation of personal violence. A close relationship with contributors may make this difficult, but as long as the treatment is fair, and as long as there was no trickery involved in obtaining testimony, people will probably take less offence than the historian would expect. In the last resort, the only course is a firm but not abrasive insistence on the right to take a point of view and not to be an uncritical recorder.

Large numbers of extracts inevitably pull an account towards pure description, and some books contain none at all. Mainstream historical writing takes it for granted that only a small part of the evidence on which an argument is based will be quoted directly and it is worth noting that George Ewart Evans' *Ask the Fellows Who Cut the Hay,* which was so influential in establishing oral history in this country, has no direct quotations, because he had no access to a tape recorder at that time. If it is clear that the arguments put forward are based on sound evidence, there is no intrinsic harm in this, but it seems a shame not to use the power that is often present in eye-witness accounts as long as they are reliable. This has to be objectively assessed, but since it is good practice to validate any piece of historical evidence as far as possible, this is not a constraint unique to the oral historian. We have already discussed the limitations of memory as a guide to a single, unusual event from decades ago and have seen that this needs more caution than recall of a routine that was widely accepted. I would thus confidently expect a high standard of accuracy from an ex-horselad about the detail of farming practice on East Riding farms.

I would not, however, expect former horselads to have more than a sketchy knowledge about the operation of the farms as businesses, unless they had later become farmers themselves, like Mr Johnson, or had been particularly involved in management as foremen . They were workmen and the farmer kept his financial affairs to himself. Indeed, when I came to prepare my index of subjects covered in my tapes, it was remarkable how little farmers were mentioned at all and how utterly inadequate any picture of them would have been if it rested solely on this material. Anyone who has worked both manually and as a manager knows how different the perceptions of the running of a business are on different sides of the fence. Large farmers would be the best source for business information, but they would have deficiencies in their knowledge of how to actually perform particular operations since they rarely got involved in work in the fields.

Generalisations from memory about, let us say, the percentages of people in an area who voted one way or another, or who were of one religion or another, are unlikely to be factually accurate. Take present-day impressions about the extent and significance of immigration as an example. They are usually the product of strong views and the disinformation that is constantly being produced, and I would doubt if one in a hundred people has any idea of the percentages of the different ethnic groups that make up our current population nationally or locally, or of the rates at which immigration has proceeded since the war. I certainly do not have such information at my fingertips, so I would find nothing surprising about anyone admitting the same: the problem is that many people would offer an impression they firmly believe to be true. Statistics are much more quickly, easily, and reliably derived from official sources and it would be perverse to seek them in any other way if we needed accuracy. On the other hand, precisely because there are so many erroneous views and because it is a subject on which such strong views are held, people act on the basis of their beliefs, not the facts. It would be quite impossible to understand the support among the German people for Hitler's persecution of the Jews purely by looking at whether there really was a Jewish conspiracy, or at Jewish population levels. The crucial thing is what German people came to believe, so we must seek to understand those beliefs and how they arose in the context of the times. Contrasting and combining perception and statistics is what moves us towards a real explanation, not rejecting either out of hand.

No source anywhere offers us unalloyed truth, and oral testimony is no worse or better than any other source in itself. It is more appropriate in certain circumstances, it is on a level in others, and sometimes it is worse. There are, however, practical considerations that are unique to this type of evidence, or which occur elsewhere only occasionally and on a small scale. Most obvious is the question of copyright in the material and of the rights of the contributor to payment for use. My position on payment is that, when contributors give material freely to collectors who clearly state their intention to publish, together they put that material into the public domain. The collector acquires tacit rights to use the material first, within a reasonable time, but there should be no question of it becoming their property or of their charging for access or use, beyond asking for fees for legitimate services such as photocopying or staff time spent on lengthy searches. No law prevents charging, or the sale or purchase of oral material, but honesty, accuracy, and openness are simply incompatible with it. Put at its crudest, if collectors are seen to be selling material, they will also be expected to pay for collecting it.

Copyright does exist in oral material, but it is hard to state unequivocally who holds it and how it should be handled. It has caused a great deal of heart-searching, but the legal position remains unclear even though the *Copyright, Designs and Patents Act* of 1988 has clarified many other muddles in bringing British practice into line with Europe. The crucial element is the status of reminiscences as intellectual property, and this is nowhere dealt with directly. An analogy with journalism suggests that anything collected which was not previously written down cannot be the subject of a claim, but on the other hand, a long verbal memoir could be considered to be a conscious literary creation in itself, and therefore the unequivocal intellectual property of the contributor. Alan Ward's *Manual of Sound Archive Administration* (1990) is the definitive guide to good practice for the foreseeable future, and he is clear that it must be assumed that each contribution is a literary creation. This is sensible, since to assume the reverse runs the risk of serious consequences if it proves not to be correct. The contributor therefore does have legal claims over the contribution, which must be respected. An analogy with photographs and films, which handbooks on copyright law regard as valid, suggests that any rights the collector has depend on their own status within the project. The person or body who organises a recording session has unequivocal rights over it, so a collector working for a large project is merely an agent and has none. There are many handbooks to the way the law works in practice, such as *Law and the Media: An Everyday Guide for Professionals* (1989), by Tom Crone.

Very little dispute has ever actually arisen and raising the question of copyright is really a matter of doing a job properly. All collectors worry about the possibility of being challenged by a contributor over the use made of their memories, but for the ordinary collector, copyright is a sword of Damocles that shows no sign of falling as yet. No contributor ever asked me about copyright, and under the old law I did not raise it with them because I felt that this in itself suggested that the copyright did have a value worth protecting. I now regret this, and it makes passing tapes over to an archive a more uncertain business than it would be with a signed release giving clear authorisation. The need for legalities is clearly much greater when working with the top layers of society, for they are used to thinking in these terms, and there is the possibility that some books might make real profits, which ordinary history books never do. Most collectors now use printed forms that both collectors and contributors sign before recording begins, or as part of the process of winding up a session, and a copy of which is left with the contributor. These clearly assign copyright to the collector or the institution they represent, and a common format is the one used by the Kirklees Sound Archive, which reads:

> The purpose of this deposit agreement is to ensure that your contribution is added to the collections of Kirklees Sound Archive in accordance with your wishes. Contributions of photographs are listed on the reverse of this form.
> 1. Can Kirklees Sound Archive use your contribution:
>   (a)   for public reference purposes (Libraries/Museums)
>   (b)   for educational use (schools etc)
>   (c)   for broadcasting (radio/TV)
>   (d)   as a source that may be published
>   (e)   in public performance
> 2. Can we mention your name?
> 3. Are you prepared to vest your copyright in the information in the recordings to Kirklees Sound Archive?
> 4. If you wish to apply a time restriction before your contribution is released please state for how long.

Institutions have more reason than individuals to adopt a formal approach to the assignment of copyright because of the quantity of tapes and the numbers of collectors they deal with. In addition to this, their function of allowing third parties access to tapes might invalidate any implicit consent that existed as part of the personal relationship between collector and contributor. Rights may be claimed by relatives after the contributor dies, moreover, for copyright is property and can be inherited. It runs for fifty years after the death of an author. My museum experience suggests that relatives may be more sensitive on behalf of a contributor's reputation and image than the contributor was, through seeing or imagining implications for the family as a whole. Some will obviously see the recording as a tribute to someone they cared for, but others will see it as a nuisance they would rather do without. Never forget that a good recording is bound to contain personal information and this can be seen as a threat. Anonymity, whether total or achieved by the use of false names, as Theodore Rosengarten did, may protect against such fears, especially for tapes in a local archive which could embarrass or annoy many people. In local publications it is common not to attribute quotations for this reason, and it is probably sensible to run such a project on the assumption that all names will be withheld in all circumstances. Certainly, where confidentiality has been directly requested by the contributor, this must be respected unless you openly refused at the time. Again, it is important not to get this out of perspective, however. No-one has ever asked me to keep their name completely secret, though I have been asked to turn the tape recorder off during particular stories, or to keep sections of a recording confidential. There are many sides to this question, and the answers in different circumstances will themselves vary.

One man told me he gave drugs to his horses to make them eat better and look better. All horselads felt that their personal reputations depended on the condition of their teams, and they would go to great lengths to get special foods for them, including pilfering treats like cattle cake, wheat, and barley from the farm outhouses. Farmers usually turned a blind eye to this. Drugging, however, was mostly abhorred, both because a horse suffered badly if it was deprived of the drugs, and because any lad who inherited such a horse at Martinmas was in for a very difficult time as it went downhill due to withdrawal symptoms. This man did not move around a lot, and he had seen a horse killed by feeding it wheat, so he felt that drugging was actually less dangerous than such tactics. He knew that his workmates might take it badly if they found out, and he had to bury his drugs in the garden whenever he went home at Martinmas, for his father searched his sons' belongings looking for anything like this. Half a century on, he was willing to talk about what he had done, but he had no wish even then to be publicly identified. By respecting his wishes, I uncovered something that was widespread but fairly well hidden, unlike the other tricks all lads got up to in search of better teams and of which they were not in the least ashamed.

Some historians avoid using names not to protect contributors, but either from a desire to depersonalise the oral material, or because they see the reiteration of names as disruptive. Identifying contributors directly or by pseudonym is something I believe in, however. I see my extracts as personal testimony, and the reader can evaluate it and what it signifies better by getting a sense of who is talking and what sort of person they are. The use of code numbers or letters in the text frequently seems to me to go with a desire to treat the oral material in a pseudo-scientific fashion that it will not bear since samples are too small and not random. It also seems to voluntarily surrender the unique quality of oral history, its humanity. I feel, too, that the testimony was the contributors' and they deserve the credit that accrues from it, just as few authors wish to publish anonymously. In any case, any article or book meant to be read by scholars must make clear the source of individual quotations. An indication of the tape from which each extract comes must be clear and detailed enough to allow it to be followed up swiftly. The reference should give either the relevant page of a transcript if such exists and is accessible, or, if not, the tape collection, the tape's number or code, and the side from which the extract comes.

Honest working practices are essential in any branch of history but bad practice is particularly likely to cause trouble in oral history because we are dealing directly with people. Using detailed autobiographical knowledge against the wishes of contributors; attaching their names to statements that are bound to embarrass them if made public; misleading them about your intentions; editing material to alter its meaning – all these are bound to cause justified accusations of bad faith. This does not mean that everyone must be handled with kid gloves, however. Someone in Alexander Harrison's position would have to stand by agreements made with the O.A.S. terrorists who told him about their part in the French struggle to hold on to Algeria, but they must have been willing to face the general disapproval that publication would bring to them or they would not have agreed to talk to him with a recorder running. This is a case of facing up to a difficult subject rather than tricking contributors. There is really no need to risk doing so, because the rewards of working with contributors rather than against them are so high. There is something unique about the actual words of participants in events, even if they are set down on paper rather than played back on a tape recorder, and they can be used in so many ways that there is something everyone can do.

NOTES AND REFERENCES

1. P. Roberts, S. Weston and C. Weston (eds), 1987, *Windybank: It's What You Make It!*, Artivan and Windybank Community Association, introduction.

CHAPTER ELEVEN
The Hardware

Having taken the tape recorder for granted so far, the moment has finally come when we need to look at it for itself. Using one can still be a real psychological barrier for new collectors, but there is absolutely no reason to worry about it in this day and age. Today they are to be found in virtually every house, whereas they seemed like technological miracles when George Ewart Evans first used one in 1956. The BBC then loaned him 'a Midget recording unit, and an engineer to instruct me in its use. This portable tape-recorder caused a revolution in outside broadcasting. Previously, to record someone outside the studio was an expensive exercise requiring a special van and two or three personnel.'[1] A modern tape recorder in contrast is one of the simplest electronic machines available and most work extremely well. The main controls on all machines are standardised and anyone who can press a button can work one, so there is absolutely no need to be a technician to run a successful session. It is simply a matter of finding out by experiment how your particular recorder does its job best and of putting the contributor at their ease while recording goes on. The two things are linked, for setting the right atmosphere depends on your confidence that you know what you are doing, linked to causing the minimum disruption, but the familiarity of recorders means that the presence of the machine should not be too much of a distraction.

If the aim is the best possible result, then it is necessary to look on the room where the session will take place as a temporary recording studio. If it is unsuitable in any way, furniture may have to be rearranged and it may be necessary to move to another room to get the right conditions. In my opinion, this can easily unsettle and perhaps annoy your contributor while attracting attention to the recorder as the crucial element in the session, which may do more harm than good. I

prefer to explain the recorder as my notebook: a device that allows me both to give my full attention to what is being said and to forget nothing as the conversation moves on. Different oral historians take different positions on this, a few insisting that a poor recording is useless, while most are much more tolerant. Certainly, as a beginner, it is necessary to be realistic about what you can achieve, or you may feel that you are wasting your time and that of the contributors. Top quality – suitable for broadcasting, let us say – is something that professionals achieve through the use of expensive equipment and long practice, and there is no shame in failing to reach such a standard. Your goal should be to make the best tape you can. No-one should be happy with persistently poor results, but if you identify faults and try to correct them as you go along, you will see a steady improvement.

There are some things you should always watch out for, such as a room right by a busy road, where traffic noise spoils a recording as it seems to be amplified and to overwhelm voices. Kitchens or other rooms with hard surfaces tend to distort recordings, and it is worth testing this out in your own home. Radios or televisions obviously have to be turned off, and noisy parrots or any other cause for real worry have to be dealt with as politely as possible. In some circumstances, it may even be impossible to use the recorder. One ex-farm servant, Mr Appleyard, was a lorry driver when he contacted me and he suggested that I should meet him at work. We therefore talked in the cab of a heavy tipper waggon while he made several round trips, moving earth from a building site. The noise interfered with normal conversation so there was no question of recording what was said. I wrote out everything we had discussed to the best of my ability at the first opportunity, and, while such a record cannot compare to a proper tape, it contained some valuable information and a relationship had

---

Plate 11.1   A one to one session in 1987 where Mr Lajszczuk talks about his past life in the Ukraine, and what living in Bradford for the past forty years has been like. The room is a fascinating blend of Englishness and Ukrainian, symbolising the gulf that such people have to bridge within themselves. This was one of the Bradford Heritage Recording Unit's sessions, and they later followed them up by visiting the Ukraine to find out what life is like there now.

Note that no attempt has been made to turn the house into a recording studio. Both men are sat in easy chairs and the tape recorder is out of the way, though not hidden. The clip-on microphones, one for each of them, make for clear recording at all times. The recorder in use here is the Uher, the old standby which I used for all my East Riding work, and they still produce an excellent quality. The reason why most people buying new equipment today would not buy them is their size and the difficulties open reel tape can cause.

been established, so that the next time I met Mr Appleyard, I did so at his house.

Normally the most crucial factor in getting a good recording is the placing of the microphone, which should never be too close to the recorder as it may either pick up the motor noise or produce a high-pitched squeal of feedback, or both. Using a built-in microphone is therefore best avoided as there is almost inevitably a low hum of motor noise in the background at the very least. On cheaper machines this may make it quite hard to hear voices clearly. The best distance to position a microphone from the mouth of a speaker is usually put at just over two feet, but it is better to try and get closer. A large microphone can be held in the hand, or put in a rest, or stand, on a piece of furniture, but the easiest type to handle is the clip-on sort used extensively in television interviews. It is tiny, out of sight, and is always the right distance from the mouth. Such microphones can also be hand held if this is necessary for any reason, or attached to a wall or furniture with no difficulty as they are so light.

Using a second microphone for yourself means that your part of the session is always as clear as the contributor's. On a stereo machine this just means plugging one into each of the two channels, but with mono they must be wired to a common jack plug. In recording a group, a large microphone placed centrally will probably be needed. I was once shown round his workshop by a wheelwright and again a large microphone, held in the hand, is the best for such a situation. Foam plastic caps that cut out noise made by the air rushing past the microphone are available very cheaply. If you have a Dolby B switch on your recorder, use it, as it reduces hiss on the tape itself. Experiment to make sure what works best, ideally by persuading someone to help you by playing the part of a contributor and running short sessions in different types of rooms, trying various positions for the microphone or machine. All recorders have a recording level indicator that shows when you have the volume set too high, usually because a needle swings into a red zone most of the time that anyone is speaking. Keep an eye on this at first, but once things are going well, the machine can be ignored except for turning over or changing the tape.

Mains power should always be used for transcribing because this uses batteries up very quickly, but it can cause problems if used for recording. Batteries are more convenient for this, and now that it is possible to buy rechargeable versions from ordinary shops they are less expensive than they used to be. More expensive machines have their own rechargeable packs. Using mains power in other people's homes means carrying an extension lead in case the sockets are few and far between, and having an adaptor or a special multi-purpose plug to cope with the old round-pin sockets that are still to be found in old houses. These plugs can be altered to fit any socket, but they are not the easiest things to manipulate, and messing with one of them is not the ideal start to a session. It is polite to offer to pay something for any power used, even though the amount will be very small. I much prefer to be in a position to sit down, put the machine down, switch on, and start recording. Use a new or freshly-recharged set of batteries at the start of a session, and always have a spare set handy for unforeseen circumstances. Fit them before you set off and check that they do work. If there is a meter showing the level of the charge, check it when you change tapes.

It is also sensible to put the tape in beforehand and to record a few words to check everything is all right. It is all too easy to arrive without something vital if you make no routine checks – I have done it myself. There is no better way to make yourself feel thoroughly stupid than to have to admit that you won't be recording the session after all because you don't have the microphone/ batteries/ tape, or because the machine won't work. Always carry at least two spare tapes, both to be sure you can cope however long the session lasts, and in case there are any mishaps. Keep an eye on the time, or on the tape if you can see it during recording, so that you know when to turn the tape over or change it for a new one. Some recorders have a warning that sounds as the tape runs out, or else you can hear that it has happened from the change in the operating noise, but otherwise it is easy to forget, and then you may lose irreplaceable material unless you can go over it again. If the loss is substantial this will be harder than where a contributor is in full flow and carries straight on through a tape change. Since it should only take a few seconds to get the recorder going again, I would normally accept the loss of a few words, unless they were very important, to avoid putting the contributor off their stride.

Advice about particular recorders is generally pointless since some of it would inevitably be obsolete by the time this book has been in print for a year or two. It is worth making some general points about what to look for, however, and there are one or two machines so widely used that they are worth naming. When I started recording, it was taken for granted that cassette tape was unacceptable, and reel tape was the norm. The Nagra, and below that, the Uher remain the machines for really top quality recording. This is advisable for the intricacies of dialect where every nuance of sound must be recorded accurately, for instance, and they are used by the BBC for this reason.

Reel tape is the most solid tape available, which also means that it may last longer in an archive than the thinner cassette tapes. Such reel-to-reel recorders are, however, very expensive, because the market for them is so small, and reel tape is difficult to handle, particularly in loading. If it is not stored and transported carefully, it easily falls off its spool into a tangled mess. Moreover, whereas cassettes can be played and copied on all domestic equipment, reel tape requires a heavy investment in extra equipment for such things. Most collectors who continue to use reel tape copy their sessions on to cassettes immediately to make working copies, and hold the reels in reserve as master tapes, but even this involves linking a reel machine to a cassette machine, and precludes the high-speed copying of which many domestic cassette machines are now capable.

The consensus now is that for all normal purposes there is nothing wrong with cassette recorders or good quality cassette tapes, which only means using the branded tapes available in chain stores. They meet any reasonable criterion as a secure storage medium. They are the obvious choice for any new project and there is no point in thinking of anything else unless there are compelling reasons to do so. The leading professional standard machines are currently made by Marantz, and they cost two thirds or a half of the price of the Uher. Sony make similar good quality machines, but they are not as widely used. In fact, even though the tiny personal cassette recorders that are everywhere today are usually of low quality, the Sony Pro Walkman invariably gets enthusiastic reviews even in the hi-fi press, and it both records and plays back at a very high standard. It is now widely used by television and radio journalists, and since their jobs depend on getting good recordings, this is a powerful recommendation. It can be run off the mains and plugged into large speakers when required and yet it fits in a pocket, so this is something to look at seriously, especially as it is perhaps half the price of the Marantz.

The next decade seems set for a further explosion of quality improvements in recording technology. The Digital Audio Tape format already offers higher quality recording and a more secure storage in the long term than conventional tape, but it is expensive and has not really taken off commercially, so there are very few machines available. Like reel tape, it is not compatible with standard equipment and, given these drawbacks, it is doubtful if the extra recording quality is really relevant where speech alone is concerned. Digital Compact Cassettes are currently being launched and have the quality associated with digital recording, but again the cassettes cannot be played back on standard machines. They are bound to be expensive at first and no-one can say that they will not also prove to be a white elephant, so an ordinary recording project should not get involved. More likely to revolutionise things in the longer term is the steady move towards recordable compact discs. These are, of course, much better as a permanent record than any tape can be. They will be relatively expensive at first, of course, but at the very least many existing tapes can be copied onto them for security, and there seems little doubt that they will appear soon in an affordable form. This seems to further undermine the case for continuing to use reel tapes, or any other awkward-but-secure format, for there will then be no need to take account of the strength of the original tape, only its recording quality.

Camcorders need consideration as well since they are getting cheaper, smaller, and more automated all the time. They already compare in price with medium-range tape recorders and sooner or later they are bound to have a big impact, for much communication is visual, through facial expression, body language, and gesture, and a video tape is therefore inherently far better than an audio tape. For capturing folk dances, folk song, or any event, they are clearly essential. The actual tapes are as robust as audio tapes, and they record and reproduce sound well. The drawback for conventional sessions is that the contributor is likely to be much more self-conscious than with a tape recorder, and that the collector has to be more careful in setting up the session to ensure that a passable recording is made, with the contributor on camera at all times. Few contributors move around, however, and practice beforehand allows a quick estimation of whether there is a piece of furniture that will serve as a suitable base or if more elaborate arrangements are necessary. This recreates some of the difficulties of using audio recorders several decades ago, so currently the audio format is probably best for ordinary purposes, as long as it is not blindly taken for granted. The Oral History Society held its first video workshop as long ago as 1982 and there has been a great deal of activity since, so this is a thing of the present rather than the future.

Good quality audio recorders can be purchased through the specialist hi-fi shops that exist in all cities and many towns, though it will probably be necessary to order from a catalogue as portable recorders are not in great demand. Chain stores are unlikely to be able to supply them at all, even by order, and in any case, you cannot expect the same level of knowledgeable advice from their young sales staff who sell the whole range of consumer electrical goods. Specialist shops should also offer better backup facilities, but it is worth looking round for local firms who specialise in repairing recorders as they can save a great deal of money for a project as its machines get older and need maintenance. It is wise to do some research yourself into what you want before going, of course. Recorders are used by talking newspapers for the blind, by local radio, by schools, and by many other organisations, and a polite request for help will usually get a good response. They are likely to be the best source of up-to-the-minute advice, though it is important to stress what you want the recorder for and what you can afford, so that you are not directed to something that is needlessly complex or expensive. In the final analysis, the choice is yours, so insist on testing the machine you intend to buy before taking it home if you are in any doubt about its suitability. Recorders are the most crucial items of equipment you will buy and are worth taking trouble over.

Reliability and reasonable quality can now definitely be obtained without spending a fortune, for, as in all things electronic, progress over the past three decades has been continuous and rapid. Avoid paying for a trademark or for facilities you will never need, like stereo, if you are purchasing a recording machine and there is a cheaper mono equivalent. If money is really tight, the cheap end of the market is one where it is vital to tread warily, because now that music centres with built-in cassette decks have become standard, High Street shops only stock the ordinary personal stereo type and those used in loading programs onto home computers. They are generally very cheap, but you only get what you pay for, so only necessity should make you look at such machines for recording purposes. There is nothing good about using a poor machine for the sake of it – in a kind of reverse snobbery, for example – but equally no one should refrain from recording because they cannot afford a good one. If a very cheap machine really is all you can afford, it will make audible and transcribable tapes, and that is better than making none at all. 'Ten Inches into Six Feet – Low Budget Recording for an Oral History Project', which appeared in *Oral History* in Spring 1988, gives advice for groups with low budgets, but even as the article was printed, obsolescence was already claiming some of the machines named. A good microphone will bring out the best in even the cheapest machine, so ask for advice on this and don't go for the cheapest to save a few pounds. Electronics shops like Tandy will usually have the best ranges to choose from, and they are also the best places for accessories of all types.

Photography provides an instructive example of what can be achieved by sheer dedication rather than expensive equipment in the case of Jack Hulme, three of whose photographs have already appeared in this book. He was born in 1906 in Fryston in West

Plate 11.2   Because Jack Hulme was a member of the Fryston community and because he was literally always taking pictures, people virtually ceased to notice him and he was able to produce pictures like this that no professional could have achieved, even had they been interested. To anyone researching how the poor actually lived in the 1930s, when this was taken, this kind of intimate study is invaluable. Had he felt that photographs could only be taken with expensive equipment, Jack Hulme would never have started.

Yorkshire and bought a cheap camera when he was fourteen, a second-hand Box Brownie costing half-a-crown. He took photos continuously from then on, virtually up to his death in January 1990, creating a unique and fascinating archive of over 10,000 images of ordinary life in a mining village only about one square mile in size. Many are portraits and wedding photos, but besides them, he said, 'I took pictures nobody else would bother with because they thought the subjects weren't important enough.'[2] Fryston is not the sort of place to figure in the negatives of a professional photographer, and, as one of the community, he was able to capture all sorts of mundane views, like the one shown here, as well as the more obvious celebrations and public events that might have attracted outside attention. In recent years the value of his efforts has been recognised, with examples published in book form as *World Famous Round Here: the Photographs of Jack Hulme*, and displayed in several galleries. The title is one of his own comments, made near the end of his life: ' "It's all right," he explained to someone watching him being photographed outside his house, "I'm Jack Hulme. I'm famous, you know. World famous round here."[3]

Had anyone convinced Jack Hulme that photography with a simple camera was pointless, there simply would be nothing in the historical record where his photographs currently stand. He went on to better cameras, culminating in a Leica his first wife bought after scraping together the enormous sum of £91 in 1941, but otherwise he still operated on a shoestring, using an enlarger made from a vacuum cleaner, for instance. He developed his technique through endless practice and many of his photographs are excellent even apart from their subjects. A community group or an individual, interested in preserving a record of their community through oral history in an analogous way today, should take courage from this example and plough on regardless. After all, if the tapes are poor, they can still be transcribed, and if one or two are actually useless, what harm has been done? No-one else was prevented from making a better job and it was worth trying. If it is a success, it is possible to improve your equipment and methods as you go along, just as Jack Hulme did.

A community project that presents a coherent, sensible case has a good chance of getting a small grant to help them with essential equipment from the local council, local charities, or bodies such as the Lions or Rotarians. A tape recorder is the ideal item to ask for help with as most grant-givers like to pay for a single piece of equipment that has a clearly identifiable purpose. They will rarely, if ever, contribute to the running costs of a scheme and are also reluctant to fund such things as the bulk purchase of tapes or paper, though, if a good relationship develops out of the initial application, this may be worth a try later. A few phone calls and letters are a very good investment at this stage, and do not be frightened to ask for a realistic sum of money. While there will probably be no question of getting many hundreds of pounds for a new and untried project, donors often prefer to hand their money out in amounts big enough to matter, even if only to avoid the administrative fuss of making tiny handouts. Others may refuse to give everything asked, but offer a percentage, and as long as the original sum is not obviously inflated, the more you ask for, the more you can get.

Where several collectors will be at work, consider whether two ordinary machines will be more useful in the long run than one excellent one. Sharing one means that only one collector can record at any one time, and with travelling time and the need to pick it up early or keep it overnight after a late session to take into account, there will be great difficulties in keeping everyone happy. If the only machine is also used regularly for transcribing, a bottleneck is inevitable. It may be possible to save money by buying different types for recording and transcribing, though it is best to avoid a proliferation of types. Personal stereo cassette players make a very cost-effective playback system, as long as they can be run off the mains. Ordinary domestic equipment can also be used to copy tapes and to transcribe from if money is short, but the practicalities of this need to be evaluated at the start. Access to a tape copier is certainly essential to avoid use of the original tape with all its risks of deterioration, loss, and damage. Even relatively cheap music centres now have these, often including a high-speed copying ability which is a great time-saver.

In ensuring the survival of tapes, there is no better course of action than instantly making a working copy from the original, which can then be put away and only brought out if another copy is needed. Test out any copying system for loss of quality, however, and see that everything works correctly before committing yourself to it. Also ensure that copying is done promptly and carefully so that tapes are not left unlabelled, do not end up in the wrong cases, or worst of all, that originals are not taped over. Protect tapes as soon as possible after recording by breaking off with a knife the two small plastic tabs which are to be found on the back edge of all cassettes, leaving square holes like those on pre-recorded tapes. It is impossible to record onto a cassette with these holes, which should prevent any tape being wiped by accident. If there is a need to remove this protection, the holes have only to be covered with sticky tape. Originals should be kept in a locked storage unit with access clearly restricted to the minimum number that is acceptable, and they should never be cut up for editing under any circumstances. Security is required not because of any risk of theft, and this should be made clear to all involved, but because these tapes are literally irreplaceable in the sense that they are the originals. Allowing free access more or less guarantees that people will borrow them 'just for an hour' now and then when they cannot get hold of a copy for one reason or another, and this in turn will lead to loss or damage.

Tapes are likely to form the biggest single running cost of a small voluntary project so there is always a temptation to look for savings here. Re-using them after transcribing their contents may seem like an effective economy, but even if complete transcripts are made, once the original tape is wiped, the transcripts cannot be authenticated and the sessions are no more reliable as a historical source than those the Reverend Morris conducted with William Blades seventy years ago. Complete transcribing is unlikely in any case, and there is no way of knowing what people in the future will be interested in. Even selective wiping risks destroying evidence that might have been valuable. Thus, television and radio programme makers began by keeping only a small selection of their output, and even in 1975 *Oral History* reported that,

> In November and December, BBC 2 broadcast ... five programmes on 'The Black Man in Britain 1550-1950'. Four of these were largely based on oral material collected by Michael Phillips and Tony Laryea; two on the black communities of Cardiff, Liverpool and Manchester before the First World War, and one on the African and West Indian nationalist groups in Britain during the 1930's and 1940's. Given the serious neglect of the social history of black people in Britain, and the very considerable research which went into the making of these programmes, it is deeply disturbing to learn that all the unused film collected for these programmes has already been destroyed, and the future of even the programmes themselves is uncertain.[4]

Videotape was expensive in the early days of television and had to be re-used, but a lot of destruction occurred just because no-one recognised the value of what had been recorded, for it was assumed no-one would ever want to see most programmes again once they had gone out. Now the archive material that does survive proves the reverse and there are few who do not regret the old policies, for it is a valuable source of programmes, and even of revenue since classic items can be sold on tape. Radio One has discovered that live sessions recorded by rock singers and groups in their early days now form an invaluable and unique archive, and their current histories of different types of popular music are often classics of contemporary history recording. Even a community project recording its own members for some clear and immediate aim, such as the production of a leaflet, should learn from these mistakes and look on the tapes they produce as archive material.

Cheap tapes are not a way of avoiding this dilemma, for they are usually poor ones. All tapes consist of a backing coated with a substance sensitive to magnetism, so that a pattern can be electrically created on it. It is this pattern that holds the sound and any imperfections or any decay in it, or any damage to the tape, will impair the recording, or even destroy it. Obscure brands can have insubstantial backings and magnetic coatings that come off easily, and then they record badly, deteriorate rapidly, or fill the recorder with dust, or all three. There are suppliers who sell bulk tape of reliable quality, or a local supplier may allow you to buy in bulk at a discount, or even at cost price if they are approached in the right way, but do not be tempted by unknown types, however good an offer seems. Most districts have a talking newspaper for the blind, whose address the reference library should have, and they may be able to give details of how to get good tapes locally at the best prices, or try one of the Oral History Society contact network.

There are three types of tape generally available: ferric oxide (known as ferric), chromium dioxide (known as chrome), and metal, and generally the cost rises in this order. Metal tapes are generally very dear indeed. All are usable, but the advantages of the dearer types really rest in allowing a wider range for high-fidelity reproduction of music. For speech this is really irrelevant, and cheaper recorders may only be able to use ferric tapes. On older machines it is necessary to set a switch to the appropriate setting for each type, but modern ones do this automatically from a code on the cassette. Tapes perform slightly differently on different machines, so if your results are disappointing, you could try switching types. *Which* magazine regularly tests tapes, and it may be worth consulting their result tables, but it is clear from them that all reputable tapes perform adequately at the very least. Playing times are normally thirty, sixty, ninety, or one hundred and twenty minutes depending on the code number of the tape: a C60 plays for 30 minutes per side. C120s appear cheapest per minute, but in order to fit the extra tape into the cassette, it has to be thinner, making it weaker and less stable in the long term. For ordinary use this may not be noticeable, but in the long run it could make a difference. C30s give the strongest tape but the frequency of tape changes and the number of tapes that would be needed to cover the average session is too high to be practical. With longer tapes, sessions will rarely fill them exactly and there may be a temptation to start the next one immediately after the last. There is a great risk of confusion in this, even with the same contributor. It is easier all round to index, transcribe and edit tapes which each contain only one session.

Do not overlook the straightforward need for good housekeeping in ensuring the survival of tapes and their continued usefulness. Their contents need to be readily identifiable for those who, years from today, do not have your personal knowledge, so write down immediately on each tape whose voice is on it and when it was made, then duplicate the information on the tape box. The most lasting way to ensure that a tape can always be identified is to record at the start or end of each tape a short statement of who you are, who the contributor is, and the date. If it is to be at the start, where it is most useful, it is best to leave space and record the statement after the session as it makes an off-putting start to a session to do it on the spot. This can always then be matched up with the file of your contributors' details that you should have made. Tapes do not need special conditions to keep them at their best, but they should be kept dry and somewhere near a cool room temperature, in an environment that is not dusty and not liable to sudden temperature changes. If they get damp they can become mildewed, which may damage the recording head if they are played. This reinforces the case for keeping them in cupboards if they are not in frequent use.

Since information is coded onto the tapes magnetically, they must be kept away from magnets, which may wipe them completely. This includes the magnets in loudspeakers and many other electrical appliances. In fact, since the act of recording creates a weak magnetic field on the tape itself, when it is tightly pressed together it is possible for the magnetism of one section of the tape to interfere with what is on the next section, a phenomenon known as *print-through,* where the contents of one side seem to merge with the other and spoil both. Until recently this was attributed mostly to the cumulative effect of leaving tapes undisturbed for long periods, and it is true that it is a good idea to run through stored tapes at least once every two years or so, since this leaves the tape wound in a slightly different configuration. In fact, the real danger occurs during recording if the record level is set too high.

There is really no more to it than that, and even if the technical side sounds a little daunting when it is all laid out together, in practice you will find things are never as bad as you had feared, as long as you prepare yourself in advance and take a few simple precautions. Buying the right equipment is a matter of doing your homework first, assessing what you can spend, and increasing it from grants if possible. Make realistic decisions about the right mix of machines for your purposes. Thereafter, the secret of success is not eliminating all mistakes and accidents, for this is impossible, but learning how to head them off and having routines for coping if they cannot be prevented. Keep equipment in a safe place, insure it, and have a proper booking system so that collectors always know where they stand on its availability. Then, everything always seems to run well and everyone thinks you are infallible despite your own knowledge of all the things that really have gone wrong. Getting ever better recording quality is about learning from experience, and that means everyone has to make a start before they can become an expert.

NOTES AND REFERENCES

1. G.E. Evans, 1987, *Spoken History,* Faber, p. 4.
2. R. Van Riel, O. Fowler, H. Malkin (eds), 1990, *World Famous Round Here: the Photographs of Jack Hulme,* Yorkshire Art Circus, back cover.
3. *Ibid.,* introduction.
4. *Oral History,* Vol 3, no 1, 1975, p. 8.

CHAPTER TWELVE

Oral History: A Survey

It seems appropriate to close with a few comments on the state of oral history at the moment. I have stressed throughout that I see it as part of the wider field of history and that the value of differentiating it stems entirely from the need to challenge the limits of conventional definitions of history. It links naturally to other disciplines such as anthropology, sociology and psychology, weakening the barriers between history and a wider view of human experience rather than building new ones within history. How successful is this challenge, and do its results promise to be lasting? The crucial test will really be over when people cease to see oral history as special, except in the way that the use of statistics in history, say, is special, for any particular source gives a flavour to what is being examined, and dictates that certain perspectives will influence the conclusions reached. When historians no longer feel the need to include sections in the introductions to their books justifying their use of oral sources, its future will be assured. As long as any history is written, some of it will then be purely oral history and some will be based partly on oral evidence. Fashions will no doubt cause its significance to rise and fall over time, but it will be accepted alongside documentary evidence as part of the available material from which it is natural to work.

In these terms oral history shows signs of having created a genuine bridgehead. We are no longer talking about the activities of a few individuals, often unaware of others working in the same way as themselves, as George Ewart Evans was for years. In *Spoken History* he described his feelings in the early 1970s as activity exploded and the actual title 'oral history' was imported from the USA: 'I felt a bit like the Frenchman in Molière who had been speaking prose all his life without knowing it'.[1] The Oral History Society has been successful in bringing people together, both historians and those for whom oral history can be useful though they themselves are not historians. It is more active in this way than most historically-based groups, and its journal acts a noticeboard for what is happening across the country in a way that few other journals attempt. It shows there are local oral history groups working in most parts of the country, and its network of advisors offers newcomers an obvious contact point with those already at work. Museums as a whole accept oral recording as a fundamental part of their remit, valid for its own sake and for the life it can bring to displays. Schools increasingly make use of it and the national curriculum gives it a place. Reminiscence therapy, to give it its most common name, has taken off on a truly staggering scale among those who work with the elderly and has become central to some aspects of this type of work. Existing archives are increasingly accepting tapes, and specialist archives, most notably the National Sound Archive, have been set up. Academic historians are using oral history and history students in higher education are being brought into contact with it as part of their training.

The danger now is therefore not oblivion, but there is still a real risk of being allocated a permanent second-class status, preserving a distinction between real history and oral history. In just this way the study of material culture has been recognised so far that most districts of this country have at least one local museum, and the total number of staff employed in museums is now impressive, though inadequate for the tasks they undertake. Museum studies have a toe-hold in the universities. Most museums hold large reserve collections for the use of present and future scholars, as well as their displayed collections. However in my time in museums the number of such enquiries I received was very small, although I have worked with collections covering wide fields in several institutions. The great national museums and a few regional ones stand apart from the rest and are taken seriously, though even here it is only in certain subject areas that museums are seen as having anything to offer apart from dusty relics that tell a serious historian nothing. The current primacy of the heritage industry threatens to undo much of the good undoubtedly done in the last few decades by turning the collections into theatrical props and the curators into managers. Material culture lacks direction and cannot realise its potential, which is symbolised to me by the widespread belief that a choice must be made between being popular and being serious. This is spurious: collections, including oral material as well as objects, can be put to many uses, and an institution can offer services and displays on many levels. My own experience is that large and increasing attendances can be gained without sacrificing truth or objectivity, but this does not seem to be fashionable.

Oral history runs the risk of replicating this experience, getting so far, but then hitting a glass ceiling. It also is subject to the attraction of the heritage industry, which wants the past always to have been pleasant, or if unpleasant, enjoyably so: people relishing hardship and bad working conditions because they were a necessary part of a strong community. To advocate breaking out of this is not to advocate sawing off its roots in local history and moving into elitist isolation, but to create a continuous band of collection, study, and use on all possible levels and in styles appropriate for the audience and subject. My talks on farming with horses, which I give to all sorts of groups, are popular and I appreciate the numbers of people who approach me at the end and say that they really enjoyed hearing about something that was part of their own past, or that of someone they know or to whom they are related. I adapt what I say to my audience without ever feeling that I only act as a historian when addressing other historians, and I do not have to pretend that the East Riding was some sort of rural idyll to hold non-professionals' interest.

Oral history's success in getting staff, funds, and buildings devoted to its exclusive use is still slender and easily lost. The great surge in oral history activity was based upon the funding that became available in the 1970s and 80s under national job creation and training programmes. Heritage activities were seen (often inaccurately) as a non-political way of utilising unemployed people. They were widely acceptable because the results were popular where schemes were run well, and because the scale of such projects was compatible with the limited money available to buy machinery and materials. Oral history, either on its own or as part of larger packages, was suddenly able to set to work large numbers of collectors. I myself did some recording on one of the first such schemes at Beamish Museum in 1974, and the extract from Mr Orr reproduced in Chapter 2 is one of the fruits of that. Later I set up and ran a highly successful local history scheme based at Red House Museum in Gomersal, West Yorkshire, while working for Kirklees Metropolitan Council, in the heart of the Luddite country. This scheme metamorphosed several times, and, having linked up with other initiatives, it still survives in a sense, for Red House is now the home of the Kirklees Sound Archive with a full-time sound archivist. She is the entire staff, however, and this experience can be replicated right across the country. The nearby Bradford Heritage Recording Unit once had thirty workers, most of them part-timers, but now has one person to keep things going, and they work only two days a week.

There is little or no sense of public need attached to spending on oral history at any level and what little money now goes into training the unemployed does so in ways that usually exclude this type of scheme. In these times of cuts, local authorities who were willing to spend some of their own money alongside windfall grants from the government usually withdraw their support as soon as the outside money vanishes. Kirklees is highly unusual in having retained even one full-time worker in a permanent post. In Leicester, despite a council pledge to continue an MSC oral history archive, 'the tapes have been locked away in the Central Reference Library, equipment and files have been boxed up,'[2] and yet, when this occurred in early 1990, Leicester was bursting with enthusiasm for oral history in terms of volunteer groups making tapes. A year later the North West Sound Archive itself was threatened with closure, and though Lancashire County Council stepped in at the last minute to guarantee the salaries of two and a half staff members, running costs were not covered. Any permanent posts are better than none, of course, and none existed thirty years ago, so this is not cause for unmitigated gloom. Those in these posts receive real, if low, salaries and some degree of job security, whereas the old system paid very low allowances and rarely employed anyone for more than a year at a time. The fact is, however, that the boom time is over and the task now is the consolidation of the hectic collecting of those years, and the protection of the real gains made.

If this permanent structure is to function to best effect it will be as an enabling and preserving network, doing the jobs that cannot be done by voluntary groups. They can provide the collectors and do all the publishing they wish to with the results, while the tapes and transcripts go to places where their long term future is as secure as it can be. More ambitious publications can also come at this level, especially as oral history is genuinely popular and both tapes and books can expect to be self-financing if properly handled. On the basis of this accumulating source material, more academic histories will be possible, and better ones as well. It will eventually be impossible to exclude oral history from serious consideration. This does not mean that all opposition to it will cease, or that all doubts will be overcome. There is not a single source in history that cannot be queried and that does not have its detractors. For all the successes in recent years of statistically-based history (cliometrics to its adherents) – and they have been considerable – there are plenty of historians who have a complete aversion to this method of working, and others, including myself, who have reservations about its wilder claims. If oral history can get to that level of acceptance, that is all that can be looked for.

It is not there yet. In 1991 Professor Michael Turner's review of a new edition of *The Whistler at the Plough,* by Alexander Somerville, included the comment that the book's fate 'depends on the value historians attach to anecdotal evidence (which gains some kind of scholarly legitimacy by being called oral history).'[3] Admittedly this concerns oral material unvalidated by tape recordings, but the attitude that is revealed to oral evidence in general is what matters. George Ewart Evans never managed to secure any outside funding at all for his work, despite many applications for grants, and he financed it personally from his income as a writer. Though he built links with certain academics and institutions, they signified personal linkages of common feeling rather than widespread acceptance, and it is still true that there is a great deal of mistrust of oral methodology among academics. *Oral History* can be quite hard to find, for history departments rarely regard it as one of the important historical journals and ordinary libraries regard it as too specialist.

I am also aware how many people do still barely know that oral history exists, and how many of those who vaguely recognise the title have little idea of what it really involves. Most elderly people still do believe that nothing interesting ever happened to them. Those who are fully aware of oral history are usually very keen on it and either involved or eager to become involved as soon as time permits. There is therefore a danger that oral historians will become an enclosed group, not through desire but simple practicalities of the way history operates and is funded in this country. The history on which I have concentrated in this book has been the social history of ordinary people, and it is their history, however much academic historians become involved, so it must remain open to them. It is still eminently possible to set up successful schemes and groups, and there is endless material for them to tape. In 1988, for instance, a grant from the Hervey Benham Charitable Trust allowed Bob Little to be employed for two years as a research officer in Colchester, based jointly in Essex University and the Colchester Institute. He interviewed elite figures in the local community, and after the training sessions he ran for volunteer workers, a group of thirty of them constituted themselves as the Colchester Recalled Oral History Group, with an active programme of interviewing a wider range of people.

I started this book by stressing the inherently democratic nature of oral history, but along the way I also warned that it is far from inevitable that this will determine the way oral material is actually used. I think this is a good note on which to close as well. Our society still passes traditions down from one generation to the next, but the mechanism for doing so is not what it was, and the pace of change in our lives threatens to overwhelm our capacity to keep adapting the messages of the past to the needs of the present. We will keep doing so, of that I have no doubt, and the stable communities that emerged from the social disruption of industrialisation in nineteenth-century Lancashire are a clear warning not to give way to gloom and despair about ordinary people's ability to rebuild new structures from the disjointed sections salvaged from the old. Even so, we do now live in a different world and much that was normal even one generation ago can be nearly meaningless today. If we want to preserve memories of the obsolete, we have to do something about it. It is natural to turn to the elderly and draw on their experience, and it is natural that the young should provide an audience for their stories. We are just having to adapt the way we do it. Let us also ensure that the widest range of approaches is used as we try to catch it all, and let us ensure that it is passed along to the next generation in an accessible and relevant form.

NOTES AND REFERENCES

1. G.E. Evans, 1987, *Spoken History,* Faber, p. 34.
2. *Oral History,* Vol 18, no 1, Spring 1990, p. 4.
3. M. Turner, Review of A. Somerville, *The Whistler at the Plough,* in *Agricultural History Review,* 39, 1991, p. 89.

Further Reading

WHAT IS ORAL HISTORY?

Robert Perks, *Oral History, An Annotated Bibliography* (The British Library: 1990), is the nearest thing that exists to a complete list of oral history books: 2,132 titles are listed, including many foreign works. Many are articles or pamphlets published locally, so it is not as overwhelming as it may seem, but it does show the scale of oral history publishing over the last two decades. It is a very useful guide, with short notes on each title to give some idea of its contents, and a thorough subject index that allows many of the issues raised in this book to be followed up with ease. It is not complete, for many local publications inevitably did not come to the attention of the compiler, and it is already out of date, of course. Not all the books used here are in it either, showing the difficulties of trying to be exhaustive, and many that are in it will not be easily obtained.

The original textbook of oral history was Paul Thompson's, *The Voice of the Past: Oral History* (Oxford University Press: 1978, 2nd edn 1988). This is a comprehensive look at the nature of oral history from an academic point of view, together with advice on different types of project. It is the logical next step after this book, along with Trevor Lummis, *Listening to History: the Authenticity of Oral Evidence* (Hutchinson: 1987), which, as its name suggests, is largely concerned with the nature of oral testimony.

The journal *Oral History* has featured prominently in the text and it is by far the best guide to new books and work in progress. It regularly prints articles on the practice of oral history as well as on its results. Individual editions take a particular topic, sometimes practical such as community publishing (autumn 1992); education (spring 1992); reminiscence work (autumn 1989); etc, and sometimes thematic, such as family history (autumn 1975); black history (spring 1980); the crafts (autumn 1990); etc. Early editions cover the development of oral history in Britain and elsewhere in a series of articles. Smaller magazines and newsletters that are published at many levels publicize themselves in it, such as *By Word of Mouth,* the Scottish Oral History Group's newsletter. The National Sound Archive have just begun publishing a free bulletin, *Playback,* which is free on application to the British Library National Sound Archive, 29 Exhibition Road, London SW7 2AS.

George Ewart Evans' work on BBC radio and his books were popular in Britain long before oral history was seen as a special form of history, or the very name had been applied here. His influence on most early workers, and many others others since, can hardly be overestimated, and, since it was all achieved outside the history profession, it is an inspiring example for any amateur. He wrote many more books than those included in the text, and in *Where Beards Wag All: The Relevance of the Oral Tradition* (Faber: 1970, 2nd edn 1977) and *Spoken History* (Faber: 1987) he discusses most clearly his own distinctive approach to oral collecting and the connection between oral testimony, material culture, and folklore.

The links with the media can be further seen in books like Theo Barker's, *The Long March of Everyman* (Deutsch/BBC: 1975, 2nd edn 1985), which was originally broadcast as a series of 'sound symphonies' drawn from interviews and the BBC archives. Charles Allen's, *Plain Tales from the Raj: Images of British India in the Twentieth Century* (Deutsch/BBC: 1975) attracted a wide audience when broadcast on Radio Four, and two other series followed on Africa and the South China Seas. In 1981 the Imperial War Museum issued some of it on tape. Steven Humphries' work is mentioned in the body of this book, but it is worth noting that he continues to prepare stimulating series on sensitive subjects for television, and they have convinced many of the value of oral testimony, as well as showing how vision further improves its immediacy. For those interested in oral history as drama, Age Exchange Theatre Company have published a whole series of booklets that derive from touring plays based on reminiscence, such as *My First Job* (Age Exchange: 1984).

An example of the wide scope oral history can have is that by David Edge and Michael Mulkay, *Astronomy Transformed: The Emergence of Radio Astronomy in Britain* (Wiley: 1976). The success of this book in setting aside the normal neat view of scientific progress and showing that things really happened in much messier ways, with personalities and rivalries counting for a great deal, was based on careful preparation before interviews and a double-handed interview technique designed to challenge contributors without alienating them. Elite oral history is dealt with in detail in Anthony Seldon and Joanna Pappworth, *By Word of Mouth: 'Elite' Oral History* (Methuen 1983), including advice on interviewing techniques that work in this setting.

PEOPLE AND PLACES

It is hard to select anything for special attention from the mass of local publications based on oral history, but Marie Hartley and Joan Ingleby's, *Life and Tradition in the Yorkshire Dales* (Dent: 1976) was very influential in its powerful combination of oral recollections, old photographs, material culture, and landscape in evoking a distinctive regional way of life. A series of similar volumes followed for different areas. The Centerprise Trust's, *Working Lives: A People's Autobiography of London* (Centerprise Trust: vol 1, 1976, vol 2, 1977), together with other booklets, is an impressive cumulative project from London. Check your local studies library for your area's equivalent. The work of Studs Terkel in Chicago is also worth mentioning here as it forms a long and extensive record of the ordinary experience of life in an American city that has always been widely accepted as having exceptional value. Not all his books will be available, but those that are, like *Working: People Talk About What They Do All Day And How They Feel About What They Do* (Wildwood, NY, 1974/Penguin, 1985), are well worth reading even though they are not about this country.

LIFESTYLES AND LANGUAGE

Because folklore has been such a marginal subject in academic terms there are very few modern books that give a serious overview. R. Dorson, *Folklore and Folklife* (University of Chicago Press: 1956, 2nd edn 1972) is probably the best available, while E. Estyn Evans, *Irish Folk Ways* (Routledge & Kegan Paul: 1957) is a fine example of what a purely folkloristic work can achieve, as is Trefor M. Owen's, *Welsh Folk Customs* (XXXX: 1968) for Wales. A study of a rural community from a very contrasting point of view is Ian Carter, *Farm Life in North-east Scotland, 1840–1914: The Poor Man's Country* (John Donald: 1979). Robert Burchfield, *The English Language*

(Oxford University Press: 1985) is an accessible study of English as a whole, and of its development over the centuries since it was first spoken on these islands. Good books on dialect are much easier to get hold of than for folklore. A good introduction is Peter Trudgill, *The Dialects of England* (Blackwell: 1990). *The Linguistic Atlas of England* (Croom Helm: 1978), edited by Harold Orton, Stewart Sanderson and John Widdowson is a monumental study of English dialects in action, but only covers country districts. The three volumes of *The Linguistic Atlas of Scotland* (Croom Helm: 1975–86), edited by J. Mather and H.H. Speitel, cover the Scots dialects and later volumes will do the same for Gaelic.

ALTERNATIVE HISTORY

Despite the work done with ethnic groups, there is not a great deal published in such a way as to be accessible to the general public. Caroline Adams, *Across Seven Seas and Thirteen Rivers: Life Stories of Pioneer Sylhetti Settlers in Britain* (THAP Books: 1988), which covers the 'Lascar' seamen and their families who have lived in British ports for three centuries, is a good example of what could be done. *Women's Words: The Feminist Practice of Oral History* edited by Sherna B. Gluck and Daphne Patai (Routledge: 1991) is an attempt to draw together the whole question of what this way of working can do and has done for women. Mary Chamberlain, *Fenwomen: a Portrait of Women in an English Village* (Quartet: 1975/Virago: 1977) is a rare study of women in rural society, and Carl Chinn, *They Worked All Their Lives: Women of the Urban Poor in England, 1880–1939* (Manchester University Press: 1988) has been widely praised.

STARTING OUT AND GATHERING MATERIAL

Short guides to running sessions are: Robert Perks, *Oral History: Talking About the Past* (The Historical Association: 1992); Paul Thompson and Robert Perks, *Telling it How it Was. A Guide to Recording Oral History* (BBC: 1989); Steve Humphries, *The Handbook of Oral History: Recording Life Stories* (Inter-Action Imprint: 1984), and Ken Howarth, *Remember, Remember: Tape Recording Oral History* (Pennine Heritage Network: 1984); but none of these are widely available through bookshops and libraries. For teachers, the work of Sallie Purkis is probably the most relevant and easily available, such as *Oral History in Schools* (Oral History Society: 1981), *Thanks for the Memory* (Collins: 1987) and *A Sense of History: Key Stage 1 Evaluation Pack* (Longman: 1991), which is specifically concerned with primary school teachers and the national curriculum. The prime example of what can be achieved in the right setting is Eliot Wigginton (ed), *The Foxfire Book* (Doubleday, NY: 1972), and thereafter annual additions, published by Anchor Press/Doubleday, entitled *Foxfire 2* (1973), and so on. These are compilations from a school magazine from the Southern Appalachian district of the USA, collected by students in a desperately poor area who had been virtually written off by the educational system, but who became intensely motivated by the chance to explore the strong folk-culture of their area. For reminiscence work, an important study is Peter Coleman, *Ageing and the Reminiscence Process: Social and Clinical Implications* (Wiley: 1986), showing its value and its limitations.

Index

225